Racquetball

STEPS TO SUCCESS

Dennis Fisher

Human Kinetics

Library of Congress Cataloging-in-Publication Data

Fisher, Dennis, 1951-
  Racquetball : steps to success / Dennis Fisher.
      p. cm.
  ISBN-13: 978-0-7360-6939-7 (soft cover)
  ISBN-10: 0-7360-6939-9 (soft cover)
  1. Racquetball. I. Title.
  GV1003.34.F57 2007
  796.343--dc22

                        2007026208

ISBN-10: 0-7360-6939-9
ISBN-13: 978-0-7360-6939-7

The Web addresses cited in this text were current as of September 2007, unless otherwise noted.

Acquisitions Editor: Jana Hunter
Developmental Editor: Cynthia McEntire
Assistant Editor: Scott Hawkins
Copyeditor: Tom Tiller
Proofreader: Anne Rogers
Graphic Designer: Nancy Rasmus
Graphic Artist: Francine Hamerski
Cover Designer: Keith Blomberg
Photographer (cover): © Bongarts/Getty Images
Photographer (interior): Neil Bernstein
Photo Office Assistant: Jason Allen
Art Manager: Kelly Hendren
Illustrator: Tammy Page
Printer: Sheridan Books

We thank Brigham Young University in Provo, Utah, for assistance in providing the location for the photo shoot for this book.

Human Kinetics books are available at special discounts for bulk purchase. Special editions or book excerpts can also be created to specification. For details, contact the Special Sales Manager at Human Kinetics.

Printed in the United States of America   10 9 8 7 6 5 4 3 2 1

Human Kinetics
Web site: www.HumanKinetics.com

United States: Human Kinetics
P.O. Box 5076
Champaign, IL 61825-5076
800-747-4457
e-mail: humank@hkusa.com

Canada: Human Kinetics
475 Devonshire Road Unit 100
Windsor, ON N8Y 2L5
800-465-7301 (in Canada only)
e-mail: orders@hkcanada.com

Europe: Human Kinetics
107 Bradford Road
Stanningley
Leeds LS28 6AT, United Kingdom
+44 (0) 113 255 5665
e-mail: hk@hkeurope.com

Australia: Human Kinetics
57A Price Avenue
Lower Mitcham, South Australia 5062
08 8372 0999
e-mail: info@hkaustralia.com

New Zealand: Human Kinetics
Division of Sports Distributors NZ Ltd.
P.O. Box 300 226 Albany
North Shore City
Auckland
0064 9 448 1207
e-mail: info@humankinetics.co.nz

Racquetball

STEPS TO SUCCESS

◨ Contents

Climbing the Steps to Racquetball Success   vii

The Sport of Racquetball   ix

Key to Diagrams   xxvii

Step 1   Forehand   1

Step 2   Backhand   17

Step 3   Serve   33

Step 4   Return of Serve   57

Step 5   Front-Wall Shots   77

Step 6   Side-Wall Shots   95

Step 7 **Ceiling Shots** 107

Step 8 **Back-Wall Shots** 119

Step 9 **Court Positioning** 135

Step 10 **Shot Selection** 147

Step 11 **Game Management** 157

Step 12 **Doubles, Cutthroat, and Outdoor Court Games** 165

About the Author 177

◪ Climbing the Steps to Racquetball Success

Beginning and intermediate players, as well as teachers and coaches, will find *Racquetball: Steps to Success* an invaluable asset for building the necessary foundation or adding to what the player has already accomplished to enjoy this sport.

The steps to success are arranged in a precise order—one skill or stroke at a time. Beginners should start with the grip and progress to the forehand and backhand strokes before advancing to specialty shots such as the pinch, ceiling ball, and off-the-back-wall shots. Advanced players can start with the skills they wish to refine and add to their game repertoire. All explanations, pictures, and illustrations provide the tools to assist in building a strong foundation so each player can develop his or her own style of play.

This book not only offers thorough explanations of fundamental and specialty shots, but it will also give the beginner and advanced player insight into how, when, and why to hit each shot. Players will learn to analyze opponents, rallies, and game and match situations to minimize errors and maximize success.

For teachers and instructors, *Racquetball: Steps to Success* provides an all-inclusive instructional package. The detailed information, drills, and scoring methods are easily adapted to existing instructional curriculum. Players and teachers also will find useful information on the history of racquetball, equipment, etiquette, basic rules, and web-based resources. This teaching resource also features a detailed time-proven sequence of information cues in executing a full range of racquetball shots, as well as strategy, self-paced drills, and methods for evaluating students.

As a coach to amateur, elite, and professional racquetball players, I constantly pick the brains of my mentors and colleagues to find new solutions to age-old problems and time-tested methods for improving player performance as quickly and efficiently as possible. *Racquetball: Steps to Success* is a collection of years of study in the art of racquetball and the skills, strategies, and drills used to coach successful players at all levels. Any coach will find a fresh or new approach, idea, or drill that will help his or her players improve.

Regardless of whether you are a beginning or competitive racquetball player, you will improve your performance and find a greater love of the game as you develop increased competency in your skills and strategies. *Racquetball: Steps to Success* empowers you with a progressive game plan for developing and improving your racquetball skills and gaining more confidence on the court. This is best accomplished by following the systematic approach provided. Follow the same sequence for each skill as you work your way through every step:

1. Stroke instruction. Carefully read and study all explanations, illustrations, and pictures for each skill. Next formulate a mental image of how to perform the skill.

2. Drills. Perform each drill in the given sequence. Do not move on to the next segment of the sequence until you are confident of your performance.

3. Success checks. During each drill, concentrate on each component of the skill. Review the success checks as needed as a reminder of what to focus on.

4. Score your success. Grade yourself on each drill. Repeat each drill until you attain your goal. Repeat the drill and score your success as often as you want. Don't worry about getting a perfect score—perfection is not the object; learning is. It will be helpful to have a qualified observer such as a teacher, coach, or skilled player evaluate your technique, if possible.

5. Missteps. Common errors in stroke mechanics and execution are made by all players at all levels. Missteps are a way of identifying and correcting them and may increase your learning curve. Reviewing these prior to performing the drills may assist in avoiding some of the obvious and common errors altogether.

6. Success summary. At the end of each step, a success summary briefly outlines the most important teaching and learning objectives. Each step wraps up by asking you to rate your success by adding the points you earned in each drill. The total score will assist you in knowing whether you have accomplished your goal and are ready to move on to the next skill or need more practice.

Use *Racquetball: Steps to Success* to assist you in becoming a better player. The steps will aid you in learning the game and increasing your skills. Coaches and instructors will learn ways to teach the game using key techniques and valuable evaluations or coach with proven player-development techniques. Even advanced players will benefit from drills that will hone their shot-making skills and on-court tactics for a more competitive advantage.

Everyone plays racquetball for different reasons. For some it is a means of recreation, for others it is exercise, and yet someone else may like the adrenaline rush that comes from being competitive. Regardless of your aspirations or reason for playing this wonderful lifetime sport, *Racquetball: Steps to Success* will help you become the player you want to be.

◨ The Sport of Racquetball

Welcome to the greatest game on Earth. From the moment I was introduced to racquetball, I couldn't get enough. At the time of my introduction, I was a competitive tennis player, living from one tournament to the next. That soon changed with the challenge of this year-round game. I especially love this game for the friendships I have developed through playing, teaching, and coaching. I am an admitted competitive sports junkie. At one time or another, I have competed in all stringed racquet sports, baseball and softball, swimming, triathlons, track and field, cycling, and running. None of these, however, has been as enjoyable or stayed with me as long as racquetball.

Racquetball is fast and fun. It is played by men and women, children and seniors, and persons with and without disabilities. It is a lifelong sport that is great for recreation and competition. Racquetball is super for burning large numbers of calories in a short amount of time. It is excellent for developing eye–hand coordination and improving speed and agility. In fact, many coaches recommend racquetball as an excellent cross-training option for their athletes in traditional sports such as football, track and field, basketball, volleyball, baseball, and softball.

Racquetball is played with a racquet, a ball, and a few additional (and sometimes optional) accessories. One accessory that should be mandatory at all facilities is eyewear. The United States Racquetball Association (USAR, or USA Racquetball) and the International Racquetball Federation (IRF) have set standards and specifications for all racquetball-specific equipment and courts.

The racquet and ball have come a long way since their inception in 1949. The first racquet was a hybrid derived from rackets designed by Joe Sobek for paddleball, paddle tennis, and platform tennis. The first racquet was made of a thick wood frame using a cross-string pattern of nylon string. At the same time, the Seamless Rubber Company designed a unique ball (called the Seamco blue ball) to complement the new racquet and sport. The game of racquetball was now on its way to becoming a worldwide phenomenon. Since then, the racquet, ball, and supporting equipment have become part of a highly technical, multimillion-dollar marketplace.

According to the USAR and the IRF, the current racquet must not exceed 22 inches (55.9 centimeters) in length and must include a cord, or lanyard, securely attached to the player's wrist. The strings may be of any material that will not mark or deface the ball. The standard racquetball is 2 1/4 inches (5.7 centimeters) in diameter, weighs approximately 1.4 ounces (39.7 grams), and may be any color. Eyewear must be designed for racquetball, lensed, shatter resistant, and approved by the USAR or IRF. The soles of your shoes must be free of dirt and debris and must not mark or damage the floor.

Racquetball uses four standard courts. Indoor courts (figure 1) have four walls and a ceiling. The court is 40 feet (12.2 meters) long, 20 feet (6.1 meters) wide, and 20 feet high. Indoor courts may be made of any combination of glass, fiberboard, cement, plaster, or paneling for the walls and ceiling. Most indoor floors are inlaid wood; a few are made of cement.

Outdoor courts come in three flavors. On a one-wall court, the front wall is 20 feet (6.1 meters) wide and 16 feet (4.9 meters) high. The playing surface on the floor is 20 feet wide and 34 feet (10.4 meters) long. Three-wall courts come in two types. The long side-wall version

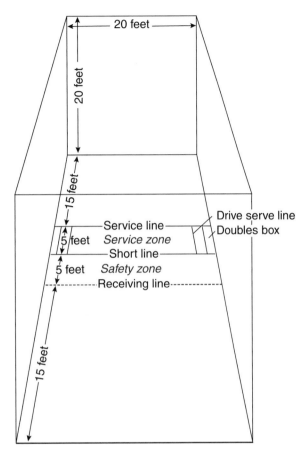

Figure 1 Indoor racquetball court.

has a standard 20-by-20-foot front wall, with side walls that are 40 feet (12.2 meters) long and 20 feet high. Floor dimensions and markings are the same as for the indoor four-wall court. The most common outdoor court, however, has a front wall and side walls that are 20 by 20 feet, with the side walls tapering to 12 feet (3.7 meters) high at the back end of the court. Floor dimensions and markings are the same as for an indoor four-wall court. Typically, outdoor courts have cement floors and walls. For the most part, the rules are the same on any court, with the exception of the way the ball is played outside the dimensions of the floor on an outdoor court (see step 12).

The game can be played with two, three, or four players. The two-player game is called *singles,* and the four-player game is *doubles.* The three-player game is a hybrid of singles and doubles called *cutthroat.* Cutthroat has many variations, but the two most common are one-out and two-on-one. A popular variation of

cutthroat among competitive players is *ironman,* in which one player competes against two players for an entire game. You will find the basic rules for these games and how to play them in step 12.

GEAR

Most universities, clubs, and recreation facilities require the same basic equipment and clothing for racquetball:

Racquet with wrist lanyard

Shoes with nonmarking soles

Shorts

Shirt

Eyewear (approved)

Glove (optional)

Ball

All gear comes in various sizes, colors, shapes, weights, and price ranges. Most people coming into this sport already own shoes, shorts, and shirts that are used in other athletic activities. The racquet, eyewear, and ball are unique to the sport of racquetball. You can purchase this equipment, at the low end, for less than $50 U.S.

Enjoyment of the game is not tied to a price tag. However, as with any sport, the medium-range to upper-end equipment is designed to provide the player with optimum balance, power, accuracy, protection, and skill advancement. As usual, you get what you pay for. An occasional player who plays a couple times per year will probably be happy with a low-end racquet and running or cross-training shoes. A recreational player who plays a couple of times a week will benefit from a medium-range to upper-end racquet, court shoes, glove, and other racquetball-specific equipment and clothing. All serious competitive players use upper-end racquets, court-specific shoes, gloves, and approved eyewear (which is mandatory in tournament play).

One of the first things any player needs to look at when considering playing racquetball seriously is the equipment. Low-end equipment will allow you to play the game but will hinder your skill advancement and, to some degree, your competitive enjoyment of the game. One equipment addition for the serious player is the glove. A racquetball glove serves two purposes: It helps prevent blisters, and it provides better control of the racquet with less fatigue of the hand.

Relatively speaking, racquetball is an inexpensive sport to get into for the amount of pleasure and exercise you get out of it. The average start-up equipment cost for the recreational player is around $150 U.S. Players may also encounter fees associated with playing at a private club or recreation center. However, some towns and cities have three-wall and one-wall outdoor courts that may or may not cost anything to use. Competitive players may spend $500 to $1,000 U.S. (sometimes more) per year for equipment, not to mention club fees, restringing costs, tournament fees, and travel and lodging expenses.

Racquet

Choosing the right equipment, especially a good racquet, will play an important part in your skill progression. When choosing a racquet, consider these factors: weight, balance, grip size, and cost.

The racquet's weight will affect how easily and quickly you are able to swing the racquet. Most adult male players use racquets that weigh 150 to 200 grams. Most competitive male players choose a racquet that weighs between 150 and 170 grams. Female players typically use racquets that weigh between 145 and 180 grams. Most competitive female players use racquets that weigh 150 to 170 grams.

Much of the choice in racquet weight and balance depends on your body build, weight, and strength. For balance, racquets come in *even-balance* and *head-heavy* versions. A head-heavy racquet helps generate more racquet head speed as the player swings the racquet, which equates to more power. Nearly all upper-end, high-priced racquets are head heavy. Typically, low-end racquets have even balance although some heavier upper-end racquets have even balance.

Racquet handle grips come in two sizes: 3 5/8 inches (9.2 centimeters) and 3 7/8 inches (9.8 centimeters), or SS and XS, respectively. As a rule of thumb, if you wear an extra-small to large glove, you may benefit more from a 3 5/8-inch grip. If you wear a large to extra-large glove, you may benefit more from a 3 7/8-inch grip. Most competitive players play with the 3 5/8-inch or SS grip (most competitive racquetball players are below 6 feet [1.8 meters] tall).

Racquet frame composition comes in two basic categories: metal and composite. Most metal racquets are made of aluminum and can be found in the low-end racquet lines. While the weight is a bit on the heavy side, metal racquets offer durability and are less likely to break. Upper-end racquets are made of myriad materials such as graphite, titanium, Kevlar, fiberglass, and plastic. It is also worth your time to consider frame construction and vibration. If possible, find a way to test a racquet to see if it fits your style of play before purchase.

Shoes

After the racquet, court shoes are the next most important piece of equipment. For most players, good indoor court or cross-training shoes—such as basketball, volleyball, or indoor fitness shoes—will work. Tennis-specific shoes will also work; however, they have extremely hard soles and don't grip as well on the wood court surface.

One type of shoe *not* recommended for racquetball is the typical running shoe. A good semisoft sole with a breathable mesh upper is desirable for most competitive players. All major racquetball manufacturers make racquetball-specific shoes.

Eyewear

Let me say this about eyewear—get it and wear it! Currently, eye transplants are not a medical option, and a racquetball can permanently damage an eye. A racquetball can be hit upward of 150 miles (240 kilometers) per hour by an inexperienced player who has little control of the racquet or the flight of the ball. Inexperienced players also have little anticipation of where to move on the court to avoid getting in the way of the opposing player's racquet or the ball's path. Because the ball can be hit either forward or backward (off the back wall) to keep it in play, the inherent risk exists to be hit by the ball. Being hit in the face is uncommon, but it does happen. Given the unexpected tendencies of the inexperienced player, coupled with a lack of control and the speed of the ball, it makes sense to wear approved protective eyewear on the court at all times. Eyewear is the least expensive piece of equipment, other than balls and gloves, but it is the most important in terms of safety.

Type, size, shape, and color of eyewear are personal choices. Be sure the eyewear is comfortable and fits the size of your face and head. All racquetball-specific eyewear comes with a safety band that can be attached to the temples and goes around the back of the head to ensure the eyewear doesn't come off during play. Be sure to get eyewear designed specifically for racquetball that bears either a permanent, physical stamp of the appropriate "ASTM F803" citation on the frame itself or the Protective Eyewear Certification Council (PECC) seal of approval for the ASTM standard. This is especially important if you plan to compete in USAR- or IRF-sanctioned events: Approved eyewear is mandatory for sanctioned competitive play.

Gloves

Gloves come in sizes from junior to extra large. Glove composition includes combinations using synthetic leather, Lycra, nylon, and natural leather. Gloves made with natural leather will last longer than those made with synthetic leather. Softer leathers, such as deerskin or cabretta, generally make for more comfortable gloves and reduce blistering. All major racquetball manufacturers make racquetball-specific gloves in a wide range of sizes, compositions, and prices.

Regardless of your level of play and your investment in equipment, racquetball is fast, fun, and addictive.

BASIC RULES OF PLAY

At its highest levels, competitive racquetball features many official rules and guidelines to keep the game fair. The beginning recreational racquetball player needs to have a grasp of the basic rules to keep the game simple, enjoyable, and safe. Official rules can be obtained through USA Racquetball (USAR) or the International Racquetball Federation (IRF). See the resource list at the end of this chapter (page xxvi) for contact information for these organizations.

The objective is to win each rally by serving or returning the ball so the opponent is unable to keep the ball in play. A rally is over when a player or team is unable to return the ball before it touches the floor twice, is unable to return the ball to the front wall before it touches the floor, or when a hinder is called (hinders are discussed on page xv).

Serving and Scoring Points

Only the server or serving team scores points. The serving side receives 1 point when a serve is not returned (an ace) or when the serving player or team wins a rally. In singles, if the serving player loses the serve, it is a *sideout,* and the server and receiver change roles. In doubles, when the first server loses the serve, it is called a *handout*; when the second server loses the serve, it is a *sideout,* and the serving team and receiving team change roles. (Doubles play is covered in more detail in the doubles section of the rules.)

The server puts the ball in play with any legal serve from any place within the service zone or box. Neither the ball nor any part of either foot may extend beyond either line of the service zone when the server initiates the service motion. You may step on but not completely over the lines. When finishing the service, the server must have some part of both feet on or inside the front or service line until the served ball passes the short line: The server is not allowed to step over or past the short line until the ball passes the short line.

The server continues serving until he or she hits an out serve, commits two consecutive fault serves in a row, or the server (or serving team) is unable to keep the ball in play during a rally. (Out serves and fault serves are discussed a bit later.)

The first player or team to win two games wins a match. The first two games of a match are played to 15 points. If each player or team wins one game, a tie-breaker game is played to 11 points.

The server may serve down the wall only if he or she starts and remains outside of the 3-foot (0.9-meter) drive-service zone. If the serve begins in the 3-foot drive-service zone, the server may not hit a drive serve to that side of the court. The drive-serve zones are not a factor for cross-court drive serves or for the hard Z, soft Z, lob, or half lob serves (see step 3, Serve).

Defective Serves

A serve that doesn't follow the rules results in either a re-serve or a penalty.

A dead-ball serve results in no penalty, and the server is given another serve (without canceling a prior fault serve). Dead-ball serves include court hinders and broken balls. A court hinder is a serve that is altered in its normal path due to a wet spot or an irregular court surface. If the ball breaks on the serve, the serve is replayed. A broken ball does not cancel any previous fault serve.

Note: It is always proper to call faults on yourself in the absence of an official referee.

Two fault serves in a row result in an out (either a handout or a sideout). These are the most common fault serves:

- Foot fault. A foot fault results when the server does not begin the service motion with both feet in the service zone or steps completely over the service line (no part of the foot is on or inside the service line) before the served ball crosses the short line.

- Short serve. A short serve is any served ball that hits the front wall first and, on the rebound, hits the floor on or in front of the short line.

- Three-wall serve. A three-wall serve is any served ball that hits the front wall first and then strikes both side walls before touching the floor.

- Ceiling serve. A ceiling serve is any served ball that hits the front wall first and then touches the ceiling.

- Long serve. A long serve is a served ball that hits the front wall first and rebounds to the back wall before touching the floor.

- Screen serve. A screen serve is a served ball that hits the front wall first, then passes so closely to the server, or the server's partner in doubles, that it precludes the receiver from having a clear view of the ball. The receiver is compelled to take up good court positioning to gain that view.

A fault serve results if the server bounces the ball outside the service zone or serves before the receiver is ready.

Any of the following violations results in an out (sideout or handout):

- Two consecutive fault serves.

- Missed serve. Any attempt to hit the ball that results in a complete miss or in the ball contacting any part of the server's body is an out serve. Also, allowing the ball to bounce more than once during the serve is an out.

- Touched serve. Any served ball that makes contact with the server or the server's racquet after hitting the front wall but before touching the floor. Additionally, any ball intentionally stopped or caught by the server or server's partner.

- Fake or balk serve. A fake or balk is any noncontinuous movement of the racquet toward the ball during the serve that is preformed with the purpose of misleading the receiver.

- Illegal hit. Some examples of illegal hits are contacting the ball twice, carrying the ball (pushing or throwing it with the racquet), or hitting the ball with the handle of the racquet or part of the body or clothing.

- Non-front-wall serve. Any served ball that does not strike the front wall first is a non-front-wall serve.

- Crotch serve. Any served ball that hits the crack of the front wall and floor, front wall and side wall, or front wall and ceiling is a crotch serve.

- Out-of-court serve. Any served ball that hits the front wall first and, before striking the floor, either goes out of the court or hits an area above the normal playing area of the court is an out-of-court serve.

- Safety zone violation. If the server or his or her doubles partner enters into the safety zone before the served ball passes the short line, it is a loss of serve.

Return of Serve

The receiver may not enter the safety zone until the ball bounces or crosses the receiving line. However, the receiver's follow-through may carry the receiver or the racquet past the receiving line. A violations by the receiver results in a point for the server.

After a legal serve, the player receiving the serve must strike the ball on the fly or after the first bounce but before the ball bounces on the floor a second time. The receiver must return the ball to the front wall using any combination of ceiling, side wall, or back wall surfaces. The ball must touch the front wall before it touches the floor.

If the receiver fails to return the serve, the server receives a point.

Rallies

Only the head of the racquet may be used to return the ball. The racquet may be held in one or both hands. Switching hands to hit a ball, touching the ball with any part of the body or clothing, or removing the wrist safety cord during a rally results in a loss of the rally.

The player or team attempting to return the ball may touch or strike the ball only once during the rally or the rally is lost. The ball may not be carried (pushed or thrown off the racquet). A carry is typically noticed by the absence of a distinct ping when the ball hits the strings.

Any of the following also demonstrates a failure to make a legal return during a rally:

- The ball bounces on the floor more than once before being hit.

- The ball does not reach the front wall on the fly.

- The ball is hit into the gallery or wall opening or hits a surface above the normal playing area of the court, striking an area that has been declared out of play.

- A ball that obviously does not have the velocity or direction to hit the front wall strikes an opposing player.

- A ball hit by one player on a team hits that player or that player's partner.

- A player commits an avoidable hinder (discussed later in the chapter).

- A player switches hands during a rally.

- A player fails to use a racquet safety cord.

- A player touches the ball with his or her body or clothing.

- A player carries or slings the ball with the racquet.

If the serving player or team loses the rally, it is an out (sideout), and the opposing player or team now serves. If the receiver loses the rally, the serving player or team receives a point and continues to serve until an out (sideout) occurs.

Following a service return, the ball remains in play until it touches the floor twice before being hit, regardless of how many walls, including the front wall, it makes contact with. If a player swings at the ball and misses it, the player may continue to attempt to return the ball until it touches the floor for the second time, which ends the rally.

If there is any suspicion that a ball has broken during a rally, play continues until the end of the rally. If the ball is broken, the ball is replaced and the rally is replayed. The server resumes play at the first serve even if the ball was placed in play on the second serve. A rally is also replayed in various situations referred to as *dead-ball hinders* (discussed in the next section, along with *avoidable hinders*). Whenever a rally is replayed, the server resumes play at first serve.

Dead-Ball Hinders

A rally is replayed without penalty, and the server resumes play at first serve, whenever a dead-ball hinder occurs. It is the responsibility of the side that has just hit the ball to move so the receiving side may go straight to the ball and have an unobstructed view of and swing at the ball. However, the receiver is responsible for making a reasonable effort to move toward the ball and must have a reasonable chance to return the ball for any type of hinder to be called.

Stop play immediately whenever the ball hits any part of the court that was designated as a court hinder, such as a vent grate, door handle, or door crack. Play also stops when the normal path of the ball is altered by an irregular bounce because the ball contacts a rough surface, such as a light or vent, or strikes a wet spot on the floor or wall.

A dead-ball hinder is also called when an opponent is hit by a return shot in flight. If the opponent is hit by a ball that obviously did not have the velocity or direction to reach the front wall, it is not a hinder, and the player who hit the ball loses the rally. A player who is hit by a ball can stop play and make the call, though the call must be made immediately. It is possible that such interference may, under certain conditions, be declared an avoidable hinder.

A hinder is called if body contact occurs that is sufficient to stop the rally, either for the purpose of preventing injury by further contact or because the contact prevented a player from being able to make a reasonable return attempt. Incidental body contact in which the offensive player clearly has the advantage should not be called a hinder unless the offensive player obviously stops play. Contact with the racquet on a follow-through normally is not considered a hinder.

Another type of dead-ball hinder is the screen ball—any ball rebounding from the front wall so close to the body of the defensive player that it inhibits the offensive player from having an obstructed view of the ball. A ball that passes between the legs of a player who has just returned the ball is not routinely a screen.

It depends on if the other player is obstructed. Normally, the call should work to the advantage of the offensive player.

A backswing hinder is called when any part of the body or racquet makes contact on the backswing, or on the way to or just before returning the ball, impairs the hitter's ability to take a reasonable swing. The player attempting the return can make this call; however, the call must be made immediately. This type of interference may be considered an avoidable hinder. Any player about to execute a return who believes that hitting the opponent with the ball or racquet is possible may immediately stop play and request a dead-ball hinder. This call must be made immediately.

A dead-ball hinder can also be declared on any other accidental interference that prevents an opponent from having a fair chance to see or return the ball; for example, when a ball from another court enters the court during a rally.

Avoidable Hinders

An avoidable hinder results in the loss of the rally. It does not have to be an intentional act. Many avoidable hinders result from failure to allow the opponent a view of the ball or a reasonable chance to hit it.

Failure to move may result in an avoidable hinder. Players must move enough to allow each opponent either a shot straight to the front wall or a cross-court shot directly to the front wall at an angle that allows the ball to rebound directly to the opposite back corner. An avoidable hinder is also called when a player moves in order to prevent the opponent from taking either of these shots.

Stroke interference occurs when a player moves, or fails to move, thus denying the opponent a free, unimpeded swing at a return.

An avoidable hinder is also declared if a player moves into a position that blocks the opponent from getting to, or returning, the ball. In doubles, an avoidable hinder occurs when a player moves in front of an opponent as the player's partner is hitting the ball. Other examples include moving into the ball, moving in the way of the ball, being struck by a ball just played by an opponent, intentionally pushing an opponent during a rally, intentionally shouting or stomping, waving the racquet, moving across an opponent's line of vision just before the opponent strikes the ball, or disrupting the opponent in any other manner.

Players should ensure that the ball is dry before the serve. A wet ball that is served is an avoidable hinder called against the server.

If a player loses any apparel, equipment, or other article during play, that player is called for an avoidable hinder, unless the player has just hit a shot that was unplayable. If the loss of equipment is caused by an opponent, then a dead-ball hinder is called. If the opponent's action is judged avoidable or intentional, then the opponent is called for an avoidable hinder.

Time-Outs

Each player or team gets three 30-second time-outs in games played to 15 points and two 30-second time-outs in games to 11 points. Time-outs may not be called by either side after the service motion starts. Calling for a time-out when no time-outs remain or after the service motion starts, or taking more than 30 seconds during a time-out, results in a technical foul for delay of game. (Note: Technical fouls are not called in unofficial, noncompetition games.)

If a player is injured during the course of a match, an injury time-out is awarded. A player can call more than one time-out for the same injury or for additional injuries that occur during the match. A player is not allowed more than a total of 15 minutes of rest for injury during the entire match. If the injured player is not able to continue play after 15 minutes, the match is awarded to the opponent.

If any bleeding occurs during play, play stops as soon as the rally is over. The person who is bleeding is charged with an injury time-out and the match may continue only after the bleeding has stopped.

Injury time-outs are not approved for muscle cramps and pulls, fatigue, or anything else not caused by direct contact on the court. Injury time-outs are not approved for preexisting conditions.

Players should keep all clothing and equipment in good, playable condition and must use regular time-outs, or time between games, for equipment adjustment or replacement. If a player or team is out of time-outs when equipment changes or adjustments are necessary for fair and safe play, equipment time-outs may be awarded. Equipment time-outs are not to exceed 2 minutes.

The rest period between the first two games of a match is 2 minutes. If a tie breaker is necessary, the rest period between the second and third games is 5 minutes.

Postponed games resume with the same score as when the game was stopped. Games may be postponed due to unsafe conditions on the court that require skilled maintenance to correct, lighting problems, broken light fixtures, water, or any unsafe situation that cannot be fixed by the players in a reasonable time.

MODIFIED RULES FOR DOUBLES

Rules for singles also apply in doubles, with the following additions and modifications. A doubles team is two players who meet either the age requirements or player-classification requirements to participate in a particular division of play. If the two players on a team have different skill levels, the team must play in the division of the player with the higher level. When playing in an adult division, the team must play in the division of the younger player. When playing in a junior-age division, the team must play in the division of the older player. A change in playing partners may be made before the first match is played.

Serve

Each team must announce its order of serve prior to the beginning of play. Order of serve may be changed between games, as long as it is announced verbally before the first serve of the new game. At the beginning of each game, when the first server of the first team to serve is out, the team is out. Thereafter, both players on each team serve until the team receives a handout and a sideout or when both players lose service.

On each serve, the server's partner must stand erect, with his or her back to the side wall and with both feet on the floor inside the service box, from the moment the server begins to serve until the served ball passes the short line. Violations are called foot faults. A fault serve is also called if a served ball hits the doubles partner while in the doubles box. If the server's partner enters the safety zone before the ball passes the short line, the server loses service.

In doubles, when either partner serves out of order, the points scored by that server are subtracted and the server loses the serve. If the second server serves out of order, the first server loses serve and the second server resumes serving. If the player designated as the first server serves out of order, a sideout is called. A served ball that hits a doubles partner who is outside the doubles box results in loss of serve.

Serve Return

The rally is lost if a player hits his or her partner with an attempted return. If one player on the receiving team swings at the ball and misses it, both partners may continue to attempt to return the ball until it touches the floor a second time. Both partners on a side are entitled equal opportunity to return the ball.

MODIFIED RULES FOR JUNIOR MULTIBOUNCE

In general, the ball remains in play as long as it is bouncing. However, the player may swing only once at the ball. The ball is considered dead when it stops bouncing and begins to roll. Also, anytime the ball rebounds off the back wall, it must be hit before it crosses the short line on the way to the front wall, with the following exceptions:

- Blast rule. If the ball ricochets from the front wall to the back wall on the fly, the player may hit the ball from any place on the court, including past the short line, so long as the ball is still bouncing.
- Front-wall lines. Two parallel lines (tape may be used) are placed across the front

wall. The bottom edge of one line is 3 feet (0.9 meter) above the floor, and the bottom edge of the other line is 1 foot (0.3 meter) above the floor. During the rally, any ball that hits the front wall below the 3-foot line and either on or above the 1-foot line must be returned before it bounces three times. However, if the ball hits below the 1-foot line, it must be returned before it bounces two times. If the ball hits on or above the 3-foot line, the ball must be returned as described in the basic return rule.

All games are played to 11 points. The first side to win two games wins the match.

MODIFIED RULES FOR ONE-WALL AND THREE-WALL PLAY

Standard rules governing racquetball play are used, except for the following modifications.

One-Wall Play

In one-wall, there are two playing surfaces—the front wall and the floor. The wall is 20 feet (6.1 meters) wide and 16 feet (4.9 meters) high. The floor is 20 feet wide and 34 feet (10.4 meters) to the back edge of the long line. To

permit player movement, there should be a minimum of 6 feet outside each sideline and 3 feet (0.9 meter) beyond the long line (6 feet, or 1.8 meters, is the recommended space). The back edge of the short line is 16 feet (4.9 meters) from the wall. The service markers are lines at least 6 inches (15.2 centimeters) long that are parallel with, and midway between, the long and short lines. The extension of the service markers forms the imaginary boundary of the service line. The entire floor area inside and including the short line, sidelines, and service line is considered the service zone. The receiving zone is the entire floor area behind the short line, including the sidelines and the long line.

Three-Wall Play

On a three-wall court with a short side wall, the front wall is 20 feet (6.1 meters) wide and 20 feet high. The side walls are 20 feet long and 20 feet high, tapering to 12 feet (3.7 meters) high. The floor length and court markings are the same as for a four-wall court.

On a three-wall court with a long side wall, the court is 20 feet (6.1 meters) wide, 20 feet high, and 40 feet (12.2 meters) long. The side walls may taper from 20 feet high at the front wall to 12 feet (3.7 meters) high at the end of the court. All court markings are the same as for a four-wall court.

On a three-wall court, serves that go past the side walls on the fly are out. Serves that go past the long line on the fly, but within the side walls, are faults.

ETIQUETTE

The following straightforward rules and guidelines for etiquette and safety will help you and your partners get the most out of racquetball:

- If you ask someone to play, it's your responsibility to provide the balls.

- When it's your turn to use the court, always knock on the door or flick the lights and wait for someone on the court to open the door. Opening the door unannounced could be disastrous if someone is going after a ball in the backcourt.

- Each player is responsible for calling serves in or out as well as calling safety line violations.

- Call fault serves, violations, and hinders immediately. Don't wait until after the shot or rally to make the call.

- Don't ask spectators to make calls. It's your responsibility, not theirs.

- To avoid hitting someone, it is proper to hold up on your swing or wait to hit the ball. This is called a *hinder,* and it will be appreciated by your opponent or partner. It is better to play the rally over than end the game with an injury sustained from hitting someone with the racquet or ball.

- Good sporting behavior is always in fashion. If you are unsure whether a shot was good or the ball skipped, call it against yourself, give it to your opponent, or just play the point over.

- This is not a quiet or prim and proper sport. It is loud, with the racquet crushing the ball and the ball slamming against the wall. It is okay to yell, talk, moan, groan, laugh, and cry on the court, as long as it is not when your opponent is getting ready to hit the ball. Rallies are short. You will have plenty of time to express yourself between rallies. Outright distractions are unacceptable when someone is in the process of hitting the ball.

- Getting the ball for your opponent when it is near you is always appreciated. This is not always common practice with competitive players, but it should be.

- Expressing appreciation for a good shot is good practice. When your opponent hits a good shot, say, "Good shot."

- The server should announce the score before each serve. Calling out the score for your opponent to hear keeps everyone on track. It is easy to lose track of the score during long rallies, time-outs, and on-court socializing.

- Two items that should be mandatory at all facilities are the wrist lanyard and approved eyewear. Many players have damaged their eyes, lost teeth, and suffered soft-tissue injuries and lacerations from being hit by the ball or a racquet. Wear your wrist lanyard and wear your eyewear. It can be dangerous out there on the court, especially with novice and inexperienced players.

WARMING UP AND COOLING DOWN

Because racquetball is such an explosive game, it is important to warm up properly before getting on the court and playing. Experts agree that it is important to warm up your muscles before beginning any stretching routine. Include a 10-minute warm-up and a 10-minute cool-down for all exercise and practice sessions. You can warm up safely by jogging, cycling, or performing racquetball-specific dynamic exercises that slowly increase your heart rate to a playing rate.

Cool down after you finish your racquetball game or workout. The cool-down helps to remove lactic acid from the muscles and prepare your body for the next day's workout. Slowly decrease your heart rate through a series of static stretches that use the muscles you just worked during the racquetball game.

Dynamic stretching, static stretching, and flexibility are three important aspects of warming up and cooling down. These exercises may not improve your conditioning or strength, but they will help prevent injuries in joints, muscles, ligaments, and tendons. Additionally, they will aid your recovery so you are not as sore the next day.

Dynamic stretching is the slow, controlled movement of joints through their full range of motion; it helps reduce muscle stiffness. During static stretching, you slowly move the muscle to its full range and hold it. Static stretching helps muscles relax and increases their range of motion. Flexibility is the ability to move joints through their full range of motion. Dynamic and static stretching will help improve your flexibility if done properly.

All three of these—dynamic and static stretching and the resultant flexibility—work together to improve your ability to move quickly and efficiently on the court with minimal soreness, stiffness, and resistance. Although both dynamic and static stretching will increase flexibility, always start out slowly. Be careful not to overstretch during your warm-up. Overstretching places undue strain on your body. Start exercises slowly and build slowly.

Dynamic Stretching

Dynamic stretching helps to wake up muscles and get them ready to work hard. This involves moving your limbs through the full range of motion you will use during racquetball. Note: If muscles are extremely sore, perform static stretching before dynamic stretching to aid in joint movement and decrease the risk of damage.

When performing dynamic stretching, follow these guidelines:

- Do not force the movement or lose control of the movement.

- Gradually increase the range of the motion over a series of repetitions as you loosen up.

- Repeat the movement about 12 times. You may need to do more or fewer, depending on how tight your muscles feel.

- Spend about 5 minutes total on dynamic stretches during your warm-up.

Shoulder Circles

Stand upright with your feet slightly farther than shoulder-width apart and your knees slightly bent. Raise your arms straight out to your sides (figure 2). Lift your shoulders back, down, and then up again to your ears in a smooth motion.

Figure 2   Shoulder circles.

Arm Swing

Stand upright with your feet slightly farther than shoulder-width apart and your knees slightly bent. Keep your back straight at all times. Swing both arms continuously to an overhead position and then forward, down, and back (figure 3). Swing both arms out to your sides and then cross them in front of your chest.

Figure 3   Arm swing.

Side Bend

Stand upright with your feet farther than shoulder-width apart, knees slightly bent, and hands resting on hips. Lift your trunk up and away from your hips. Bend smoothly first to one side (figure 4), then to the other, avoiding the tendency to lean either forward or backward. Use a slow rhythm, breathing out as you bend to the side and breathing in as you return to the center.

Figure 4   Side bend.

Hip Circle and Twist

With your hands on your hips and your feet spread wider than your shoulders, move your hips in clockwise circles (figure 5). Repeat with counterclockwise circles.

Extend your arms to either side. Twist your torso and hips to the left, shifting your weight onto your left foot. Then twist your torso to the right while shifting your weight to your right foot.

Figure 5   Hip circle.

Half Squat

Stand upright with good posture, holding your hands out in front of you for balance. Bend at the knees until your thighs are parallel to the floor (figure 6). Keep your back long throughout the movement and look straight ahead. Make sure that your knees always point in the same direction as your toes. Once at your lowest point, fully straighten your legs to return to your starting position. Use a smooth, controlled rhythm. Breathe in as you squat, and breathe out as you rise.

a

Figure 6 Half squat.

Leg Swing

Stand with your right side to the wall. Shift your weight onto your left leg. Place your right hand on the wall for balance. Swing your right leg forward and backward. Switch sides.

Now, turn to face the wall. Lean forward slightly and place both hands on the wall. Shift your weight onto your left leg. Swing your right leg to the left in front of your body, pointing your toes up as your foot reaches its furthest point (figure 7*a*). Then swing your right leg back to the right as far as is comfortable, again pointing your toes up as your foot reaches its highest point (figure 7*b*).

b

Figure 7 Leg swing.

Lunge

Stand upright with both feet together. Lunge forward with your right leg (figure 8). Lunge until your right thigh is parallel to the ground and your right lower leg is vertical to the ground. Spring back to the starting position, with both feet together. Repeat, lunging with your left leg.

Figure 8 Lunge.

Ankle Bounce

For a double-leg bounce (figure 9a), lean forward, with your hands on a wall and your weight on your toes. Raise and lower both heels rapidly (bounce). Each time you bounce, lift your heels a few inches off the ground while maintaining ground contact with the balls of your feet.

For a single-leg bounce, lean forward, with your hands on a wall and all of your weight on your left foot. Raise your right knee forward while pushing your left heel toward the ground. Then lower the right foot to the ground while raising the left heel (figure 9b). Repeat in a rapid, bouncy fashion.

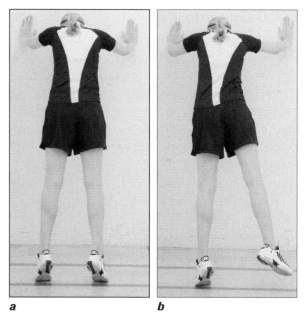

a   b

Figure 9 Ankle bounce: *(a)* double-leg; *(b)* single-leg.

Static Stretching

Static stretches cool down muscles, remove lactic acid, and get muscles ready for the next day's workout. Static stretching involves relaxing the muscles by reaching the maximum range of motion and holding the stretch.

When performing static stretches, follow these guidelines:

- Do not force the movement or lose control of the movement.
- Gradually increase the range of movement.
- Breathe easily while performing the exercises.
- Hold static stretches for 20 seconds.

Biceps Stretch

Stand upright, with your feet slightly farther than shoulder-width apart and your knees slightly bent. Hold your arms out to your sides, parallel to the ground, with palms facing forward. Rotate your hands so the palms face the rear. Stretch your arms back as far as possible (figure 10). You should feel the stretch across your chest and in the biceps.

Figure 11 Shoulder stretch.

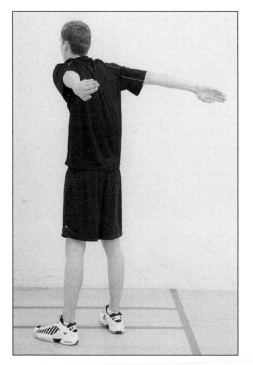

Figure 10 Biceps stretch.

Shoulder Stretch

Stand upright, with your feet slightly farther than shoulder-width apart and your knees slightly bent. Keeping your right arm parallel to the ground, bring it across the front of your chest. Bend your left arm and use your left forearm to ease your right arm closer to your chest (figure 11). You will feel a stretch in your shoulder. Repeat with your left arm.

Shoulder and Triceps Stretch

Stand upright, with your feet slightly farther than shoulder-width apart and your knees slightly bent. Lift both hands above your head. Lower your hands behind your neck and press your palms together (figure 12). Pull your shoulders down. You will feel the stretch in your shoulders and your triceps.

Figure 12 Shoulder and triceps stretch.

Hamstring Stretch

Sit on the ground, with both legs straight out in front of you. Bend the left leg and place your left foot alongside the knee of your right leg. Bend forward over the outstretched leg, keeping your back as straight as possible (figure 13). You will feel a stretch in the hamstrings of the right leg. Repeat with your left leg.

Figure 13 Hamstring stretch.

Calf Stretch

Stand upright, with one leg in front of the other and your hands flat against a wall at shoulder height. Ease your back leg farther away from the wall, keeping it straight, and press your heel firmly into the floor (figure 14). Keep your hips facing the wall and the rear leg and spine in a straight line. You will feel a stretch in the calf of your rear leg. Repeat with the other leg.

Figure 14 Calf stretch.

Hip and Thigh Stretch

Stand upright, with your feet farther than shoulder-width apart. Turn your feet and face to the right. Gradually lower your torso toward your right knee (figure 15). Place your hands on your leg to maintain your balance. You will feel a stretch along the front of your left thigh and along the hamstrings of your right leg. Repeat in the other direction by turning and facing left.

Figure 15 Hip and thigh stretch.

Adductor Stretch

Stand upright, with your feet farther than shoulder-width apart. Bend your right leg and lower your body (figure 16). Keep your back straight. Place your hands on your thighs to maintain your balance. You will feel the stretch in the adductor of your left leg. Repeat in the other direction, bending your left leg.

Figure 16 Adductor stretch.

Groin Stretch

Sit with an upright posture. Ease both of your feet toward your body and place the soles of your feet together, allowing your knees to come up and out to the sides (figure 17). Resting your hands on your lower legs or ankles, ease both knees toward the ground. You will feel the stretch along the insides of your thighs and groin.

Figure 17 Groin stretch.

Iliotibial Band Stretch

Sit upright, with your legs stretched out in front of you. Bend your left knee and place your left foot on the ground to the right side of your right knee. Turn your shoulders so that you are facing to the left. With your right arm, push against your left knee to ease you farther around (figure 18). Place your left hand on the floor for support. You will feel the stretch along the length of your spine and in the muscles around your left hip. Repeat on the other side, bending the right knee and placing the right foot next to the left knee.

Figure 18 Iliotibial band stretch.

Quadriceps Stretch

Lie facedown on the floor, resting your forehead on your right hand. Press your hips firmly into the floor and bring your left foot up toward your buttocks. With your left hand, grab your left foot and ease it closer to your buttocks (figure 19). Repeat with your right leg. You will feel the stretch along the front of your thigh.

Figure 19 Quadriceps stretch.

RESOURCES

Governing Bodies

USA Racquetball (USAR): www.usra.org

International Racquetball Federation (IRF): www.internationalracquetball.com

General Equipment Manufacturers

E-Force: www.eforce.com

Ektelon: www.ektelon.com

Head: www.head.com

Wilson: www.wilson.com

◧ Key to Diagrams

⟶	Player movement
- - - - - →	Ball movement
P, A, B, C	Player
S	Server
R	Receiver
○	First bounce
●	Second bounce
X	Bounce off wall or ceiling
A, B	Teams for doubles

Forehand

Mechanics are the foundation that every sport is built on. Without proper mechanics, an athlete would struggle to find the finesse, power, speed, and efficiency to execute any given motion or task. Proper mechanics also help prevent nonimpact injuries, leading to longer, more efficient, and higher-quality training periods and, ultimately, improved and more consistent performance.

The basic forehand and backhand strokes are the foundation of racquetball. All shots evolve from these two strokes in one form or another. It is hard to say which is used more. The answer depends on a given player's skill level as well as his or her particular strengths and weaknesses. What is certain, however, is that you cannot play the game of racquetball without both strokes.

The forehand is the first stroke taught because it is usually the easiest to learn. This is primarily because most people have thrown a ball or swung a bat, which are mechanically the same as the forehand stroke. The majority of all serves are hit with the forehand. Virtually every forehand shot, with the exception of the forehand ceiling ball, is hit with the same basic mechanics.

Power is extremely important in racquetball. The typical amateur player can hit a forehand shot around 125 to 150 miles (200 to 240 kilo-meters) per hour. Pro players can hit around 150 to 175 miles (240 to 280 kilometers) per hour. You will be able to hit a forehand harder than a backhand due to the mechanics involved and where the ball is contacted in relationship to your body.

The great power generated using the forehand stroke does come with a downside: If the stroke is not executed properly, you will eventually fall victim to elbow tendonitis or rotator cuff injury, as well as possible back problems. So, learning to perform the mechanics right should be your first priority.

As with any sport, racquetball has gone through an evolution in its mechanics, particularly in the past 10 years. Racquets are now longer, wider, lighter, and stronger, and they feature a larger hitting surface. Strings have become more structurally advanced, as well as more stable, stronger, softer, and thinner. Balls are now lighter, stronger, faster, more consistent, and available in a variety of colors.

Training techniques and equipment have evolved as well. Athletes can now train harder, longer, faster, and more efficiently than ever before.

The use of video and computers has also helped athletes improve much faster than ever before. In every sport, digital video is used to help athletes perfect mechanics; in fact, video is now the foundation for all sports mechanics. Whenever an athlete wants to improve mechanics, it is done with video analysis. With the advent of digital video, you can make a video of your mechanics, review it instantly, make corrections on the spot, and work on perfecting your strokes. Video analysis is the easiest and fastest way to see, correct, and improve mechanics.

While a trained, critical eye is often needed to see the subtleties and make the finite corrections required at the advanced level, the rookie player can still benefit from video analysis without the assistance of a trained coach or instructor. Using a video camera along with this book will give you the opportunity to see your mechanics and make some of the changes necessary to advance your game quickly. So, if you have a video camera, use it to your advantage. Record your mechanics and practice sessions so you can see what you are doing and how you are hitting the ball. This will definitely help you improve your game.

Another critical step is visualization. A coach or instructor may be able to explain and demonstrate a drill or stroke, but if you are unable to visualize yourself doing it, you may not be able to accomplish it.

Visualization is also used as a practice technique when you are unable to get on the court and hit. Many high-level athletes use visualization when they are hurt and unable to practice. This keeps the mind in the game and assists with mental and muscle memory. One caveat: Though visualization may work very well in the short run, there is ultimately no substitute for physical practice.

Throughout the course of this book you will be asked to perform practice tasks and record your results. The use of a journal (a simple composition book) to record and track training progress is a fun and easy way to see your improvement. It also helps you see where you need to work on certain aspects of your game. I like using journals as a coach, because I can see the progress of my athletes without always being on the court with them. The journal is also a great way to take notes on coaching sessions and video reviews. Additionally, you can use it to keep notes on opponents you have played and will play in the future.

GRIP

The forehand grip is quite simple. If someone hands you the racquet, butt first and perpendicular to the floor, you would simply shake hands with the racquet handle. Another way to ensure you have a proper grip is to lay the racquet on the floor and pick it up as you would remove a frying pan from a stove. Your thumb and index finger will form a V (figure 1.1) on the racquet handle.

This grip allows a flat stroke using the proper out-and-around swing mechanics. Use a trigger-finger style of grip with the thumb above the middle finger and below the index finger. You will want a firm but not overly tight grip on the handle. Additionally, you will grip the handle as low as possible, with the little finger right on the bottom edge of the handle butt. This allows for a longer reach and unimpaired wrist flexion and extension, permitting you to hit the ball with more power.

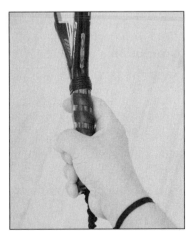

Figure 1.1 Forehand grip.

READY POSITION

The racquet should always be in the ready position (figure 1.2)—that is, in front of your body, with the racquet head up at about a 45-degree angle, your wrist at waist height, and the racquet face perpendicular to the floor and above your waist.

Figure 1.2   Forehand Ready Position

1. Hold racquet in front of body with wrist at waist height
2. Racquet head is up at 45-degree angle
3. Racquet face is perpendicular to floor
4. Racquet head is above waist
5. Body is in an athletic stance

Misstep

You have trouble getting the racquet up and ready to return the ball.

Correction

Keep the racquet in ready position. Don't let the racquet drop below your waist or to the side.

The most common error players make is not keeping the racquet in the ready position. Many players allow their racquet to drop to their dominant side or in front, with the racquet head nearly touching the floor, making it time-consuming and difficult to get the racquet up and ready for a hard-hit return from your opponent. If you have your racquet in the ready position, then when you turn to either the left or right the racquet will automatically be in position to return a ball without having to move it. Then with just a little adjustment, you will be able to get the racquet in the backswing position with minimal effort.

The key to a quick first step, as well as power and control, is your stance. Stand in an athletic position, always ready to receive the ball. This is the basic stance when you are neutral or not moving to the ball. The ready stance is similar to a basketball defensive position. Feet are slightly more than shoulder-width apart. Bend your knees and maintain a natural bend at the waist. Balance on the balls of your feet with your heels just lightly touching the floor. Knees need to be directly under your hips. When you set up to return the ball, your feet should be square to the side wall, which will allow you to execute shots with maximum power, control, and balance.

FOREHAND MOTION

The forehand stroke is likened to swinging a bat or throwing a baseball sidearm. As with swinging a bat, your arm is extended in order to generate the most power. At the point of contact with the ball, your wrist is snapped, again for maximum power. The racquetball swing is out and around, roughly like hitting a line drive in baseball rather than going for a home run.

The forehand motion begins with the backswing. Bring the racquet up from the ready position (don't drag the racquet) with your wrist slightly cocked so the racquet face is toward the side wall, close to a 45-degree angle (figure 1.3a), or facing the crack where the side wall and floor meet. Your elbow will be up slightly but below your shoulder and pointing toward the back wall, with a 90-degree angle at your elbow. Your wrist should be close to or level with your shoulder. Do not allow your wrist or elbow to be higher than your shoulder. This will place unnecessary stress on your shoulder and could eventually lead to shoulder problems.

From the backswing position, take a step toward the front wall. Your front foot points toward the corner of the front and side walls, at about a 45-degree angle to the front wall. Your elbow and back hip move forward and rotate together toward the oncoming ball (figure 1.3b).

Once your elbow and back hip begin the forward rotation, your back knee turns in toward the front wall, making it possible for your hips to continue rotating forward (figure 1.3c). Once your elbow drops and drives toward the ball along with your hips, the racquet head drops, pointing toward the back wall, and becomes perpendicular to the floor. As you continue to rotate, and your back hip, shoulder, and elbow come forward, the racquet head moves from behind you toward the ball in a flat, out-and-around swing parallel to the floor, with your wrist still in a flexed or cocked position (figure 1.3d).

Figure 1.3 — Forehand

BACKSWING

1. Bring racquet up from ready position
2. Wrist is cocked slightly
3. Elbow is up, slightly below shoulder
4. Elbow is bent at a 90-degree angle
5. Racquet face is toward side wall at about a 45-degree angle

a

STEP

1. Step toward front wall
2. Foot is at a 45-degree angle to front wall, pointing toward front corner
3. Elbow and back hip rotate forward

b

HIP ROTATION

1. Back knee turns in toward front wall
2. Hips continue forward rotation
3. Racquet head drops, pointing toward back wall

c

OUT-AND-AROUND SWING

1. Back hip, shoulder, and elbow rotate toward front wall
2. Racquet face moves toward ball
3. Swing in an out-and-around motion
4. Use flat swing with racquet parallel to floor
5. Keep wrist cocked
6. Snap wrist at ball contact

d

(continued)

Figure 1.3　*(continued)*

FOLLOW-THROUGH

1. Roll wrist forward
2. Arm and racquet continue around your body
3. Racquet ends behind your body with hand below shoulder
4. Balance weight evenly over both feet
5. Keep shoulders back, with back upright

e

To help you with the concepts of hitting out and around, staying balanced, and using your hips and shoulders to do the work rather than your arm, let's look at how a gate swings closed. The core of your body should act like a gatepost, with your dominant shoulder, elbow, and racquet acting as the gate. As the gate closes, or your arm swings around with the racquet to hit the ball, the post remains stationary. This means that once the gate closes, you continue to be balanced, as you were in your initial stance, with equal weight distributed on both feet.

The follow-through (figure 1.3e) is as important as the any other part of the stroke. Once you make contact with the ball, roll your wrist forward. This natural motion adds a slight top-spin to the ball, helping to keep the ball down after it contacts the front wall. Your hitting arm and the racquet continue around the front of your body, with your hips and shoulders facing the front wall. The racquet ends behind your body, at or below shoulder height, with the head of the racquet pointing toward the back wall. At this point you should be balanced, with equal weight distributed over both feet. If you are balanced with equal weight, you should be able to draw a fairly straight line from the top of your head through your midline to the floor. If you have more weight on your front foot, then you are too far forward and need to rotate more by pulling your nondominant shoulder back farther during rotation. Remember to rotate.

BALL CONTACT

Contact with the ball happens as the racquet comes out and around, eventually catching up with your back hip, shoulder, and elbow at the point of contact (figure 1.4). Your arm is extended, with little or no bend at your elbow. At the point of contact, your wrist is snapped forward, like snapping a whip, to produce maximum power. Additionally, both knees should be bent, with your back lower leg nearly parallel with the floor as you get low to hit the ball.

The hitting zone, or power zone, for the forehand is primarily between the inside of both knees (figure 1.5). Hitting the ball with a flat, out-and-around stroke in the middle of the power zone will send the ball directly back to where it came from, producing a straight shot. Hitting the ball with a flat, out-and-around stroke in the back of the power zone will cause the ball to go right (for a right-handed player) or left (for a left-handed player). Hitting the ball with a flat, out-and-around stroke forward in the power zone will direct the ball to the left (for a right-handed player) or right (for a left-handed player).

Keep your body at the proper distance from the ball to make contact in the sweet spot of the racquet. If you let the ball get too close to your

Figure 1.4 At contact, your arm is extended and both knees are bent.

Figure 1.5 The hitting, or power, zone for the forehand.

body during the swing, you will most likely raise your shoulder or turn your wrist, thereby pulling the ball up or pushing or slicing the ball out. You will also lose power in your stroke and make it difficult to remain balanced through the stroke, thus limiting your shot options. Conversely, if the ball is too far way from your body, you will overstep, bend at the waist, and reach to hit the ball, making it impossible to rotate your hips and shoulders properly. This will result in swinging primarily with your arm, causing you to become unbalanced, lose power, and reduce your shot options. You will have similar problems if the ball is too far behind the hitting zone or too far in front of the hitting zone.

FOOTWORK

Proper footwork is essential to making your mechanics work properly. If you cannot move to the ball and get your feet in the correct place, you will be unable to hit the ball with proper execution.

As you go through each of the forehand drills, you will use progressively skillful footwork to execute each shot. You will begin with a no-step drop-and-hit, then add a step, progress to a shuffle, and finally execute a crossover. Each drill is designed to help you learn how to move toward the ball and set up to execute the correct mechanical swing. These are the basic footwork drills. More footwork drills will be introduced later in the book.

FOREHAND DRILLS

There are a number of drills you can use to practice your forehand. I like to use a progression method that helps break down the total stroke into small pieces. Instead of trying to remember everything there is to know about the forehand and perform it immediately, you will do it in segments and concentrate on a given part of the task. As you finish one segment or task, you will add the next, and then the next, thereby building the entire stroke once you get to the end. Spending time learning the proper stroke mechanics from beginning to end will save you enormous frustration with all of the shots required in racquetball.

Visualization and evaluation are key mental factors to any athletic mechanical motion. Take time to visualize the task before you perform it and spend time evaluating it on its completion. Remember, it's not the amount of time you spend performing a task, it's the quality of your work. Perfect practice makes perfect strokes.

Perform 5 or 10 repetitions for each drill. Performing 10 repetitions will give you time to make adjustments and help build muscle memory. With the following forehand drills that are done on a court, begin in position FH1, then go to FH2, and finish with FH3 (figure 1.6). Repeat this sequence three times per drill, for a total of 3 sets of 10 repetitions at each position. Remember to record your results in your journal so you can monitor your progress.

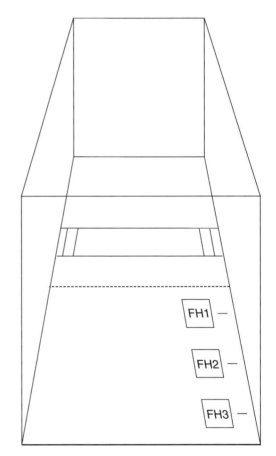

Figure 1.6 Three positions for the forehand hitting drills.

Forehand Drill 1.   *Mirror Drill*

This drill is a simple yet effective way to evaluate your stroke mechanics. It provides immediate feedback, helps build muscle memory, and can be done outside a court.

Stand in front of a mirror or large plate window. Go through the various steps of the forehand:

- Grip
- Racquet preparation
- Stance and balance
- Backswing
- Swing motion
- Ball contact
- Follow-through

As you go through each aspect of the forehand, watch your reflection and evaluate your body positioning and mechanics. Breaking the mechanics down into separate segments will make it easier to evaluate and correct errors. Once you're comfort-able with a segment, move to the next segment until you complete the entire stroke. After you go through each step, put it all together and watch your stroke in its entirety. Perform 10 repetitions of the full forehand stroke. You will need to slow your stroke in order to effectively evaluate your mechanics in the mirror. Record your evaluation and corrections in your journal.

Success Check

- For the grip, shake hands with the racquet handle. Your thumb and index finger form a V.
- Hold the racquet in ready position. Set your body in proper athletic stance.
- Execute the backswing, with elbow up and wrist cocked slightly, but with both elbow and wrist lower than the back shoulder.

- Complete an out-and-around swing, keeping your body balanced over both feet. Use the rotation of your hips and shoulders, not your arms, to generate power in the swing (close the gate).
- Stay low, with your knees bent.
- Follow through, continuing the natural rotation until the racquet is behind your body.

Score Your Success

Complete 10 repetitions of the full forehand stroke. Have a qualified observer, such as a coach or an experienced player, evaluate your technique.

    1 to 4 perfect forehand strokes = 1 point

    5 to 7 perfect forehand strokes = 3 points

    8 to 10 perfect forehand strokes = 5 points

    Your score ___

Forehand Drill 2.   Forehand Toss and Catch

This drill, done with a partner, helps you develop good footwork and eye–hand coordination. Begin by standing approximately 10 feet (3 meters) away from your partner. Your partner will have one racquetball in one hand. Stand in an athletic stance without a racquet. Your partner tosses the ball so it bounces off the floor to your forehand side. With your opposite-side (i.e., non-racquet-side) foot, step across your body and forward and catch the ball with your racquet hand (figure 1.7). Keep your eye on the ball and try to catch it in the power zone. Toss the ball so it bounces off the floor and back to your partner. Repeat.

To Decrease Difficulty

Use a wall instead of a partner. Toss the ball to the floor so it ricochets off the wall and back to the floor. Catch the ball.

Success Check

- Keep your eye on the ball.
- Step across your body and forward.
- Feet are in line with each other and squared up to the side wall.
- Catch the ball with your racquet hand in the power zone.

Figure 1.7 Forehand toss-and-catch drill with a partner.

Score Your Success

Give yourself points based on how many times out of 10 repetitions you caught the ball.

    1 to 3 times = 1 point

    4 to 7 times = 3 points

    8 to 10 times = 5 points

    Your score ___

Misstep

You are unable to catch the ball consistently.

Correction

Be sure you are focusing on the ball and watching it all the way into your hand. One of the biggest reasons for inconsistency in hitting a racquetball is failure to see the ball and racquet come together.

Forehand Drill 3.   *Drop and Hit*

Begin this drill by straddling the safety line (see the FH1 location in figure 1.6, page 8). This puts you up in the court closer to the front wall so you don't have to hit the ball so hard. Use the line as a reference for where to drop and hit in the power zone.

It's important to note a couple of safety issues before beginning the hitting drills. Be sure the wrist lanyard is securely fastened. Wear your eyewear. An unskilled player will not always be able to control the direction of the ball. Therefore, be prepared for the possibility that the ball will rebound off the front wall and hit you on the return.

All of the drills in this step are down-the-wall shots. All balls should be hit so the ball comes back to the ball-and-racquet contact location—in other words, the ball should travel a straight path to the front wall and back again.

Begin the drill by visualizing the stroke. Stand approximately 3 feet (1 meter) from the side wall and straddle the safety line, with the line centered between your feet. Check your grip and move the racquet into ready position. Get into your ready stance. Initiate the backswing. Drop the ball at arm's length so that it bounces on the safety line. This puts the ball in the middle of the power zone. Keeping your eye on the ball, begin your swinging

motion. With your knees bent and our body in a balanced position contact the ball (figure 1.8). Hold your pose at the end of the follow-through. Complete 10 repetitions.

Figure 1.8 Drop and hit. Make contact with the ball in the middle of the power zone.

Misstep

The ball hits the floor (skips) before hitting the front wall.

Correction

Raise the aimed ball-contact point on the front wall; it may be too low. Stay low in your stance and stroke, hitting out and around, not up and down. Make sure the racquet face is perpendicular to the floor, not closed or turned down, when you make contact with the ball. At the point of contact, make sure your shoulders are level in relation to your arm and racquet.

Success Check

- Use a flat, out-and-around forehand stroke.
- Bend your knees and stay low.
- The ball bounces straight off the racquet and hits the front wall at about the same height as the point of contact with the racquet.
- The ball comes directly back to the ball-and-racquet contact point.
- Your weight is evenly balanced throughout the stroke.
- Your body is balanced during the follow-through.

Score Your Success

Give yourself points based on how many times out of 10 repetitions the ball came straight back in the general location of where you hit the ball. In other words, did you hit a down-the-wall shot?

1 to 3 times = 1 point

4 to 7 times = 3 points

8 to 10 times = 5 points

Your score ___

Forehand Drill 4. *Step and Hit*

This drill is similar to the drop and hit, except that you add a step toward the ball. If you are right handed, place your left foot on the safety line (location FH1 in figure 1.6, page 8); if you are left handed, place your right foot on the safety line. When you toss the ball on the safety line at arm's length while stepping forward, the ball will be in the power zone.

Begin by visualizing the drill and the stroke. Place your left foot (if right handed) or right foot (if left handed) on the safety line. Check your grip and prepare your racquet. Get into your ready stance. Initiate the backswing. Step forward (not across) to hit the ball (figure 1.9). The heel of your front foot should be in line with the heel of your back foot. Drop the ball at arm's length on the safety line in the power zone. Keep your eye on the ball and begin the swinging motion. Make contact with the ball at a height between your waist and knees. Hold your pose at the end of the follow-through.

Figure 1.9 Step and hit. Step forward to hit the ball.

Success Check

- Use a flat, out-and-around forehand stroke.
- The ball bounces straight off the racquet and hits the front wall at about the same height as the point of contact with the racquet.
- The ball comes directly back to the ball-and-racquet contact point.
- Your weight is evenly balanced throughout the stroke.
- Your body is balanced during the follow-through.
- The heel of your front foot is in line (from frontcourt to backcourt) with the toe of your back foot.
- The toe of your front foot is at a 45-degree angle to the front wall, pointing toward the corner.

Score Your Success

Give yourself points based on how many times out of 10 repetitions the ball comes back down the wall.

1 to 3 times = 1 point

4 to 7 times = 3 points

8 to 10 times = 5 points

Your score ___

Misstep

The ball hits the back wall before the first bounce as it ricochets off the front wall, or the first bounce is deep in the backcourt.

Correction

Lower the aimed ball-contact point on the front wall; it may be too high. Stay low and hit out and around. Make sure the racquet face is perpendicular to the floor, not open or turned up, upon contact with the ball. Make sure your shoulders are level in relationship to your hitting arm and racquet.

Forehand Drill 5.   Shuffle and Hit

This drill will help you begin to use footwork to adjust your position while preparing to hit the ball. Begin with one foot 12 to 14 inches (30 to 36 centimeters) behind the safety line (the FH1 location in figure 1.6, page 8). The foot just behind the line is your front foot. Bring your back foot up to your front foot and then step forward with your front foot while tossing the ball out and forward on the safety line (figure 1.10). Hit the ball. It may take some practice to get the toss in the right location. The shuffle movement is similar to doing a side-to-side defensive shuffle in basketball. A key point to remember in this drill is to keep one foot on the floor at all times. This is not a hop; it is a shuffle.

Begin by visualizing the drill and the stroke. Check your grip and prepare the racquet. Get into ready stance. Initiate the backswing. Step forward (not across) to hit the ball. The heel of your front

Figure 1.10 Shuffle and hit. Toss the ball out and forward on the safety line.

foot should be in line with the toe of your back foot. Toss the ball forward, out, and away to put the ball in the power zone by the time you finish your step forward. Keep your eye on the ball as you begin your swinging motion. Bend your knees and stay low. Make contact with the ball at a height between your waist and knees. Hold your pose at the end of the follow-through. Complete 10 repetitions.

Success Check

- Use a flat, out-and-around forehand stroke.
- The ball bounces straight off the racquet and hits the front wall at about the same height as the point of contact with the racquet.
- The ball comes directly back to the ball-and-racquet contact point.
- Your weight is evenly balanced throughout the stroke.

- Your body is balanced during the follow-through.
- The heel of your front foot is in line (from frontcourt to backcourt) with the toe of your back foot.
- The toe of your front foot is at a 45-degree angle to the front wall, pointing toward the corner.

Score Your Success

Give yourself points based on how many times out of 10 repetitions the ball comes back down the wall.

1 to 3 times = 1 point

4 to 7 times = 3 points

8 to 10 times = 5 points

Your score ____

Misstep

The ball goes out and away from you at an angle toward the side wall or it hits the side wall.

Correction

Be sure your racquet face isn't angled out when you make contact with the ball. Hit the ball in the middle of the power zone instead of back in the power zone. Make sure your wrist snap is timed correctly. If the ball is angling away from you, your wrist snap may be too late.

Forehand Drill 6.   *Step Over and Hit*

In this drill, you begin by facing the front wall, then turn, squaring off to the side wall, step forward, and hit the ball. Facing the front wall, stand on the safety line. With your racquet and body in the ready position, turn to the right (if right handed) or the left (if left handed) by pivoting on your back foot. As you turn, bring your racquet from ready position to backswing position. At the same time, toss the ball out and forward between the safety line and short line while stepping toward the front wall to hit the ball. It will take some practice to get the toss in the right location. Possible problems in this drill include tossing the ball too far to the side and stepping over so far as to overreach to hit the ball, bending over and over reaching to hit the ball, or tossing the ball too far forward toward the front wall. Make sure you are stepping forward

toward the front wall and making contact in the power zone.

Begin the drill by visualizing the drill and the stroke. Check your grip, prepare the racquet, and get into your ready stance. Turn toward the side wall and initiate the backswing. Square off to the side wall. Step forward toward the front wall (not across) to hit the ball. The heel of your front foot should be in line with the toe of your back foot. Toss the ball forward, out, and away during your step forward to put the ball in the power zone for contact with the racquet during your swing. Keep your eye on the ball as you begin the swinging motion. Make contact with the ball at a height between your waist and knees. Hold your pose at the end of the follow-through. Complete 10 repetitions.

Success Check

- Use a flat, out-and-around forehand stroke.
- The ball bounces straight off the racquet and hits the front wall at about the same height as the point of contact with the racquet.
- The ball comes directly back to the ball-and-racquet contact point.
- Your weight is evenly balanced throughout the stroke.
- Your body is balanced during the follow-through.
- The heel of your front foot is in line (from frontcourt to backcourt) with the toe of your back foot.

- The toe of your front foot is at a 45-degree angle to the front wall, pointing toward the corner.

Score Your Success

Give yourself points based on how many times out of 10 repetitions the ball comes back down the wall.

1 to 3 times = 1 point

4 to 7 times = 3 points

8 to 10 times = 5 points

Your score ___

Misstep

The ball goes across the court or cross-court and behind you.

Correction

Be sure your racquet face isn't angled cross-court when you make contact with the ball. Hit the ball in the middle of the power zone instead of at the front of the power zone. Make sure your wrist snap is timed correctly. If the ball is moving across the court, your wrist snap may be too early.

SUCCESS SUMMARY OF FOREHAND

Now that you have completed step 1 of *Racquetball: Steps to Success*, you should have a good foundation on which to build the rest of the success step skills. You should be able to pick up a racquet and immediately grip the handle in a forehand grip. You should also have a good visual, mental, and verbal understanding of the forehand mechanics and how to adjust for inconsistencies in your stroke. All of these will carry over into the next steps as you progress. You will find the mechanics of the backhand stroke to be similar to those of the forehand. Here are several success tips to think about:

- Keep your shoulders square to the front wall unless you are getting into position to hit a ball, in which case you square up to the side wall for the shot.
- Always keep your racquet in the ready position when waiting for your opponent's return.
- Always watch the ball and the racquet come together.

Review your drill scores, enter them here, and tally them to rate your forehand success.

Forehand Drills

1	Mirror Drill	___ out of 5
2.	Forehand Toss and Catch	___ out of 5
3.	Drop and Hit	___ out of 5
4.	Step and Hit	___ out of 5
5.	Shuffle and Hit	___ out of 5
6.	Step Over and Hit	___ out of 5
Total		___ *out of 30*

If you scored fewer than 20 points, review the drills that gave you trouble. If you scored 20 points or more, you are ready to move on to step 2, Backhand.

Backhand

The backhand seems to be the one stroke that most beginners shy away from. Perhaps that's because they have never been properly introduced to it. An improper introduction has caused the backhand to be the weakest part of most every intermediate player's game. Most players simply have never learned how to hit the backhand properly or have never been empowered with the tools to improve it.

Nearly everyone has thrown a Frisbee at one time or another. The motion and mechanics for throwing a Frisbee are almost identical to those of the backhand racquetball stroke. The Frisbee is thrown with a flat, out-and-around motion, with a wrist snap (extension) at the release and follow-through. The backhand stroke, of course, involves no release, but there is a wrist snap at ball contact as well as a follow-through with the racquet.

Your backhand will define you as a player, either as one who is strong and formidable or one who has an obvious, easily exploited weakness. Now is the time to decide that you will conquer the backhand demon and tame it to your advantage.

You will notice many similarities between the backhand stroke and the forehand stroke you learned in step 1. Don't disregard the repetition here. Many aspects of the forehand stroke and skill similarities are repeated in this step, but remember this: Perfect practice makes perfect strokes, and perfect repetition is the foundation.

GRIP

The backhand grip is different from the forehand grip. One way to get the backhand grip right is to place the racquet on your nondominant hip, with the handle facing forward like the handle of a sword. Reach over with your dominant hand and draw the sword out of the scabbard. Your thumb and index finger will form a V on the racquet handle (figure 2.1).

This grip enables the same flat stroke that marks the forehand, using the proper out-and-around swing mechanics. As with the forehand, use the trigger-finger grip, with your thumb above your middle finger and below your index finger. There is, however, a slight difference in rotation of the grip handle (see figure 2.1). You will want a firm grip but not an overly tight one. As with the forehand, grip the racquet handle as low as possible, with your little finger right on

Figure 2.1 The backhand grip.

the bottom edge of the handle butt. This gives you a longer reach and unimpaired wrist flexion and extension, permitting you to hit the ball with more power.

READY POSITION

The athletic ready stance does not change from the forehand. The racquet must always be in the ready position (figure 2.2)—in front of your body, with the racquet head up at about a 45-degree angle, perpendicular to the floor and above your waist. The primary difference

with the backhand stance is that the racquet is in the backhand grip. This grip is always the grip of choice when in the neutral position because most balls will be hit to the backhand side of the court, especially if you are a weak backhand player.

Figure 2.2 | Backhand Ready Position

1. Hold racquet in front of body in backhand grip
2. Racquet head is up at 45-degree angle
3. Racquet face is perpendicular to floor
4. Racquet head is above waist
5. Body is in an athletic ready stance

Misstep

You are slow in getting the racquet up and into the ready position.

Correction

Keep the racquet in the ready position at all times when waiting for your opponent to hit the ball. Don't let the racquet fall below your waist or to your side.

Keeping the racquet in the ready position is extremely important. A common mistake made by most players is allowing the racquet head to move toward the floor, thus requiring the racquet to travel nearly twice as far to get into the backswing position. If the racquet is in ready position, you will be able to move it quickly into position when you turn to the backhand side and prepare to return a ball.

From the ready stance, it is easy to make a quick first step resulting in good power and control. You should be in the athletic position and always ready to receive the ball. Remember, this is the basic stance when you are neutral, or not moving to the ball. The ready stance is similar to a baseball shortstop's defensive position when waiting for the batter to hit the ball. Your feet should be slightly more than shoulder-width apart. Bend your knees and have a natural bend at the waist. Stay balanced on the balls of your feet, with your heels just lightly touching the floor. Your knees need to be directly under your hips. Your feet should be square to the side wall once you turn to the backhand side, which will allow you to execute your shots with maximum power, control, and balance.

BACKHAND MOTION

For the backswing, bring the racquet up from the ready position, with your wrist relaxed so that the head of the racquet is up and the face of the racquet is toward the crack between the back wall and the side wall (figure 2.3a). Your elbow should be at or just below your dominant shoulder, pointing in the direction of the ball in a line from your wrist to your elbow. Your wrist should be close to or level with your nondominant shoulder. Do not allow your wrist or elbow to be higher than your shoulder. This will place unnecessary stress on your shoulder, could create possible shoulder problems in the future, and may contribute to a pendulum (up-and-down) swing. You want to swing out and around to hit the ball, not up and down. Your shoulders should be turned slightly toward the back corner.

Figure 2.3   Backhand

a

READY POSITION

1. Athletic stance
2. Racquet up
3. Weight on balls of feet

BACKSWING

1. Raise racquet from ready position
2. Keep racquet head up
3. Elbow is up, just below dominant shoulder
4. Elbow is bent at 90-degree angle
5. Wrist is level with or just below and near nondominant shoulder
6. Racquet face is toward back corner and above shoulder

c

STEP AND HIP ROTATION

1. Step toward front wall
2. Foot is at 45-degree angle to front wall
3. Begin to turn back knee toward front wall
4. Elbow and hip begin to rotate forward

d

e

OUT-AND-AROUND SWING

1. Back hip, shoulder, and elbow rotate forward
2. Racquet head is perpendicular to floor
3. Elbow is extended, and racquet moves toward ball
4. Swing out and around
5. Stay low with knees bent
6. Racquet moves parallel to floor
7 Wrist is cocked back

BALL CONTACT

1. Contact ball just inside front knee
2. Snap wrist forward at ball contact
3. Keep eye on ball
4. Arm is at full extension

f

FOLLOW-THROUGH

1. Keep racquet flat
2. Stay low with knees bent
3. Arm and racquet continue around in front of body
4. Racquet ends just behind body, at full extension and shoulder height
5. Balance and weight are even, with shoulders back and centered over body midline
6. Shoulders are level

The swing begins with the racquet in the back-swing position and a step toward the front wall (figure 2.3b). Your front foot points toward the corner of the front wall and side wall at about a 45-degree angle to the front wall. Your elbow and back hip move forward together toward the oncoming ball. Once your elbow and back hip begin the forward motion, your back knee turns in toward the front wall, making it possible for your hips to continue rotating forward.

When your elbow drives toward the ball along with your hips, the racquet head drops, pointing toward the back wall, and becomes perpendicular to the floor (figure 2.3c). Now, as you continue to rotate, your back hip, shoulder, and elbow come forward. The racquet head moves from behind you toward the ball in a flat, out-and-around swing that is parallel to the floor (figure 2.3d). Your wrist is still cocked back.

The backhand swing uses the same biomechanical motion as throwing a Frisbee or snapping a towel. Your arm must be at full extension in order to get the most power. The wrist snap at the point of contact with the ball creates maximum power (figure 2.3e). The backhand swing in racquetball is out and around, not up and down.

The follow-through (figure 2.3f) is as important as any other part of the stroke. Once ball contact is made, the racquet face remains flat and perpendicular to the floor. Your hitting arm and racquet continue around the front of your body, with your hips and shoulders facing the front wall. The racquet ends slightly behind the hitting shoulder at or below shoulder height. The face of the racquet faces the opposite side wall. At this point you should be balanced, with weight distributed equally between both feet. If you are balanced with equal weight, you should be able to draw a fairly straight line from the top of your head through your midline to the floor and your shoulders are level. If you have more weight on your front foot, then you are too far forward and need to rotate more by pulling your dominant shoulder back farther during rotation.

BALL CONTACT

Remember the gate analogy from step 1? The core of your body is like the gatepost; your dominant shoulder, elbow, and racquet are like the gate. Ball contact occurs as the gate closes, with the racquet coming out and around and eventually catching up with your back hip, shoulder, and elbow at the point of contact with the ball (figure 2.4). Your arm will be at full extension, with little or no bend in your elbow. At the point of contact, snap your wrist forward, as if you were snapping a towel, to produce maximum power. Bend both knees. Your back lower leg should be nearly parallel to the floor as you get low to hit the ball.

The midpoint of the hitting, or power, zone for the backhand is on the inside thigh of your front leg (figure 2.5). Hitting the ball with a flat, out-and-around stroke in the middle of the power zone will create a straight shot to the front wall, bringing the ball directly back (off the front wall) to the location where you hit it. Hitting the ball with a flat, out-and-around stroke in the back of the power zone will cause the ball to go left

Figure 2.4 Ball contact during the backhand.

(for a right-handed player) or right (for a left-handed player). Hitting the ball with a flat, out-and-around stroke forward in the power zone, or in front of the forward knee, will make the ball go right (for a right-handed player) or left (for a left-handed player).

Ball proximity for the backhand is virtually the same as for the forehand, with one exception: During the backhand, the ball will be closer to your body, since your dominant arm must cross your body at ball contact.

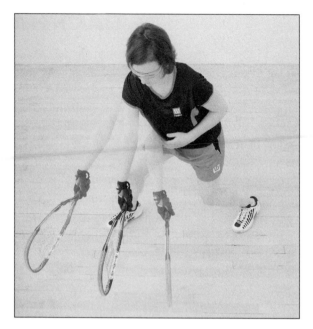

Figure 2.5 The hitting, or power, zone for the backhand.

FOOTWORK

Footwork for the backhand is largely the same as for the forehand. The only difference is that if you are right handed, you turn left for the backhand instead of right. If you are left handed, you turn right for the backhand instead of left. The footwork for stepping forward, to the side, or to the back is the same for the backhand and forehand.

Many of the drills for the backhand are also similar to those for the forehand. You will find drills incorporating footwork throughout the book. Again, repetition is necessary for muscle memory. Don't forget: Perfect practice makes perfect strokes.

BACKHAND DRILLS

Don't be concerned about remembering everything about the backhand stroke all at once; as with step 1, it is broken down so you learn it in a progressive method. Finish one segment, then move on to the next, building the entire stroke once all the segments are completed. Spending time learning the proper stroke mechanics from beginning to end will save you enormous frustration with all of the shots required in racquetball.

Be sure to visualize and evaluate each sequence in every drill, just as you did with the forehand. After each sequence, evaluate your performance. Remember, it's not the amount of time you spend performing a task—it's the quality of your work.

Perform 5 to 10 repetitions in each drill. Performing 10 repetitions gives you time to make adjustments and help build muscle memory. With the following backhand drills, begin in position BH1, then go to BH2, and finish with BH3 (figure 2.6). Repeat this sequence three times per drill, for a total of 3 sets of 10 repetitions at each position. Remember to record your results in your journal so you can monitor your progress.

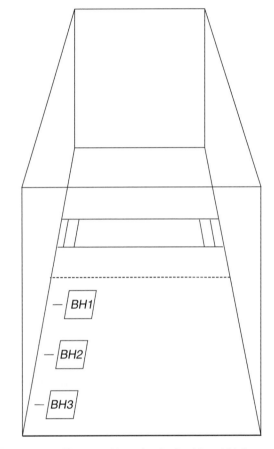

Figure 2.6 Three positions for the backhand hitting drills.

Backhand Drill 1.   *Mirror Drill*

This simple yet effective drill will help you evaluate your stroke mechanics without needing an instructor or camera. The three best things about this drill are the immediate feedback, the creation of muscle memory, and the convenience—it can be done outside a court.

Stand in front of a mirror or large plate window. Go through the various steps of the backhand:

- Grip
- Racquet preparation
- Stance and balance
- Backswing

- Swing motion
- Ball contact
- Follow-through

Just as you did with the forehand, watch your reflection and evaluate your body positioning and mechanics as you go through each segment of the stroke. Once each segment is mastered, move to the next step until you complete the entire stroke. After you have gone through all of the segments, you can put them together and see the stroke in its entirety. Slow down your stroke in order to evaluate your mechanics in the mirror.

Success Check

- For the grip, pull the racquet out of the imaginary scabbard from the nondominant side, as you would a sword. Thumb and index finger form a V.

- Place the racquet in the ready position. Set your body in the proper ready position.

- Perform the backswing, with your dominant wrist at shoulder height and your elbow at or just below shoulder height.

- Implement the out-and-around swing, keeping your balance even over both feet. Produce power by rotating your hips and shoulders instead of using your arm.

- Stay low with your knees bent.

- Follow through, using the rotation until the racquet is behind your body and you are facing forward.

Score Your Success

Compete 10 repetitions of the full backhand stroke. Have a qualified observer, such as a coach or an experienced player, evaluate your technique.

1 to 4 perfect backhand strokes = 1 point

5 to 7 perfect backhand strokes = 3 points

8 to 10 perfect backhand strokes = 5 points

Your score ___

Backhand Drill 2.   Backhand Toss and Catch

This drill, done with a partner, helps you develop good footwork and eye–hand coordination. Stand approximately 10 feet (3 meters) away from your partner, who holds one racquetball in one hand. Stand in an athletic stance but without a racquet. Your partner tosses the ball so it bounces off the floor to your backhand side. Pivot on your nondominant foot. Step forward with your dominant foot and catch the ball with your dominant (racquet) hand (figure 2.7). Toss the ball so it bounces off the floor and back to your partner. Keep your eye on the ball and try to catch it in the power zone.

To Decrease Difficulty

Use a wall instead of a partner. Toss the ball to the floor so it ricochets off the wall back to the floor. Catch the ball.

Success Check

- Keep your eye on the ball.
- Pivot and step forward.
- Catch the ball with your dominant (racquet) hand in the power zone.

Figure 2.7 Backhand toss-and-catch drill with a partner.

Score Your Success

Give yourself points based on how many times out of 10 repetitions you caught the ball.

1 to 3 times = 1 point

4 to 7 times = 3 points

8 to 10 times = 5 points

Your score ___

Misstep

You are unable to catch the ball consistently.

Correction

Focus on the ball and watch it all the way into your hand. One of the most common reasons for inconsistency in hitting a racquetball is failure to see the ball and racquet come together.

Backhand Drill 3. *Drop and Hit*

Begin this drill by straddling the safety line (see the BH1 location in figure 2.6, page 24), with the safety line just inside of your forward or dominant thigh. This puts you up in the court closer to the front wall so you won't have to hit the ball so hard. Use the line as a reference for where to drop and hit in the power zone.

Safety issues are the same as with the forehand. Be sure the wrist lanyard is securely fastened. Wear your eyewear. An unskilled player will not always be able to control the direction of the ball. Therefore, be prepared for the possibility that the ball will rebound off the front wall and hit you on the return.

All of the drills in this step are down-the-wall shots. All balls should be hit so the ball comes back off the front wall to the ball-and-racquet contact location—in other words, the ball should travel on a straight path to the front wall and back again.

Begin the drill by visualizing the stroke. Straddle the safety line, with the line on the inside of your front thigh or just inside your front knee. Check your grip and prepare the racquet. Get into the ready stance. Initiate the backswing. Gently toss the ball with your nondominant hand at arm's length on the safety line (figure 2.8). This puts the ball in the middle of the power zone. Keeping your eye on the ball, begin your swinging motion. After the ball bounces off the floor, hit it at its peak, or on its way back down, at a height between your waist and knees. Remember to stay low and bend your knees. Hold your pose at the end of the follow-through. Complete 10 repetitions.

Success Check

• Use a flat, out-and-around backhand stroke.
• Bend your knees and stay low.

Figure 2.8 Drop and hit. While in ready position, drop the ball on the safety line.

• The ball bounces straight off the racquet and hits the front wall at about the same height as the point of contact with the racquet.
• The ball comes directly back to the ball-and-racquet contact point.
• Your weight is balanced throughout the stroke.
• Your body is balanced at the completion of the follow-through.

Score Your Success

Give yourself points based on how many times out of 10 repetitions the ball comes back down the wall.

1 to 3 times = 1 point
4 to 7 times = 3 points
8 to 10 times = 5 points
Your score ___

Misstep

The ball hits the floor (skips) before contacting the front wall.

Correction

Raise the aimed ball-contact point on the front wall; it may be too low. Stay low in your stance and stroke, hitting out and around, not up and down. Make sure the racquet face is perpendicular to the floor, not closed or turned down, when you make contact with the ball. At the point of contact, make sure your shoulders are level in relation to your arm and racquet.

Backhand Drill 4.   *Step and Hit*

This drill is similar to the backhand drop and hit, except that you add a step forward when hitting the ball. If you are right handed, place your right foot approximately 2 to 4 inches (5 to 10 centimeters) behind the safety line (location BH1 in figure 2.6, page 24); if you are left handed, place your left foot in the same location. Toss the ball on the safety line while stepping forward and over the safety line. The ball will be in the power zone.

Begin by visualizing the drill and the stroke. Place your right foot (if right handed) or left foot (if left handed) next to the safety line. Check your grip and prepare your racquet. Get into the ready stance and initiate the backswing. Toss the ball at arm's length on the safety line in the power zone. Step forward over the safety line. The heel of your front foot should be in line (from frontcourt to backcourt) with the toe of your back foot. Keep your eye on the ball and begin your swinging motion. Bend your knees and stay low. Contact the ball between your waist and knees. Hold your pose at the end of the follow-through.

Success Check

- Use a flat, out-and-around forehand stroke.
- Bend your knees and stay low.

- The ball bounces straight off the racquet and hits the front wall at about the same height as the point of contact with the racquet.
- The ball comes directly back to the ball-and-racquet contact point.
- Your weight is evenly balanced throughout the stroke.
- Your body is balanced during the follow-through.
- The heel of your front foot is in line (from frontcourt to backcourt) with the toe of your back foot.
- The toe of your front foot is at a 45-degree angle to the front wall, pointing toward the corner.

Score Your Success

Give yourself points based on how many times out of 10 repetitions the ball comes back down the wall.

1 to 3 times = 1 point

4 to 7 times = 3 points

8 to 10 times = 5 points

Your score ___

Misstep

The ball hits the back wall when ricocheting off the front wall before the first bounce, or the first bounce is deep in the backcourt.

Correction

Lower the aimed ball-contact point on the front wall; it may be too high. Stay low and hit out and around. Make sure the racquet face is perpendicular to the floor, not open or turned up, on contact with the ball. Make sure your shoulders are level.

Backhand Drill 5.   *Shuffle and Hit*

This drill is the same as the forehand shuffle and hit. Begin with your forward foot about 8 to 10 inches (20 to 25 centimeters) behind the safety line (see the BH1 location in figure 2.6, page 24). The foot just behind the line is the dominant foot. Bring your back foot up to your front foot, then step forward with your front foot. Toss the ball out and forward on the safety line and hit the ball. It may take some practice to get the toss in the right location. The shuffle movement (figure 2.9) is similar to doing a side-to-side defensive shuffle drill in basketball. A key point to remember in this drill is to keep one foot on the floor at all times. This is not a hop; it is a shuffle.

Visualize the drill and the stroke. Check your grip and prepare the racquet. Get into the athletic ready stance; square off to the side wall. Initiate the backswing. Toss the ball out and away on the safety line so as to put the ball in the power zone at the end of the shuffle. Shuffle and step forward, not across. The heel of your front foot should be in line (from frontcourt to backcourt) with the toe of your back foot. Keep your eye on the ball. Begin your swinging motion. Bend your knees and stay low. Make contact with the ball at a height between your waist and knees. Hold your pose at the end of the follow-through.

Success Check

- Use a flat, out-and-around forehand stroke.
- Bend your knees and stay low.
- The ball bounces straight off the racquet and hits the front wall at about the same

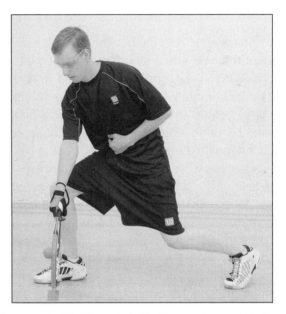

Figure 2.9 Shuffle and hit. Shuffle your feet and hit the ball.

height as the point of contact with the racquet.

- The ball comes directly back to the ball-and-racquet contact point.
- Your weight is evenly balanced throughout the stroke.
- Your body is balanced during the follow-through.
- The heel of your front foot is in line (from frontcourt to backcourt) with the toe of your back foot.
- The toe of your front foot is at a 45-degree angle to the front wall, pointing toward the corner.

Score Your Success

Give yourself points based on how many times out of 10 repetitions the ball comes back down the wall.

1 to 3 times = 1 point

4 to 7 times = 3 points

8 to 10 times = 5 points

Your score ____

Misstep

The ball goes out and away from you at an angle.

Correction

Be sure your racquet face isn't angled out or toward the side wall when you make contact with the ball. Hit the ball in the middle of the power zone instead of back in the power zone. Make sure your wrist snap is timed correctly. If the ball is angling away from you, your wrist snap may be too late.

Backhand Drill 6.   *Step Over and Hit*

Face the front wall. Pivot toward the side wall on your back foot, then step forward toward the front wall and hit the ball. Stand on the safety line (see location BH1 in figure 2.6, page 24), facing the front wall. Hold your racquet in the prep position and assume a ready athletic stance. Pivot left if you are right handed, or pivot right if you are left handed. As you pivot, bring your racquet from the ready position into the backswing position. Toss the ball out and forward between the safety line and short line as you step forward to hit it (figure 2.10). It will take some practice to get the toss in the right location. Possible problems in this drill include tossing the ball too far to the side and stepping over so far as to overreach to hit the ball, causing you to bend over and use your back and not your body core to hit the ball. Additionally, you will step toward the side wall so far as to impede your hip and shoulder rotation. Be sure to step forward toward the front wall and make contact in the power zone.

Visualize the drill and the stroke. Check your grip and prepare the racquet. Get into the ready athletic stance. Pivot on your back foot, turn your shoulders to the side wall, and initiate the backswing. Step forward, not across, to hit the ball. The heel of your front foot should be in line (from frontcourt to backcourt) with the toe of your back foot. As you begin to step forward, toss the ball

Figure 2.10 Step over and hit. Turn and step forward to hit the ball.

forward, out, and away so as to put the ball in the power zone at the end of the step forward. Keep your eye on the ball. Begin your swinging motion. Make contact with the ball between your waist and knees. Bend your knees and stay low. Hold your pose at the end of the follow-through.

Success Check

- Use a flat, out-and-around backhand stroke.
- Bend your knees and stay low.
- The ball bounces straight off the racquet and hits the front wall at about the same height as the point of contact with the racquet.
- The ball comes directly back to the ball-and-racquet contact point.
- Your weight is evenly balanced throughout the stroke.
- Your body is balanced during the follow-through.
- The heel of your front foot is in line (from frontcourt to backcourt) with the toe of your back foot.

- The toe of your front foot is at a 45-degree angle to the front wall, pointing toward the corner.

Score Your Success

Give yourself points based on how many times out of 10 repetitions the ball comes back down the wall.

1 to 3 times = 1 point

4 to 7 times = 3 points

8 to 10 times = 5 points

Your score ___

Misstep

The ball goes across the court and behind you.

Correction

Be sure your racquet face isn't angled cross-court when you make contact with the ball. Hit the ball in the middle of the power zone instead of at the front of the power zone. Make sure your wrist snap is timed correctly. If the ball is moving across court, your wrist snap may be too early.

SUCCESS SUMMARY OF BACKHAND

Congratulations! With the completion of the forehand and backhand steps, you are now ready for the rest of the steps in *Racquetball: Steps to Success*. Be sure to come back to the basics, especially the mechanics and drills, if you encounter any difficulties with the other steps as you progress through the book. These basics form the foundation for all the other shots in racquetball. And remember the success tips from the forehand section; they apply to

the backhand as well. Additionally, be sure to bend your knees and stay low during the swing, both when making contact with the ball and during the follow-through. Staying low helps to keep the ball low. If you rise during the stroke, you will most likely cause the ball to come up as well.

Review your scores for each of the backhand drills. Enter your scores and tally them to rate your backhand success.

Backhand Drills

1. Mirror Drill	___ out of 5
2. Backhand Toss and Catch	___ out of 5
3. Drop and Hit	___ out of 5
4. Step and Hit	___ out of 5
5. Shuffle and Hit	___ out of 5
6. Step Over and Hit	___ out of 5
Total	___ *out of 30*

If you scored fewer than 20 points, review the drills that were difficult for you. If you scored 20 points or more, you are ready to move on to step 3, Serve.

Serve

The serve is the one aspect of the game that you always have complete control over. You decide your exact serve location in the service zone, the ball dynamics (including speed, height, and spin), the direction of the ball based on the angle off the front and side walls, the depth of the ball into the backcourt, and where your opponent will go to return the serve. In spite of all this, the serve is often taken for granted and not given the serious attention it deserves. Therefore, make sure you are calculating in your approach to the serve.

When serving, your first objective is to get the ball in play. Second, you want to try to produce an unforced error or weak return to set up a point-winning offensive shot for yourself. Third, you want to try to get an ace serve, thereby negating your need to do anything more. Pay close attention to where the service receiver stands in the backcourt and how serves are returned. Look for weaknesses in your opponent's returns and then exploit those weaknesses to your advantage.

It always amazes me to see players step into the service zone and just serve the ball. Most don't seem to give any thought to what type of serve to use. Most of the time, the serve is to the opponent's backhand side—often a good idea—but is simply one that the server is the most comfortable with. On top of that, many players don't vary the serve with height, pace, or location.

As a coach, I encourage my players to have as many different serves as possible. I call this their bag of tricks. Having only one or two serves is like playing the game with only one or two shots. If all you have is a basic drive and a lob serve to the backhand from the same location in the service zone, it is like making only ceiling and down-the-wall shots during the entire game. No one in his or her right mind would self-limit to only a couple of shots. Likewise, you should not limit your serves options.

Given a single location in the service zone, and serving to only one side of the court, you can still hit a dozen or more different serves. Examples include: hard drive, shallow drive, deep drive, cut drive, high lob, medium lob, nick lob, off-pace drive, drive Z, high Z, medium Z, shallow Z, deep Z, off-pace jam, shallow jam, deep jam, and wraparound drive. Now, if you move just one or two feet to the left or right, you have again as many more serves to use, because the ball is now taking a different angle off the front wall into the backcourt. The only limitation is your imagination.

Learn what you can from this step. Remember, not every serve from every location is going to be taught. This step is designed to give you the basics so you can use your imagination to fill your own bag with tricks.

NO-STEP, ONE-STEP, AND TWO-STEP SERVES

A good serve rests on the foundation of good footwork. The three basic types of footwork associated with the serve are the no-step or drop and hit, the one-step, and the two-step. The one-step and two-step serves have many variations, but we primarily concentrate on the fundamental footwork for each. Experiment with the one- and two-step footwork to find what works best for your style of play.

The no-step serve is the most controlled because it involves no foot movement, only upper body rotation and arm swing. The no-step serve typically generates the least amount of power of the three footwork types. In the no-step serve, you square off to the side wall with your feet slightly farther than shoulder-width apart and in line with the front wall. This is the same position used in the drop-and-hit forehand drill in step 1 (page 10). Now, gently toss the ball in the power zone and hit the ball left or right (figure 3.1).

For the one-step drive serve, you may choose to begin in the same position as in the no-step serve: squared to the side wall with feet slightly more than shoulder-width apart. Another approach is to have both feet on or parallel to the short line. Toss the ball in the proposed power zone and step toward the front wall with your nondominant foot to strike the ball (figure 3.2).

Figure 3.2 One-step serve.

The two-step is the most common serve, especially among any of the hard drive serves. Place both feet on or parallel to the short line, with the nondominant foot forward (toward the side wall you are facing) and the dominant foot back (toward the other side wall). (For a right-handed player, the left foot will be forward and the right foot back.) The first step (figure 3.3a) is a short crossover step, with

Figure 3.1 No-step serve.

your back foot moving behind your front foot and toward the front wall. The next step (figure 3.3b) moves your front foot toward the front wall, stepping close to or on the service line, with your foot pointing toward the right front corner (for a right-handed player) or left front corner (for a left-handed player). As you make the second step you will gently toss the ball into the proposed power zone. The best time

to strike the ball is after it bounces off the floor and reaches its apex. Point your forward foot toward the front corner as you drive (push) off your back foot. Pointing your foot toward the front wall will take pressure off the knee and allow your hips to rotate toward the front wall as you strike the ball. Your dominant knee will turn in toward the front wall just as it did with the forehand stroke.

a

b

Figure 3.3 Two-step serve: *(a)* first step; *(b)* second step.

DRIVE SERVE

Although any location in the service zone may be used, only a few are typically used in making low drive serves (figure 3.4). The basic low drive serve (figure 3.5) uses the same swing mechanics and grip as the forehand stroke. As with the forehand stroke, you will rotate your hips and shoulders toward the front wall while driving (pushing) hard off your back foot to generate maximum power. Additionally, you will want to stay low in your stance and use a flat, out-and-around swing.

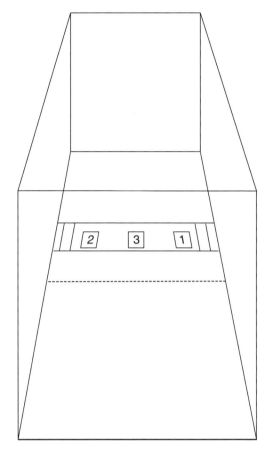

Figure 3.4 Drive serve positions.

Figure 3.5   Drive Serve (Two-Step)

READY POSITION

1. Place both feet on the short line
2. Bend your knees and get low
3. Place your racquet in the backswing position

a

36

b

c

FIRST STEP

1. Make crossover step with back foot
2. Step toward front wall
3. Don't overstep toward the side wall

SECOND STEP

1. Step toward front wall with front foot
2. Continue to stay low
3. Begin hip rotation and turn back knee toward front wall
4. Toss ball into power zone

d

e

BALL CONTACT

1. Continue to stay low
2. Keep your eye on the ball
3. Rotate hips
4. Swing out and around
5. Contact ball below knee in power zone

FOLLOW-THROUGH

1. Continue to stay low
2. Rotate toward the front wall
3. Stay balanced with some weight on both feet
4. Follow through with the racquet crossing your body to the nondominant side

During a two-step serve, the ball toss is initiated after the first step and during the second step. The ball toss is crucial to the drive serve. If the ball toss is consistent, the serve will most likely be consistent. To find the right location for the ball toss, freeze the service motion at the end of the second step (or at the end of the first step, if you are using a one-step approach). Extend your arm with racquet in hand in the power zone. This is where you will strike the ball during the serve. Toss the ball underhand (or allow the ball to roll out of your hand) for more control and to keep the ball from bouncing too high. Toss the ball away and toward the front wall (at about a 45-degree angle, in the direction of the front corner) to the proposed power zone location.

The point of impact should be below the knee on the two-step drive serve. On the one-step or no-step serve, the ball will typically be hit between the knee and the waist. The follow-through will shift most of your weight forward. This is fine for the serve; however, you will not want all of your weight forward. Keeping some of your weight on your back leg and foot will keep you somewhat balanced and help you recover from the serve and get to center court quickly.

Misstep

You hit the ball above the knee on the low drive serve.

Correction

The ball was tossed or bounced too high. Gently toss the ball or let it roll out of your hand into the power zone position.

The ball should strike the front wall approximately 12 to 18 inches (30 to 45 centimeters) above the floor, rebound to the back of the court with the first bounce hitting inside the safety zone, then finally bounce a second time before reaching the side or back wall (or *immediately* after hitting the wall). The ideal ball path to the backcourt takes an angle to reach the side wall about 3 feet (0.9 meter) out from the back wall (figure 3.6, serve A). This places the ball farthest from the receiver, thus making the return as difficult as possible. If you cannot get the ball to bounce twice before hitting the back wall, then it may wrap around the corner and set up up an easy return off the back wall. In this case, it is better to angle the ball so it comes off the back wall next to the side wall (figure 3.6, serve B).

One of the key elements to the success of the drive serve is deception. Not giving away what direction the ball will go in or what serve you are using makes the drive serve even more effective. As much as possible, you want to use racquet-face angle, not body position or a ball-drop deviation, to direct the path of the ball. If all elements of your body position and ball drop in

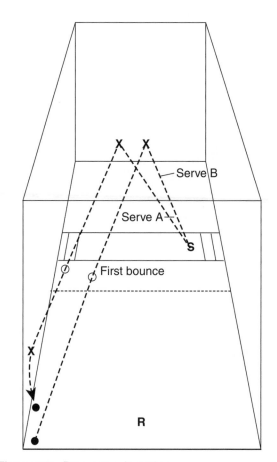

Figure 3.6 Drive serve deception.

the service zone remain consistent from beginning to end, then the only clue to where the ball will go is racquet-face angle when it contacts the ball—and this is difficult for your opponent to detect from the receiving position. So practice serves using the same service-box location, body movements, and ball drop, changing only the racquet-face angle to direct the path of the ball. If you want the ball to go right (right-handed player) you will be late with your wrist snap so the racquet face directs the ball to the right, or out and away from you. If you want the ball to go left (right-handed player) you will be early with your wrist snap so the racquet face directs

the ball to the left or crosses behind you. This same principle is true for nearly all shots in racquetball.

Two common mistakes made with the drive serve are hitting the ball too close to the body and hitting the ball too far away from the body. Both can create problems for the server but can also have different effects on the ball and thus create different looks for the receiver. In other words, these potential mistakes may or may not be a bad thing depending on your intent and the result. This is why practicing the ball toss is so crucial.

Misstep

On the serve, you don't get enough arm extension.

Correction

The ball was too close to your body. The ball must be at arm and racquet length at extension for maximum control and power.

Misstep

You have to cross over or bend over to reach the ball.

Correction

You tossed the ball too far away from your body. Control your ball drop. Don't throw the ball. Gently toss it or let it roll out of your hand into the power zone. The ball needs to be at arm and racquet length at extension for the most control and power possible.

The key to avoiding service errors is consistency, which will improve with good practice habits and skills. Remember, quality not quantity! One way to ensure consistency with footwork, ball drop, and ball-strike location is to place tape on the floor to mark the location of your feet, steps, ball bounce, and racquet-to-ball contact point.

The drive serve can be varied in many ways. The difference is typically the pace of the ball

or how hard you hit it. By varying pace you will keep your opponent off balance and actually create a different serve. Practice hitting the ball with varying pace to see how the ball reacts. Remember, you will want to use the same service motion, without deviation, to serve the ball with varying pace. Don't give away what you are doing. Deception in racquet-face angle and ball pace is the key to an effective change of serve.

Drive Serve Drill 1. *Ball Toss*

Tossing the ball for the drive serve is not necessarily a difficult thing to do. However, it can be challenging to do it with consistency so you are able to put the ball in the same location at the same height each time. In order to practice serves efficiently, you will need to develop skill with the ball toss.

Stand approximately 6 feet (1.8 meters) away from the side wall, as if it were the front wall. Now, get into your beginning low-drive-serve stance and practice the service-motion steps with the ball toss. Practicing your serve motion and toss this way makes it easy to retrieve the ball; it bounces back off the side wall so you don't have to chase it. The ball should hit the wall after the second bounce. Although you will swing the racquet to the point of contact, do not hit the ball. Make sure you are bringing the racquet to the right height and proximity to your body to make good contact.

Success Check

- The ball is at the correct distance from your body (proximity) to allow full arm extension and contact with the racquet.
- The ball is at the correct height, between the knee and floor.

Score Your Success

Complete 10 repetitions. Have a qualified observer, such as a coach or experienced player, evaluate your technique.

1 to 4 perfect steps and ball tosses = 1 point

5 to 7 perfect steps and ball tosses = 3 points

8 to 10 perfect steps and ball tosses = 5 points

Your score ___

Drive Serve Drill 2. *Dry Serves to Full Serves*

First, visualize the serve. Next, practice the footwork for the drive serve using the two-step approach in the service zone. Practice without a ball. Once you have the footwork down, incorporate the ball drop. Put together all the necessary elements and serve the ball. Using the three locations shown in figure 3.4 (page 36), practice hitting drive serves to the left and right. Begin in location 1 and progress to location 3. For each location, hit 10 serves to each side, for a total of 60 serves (3 sets of 10 to each side). Remember to stay low, drive (push) with the back leg, and hit out and around. Additionally, stay balanced at the end of the serve so you can recover quickly and move out of the service box to center court.

Success Check

- Both feet are parallel, near or on the short line.
- Knees are bent and the racquet is in the backswing position.
- Back foot steps forward.
- Front foot steps forward and toe of front foot points toward front wall corner, in line (from frontcourt to backcourt) with back foot at the end of the step.
- Ball toss is in power zone at correct proximity and height.
- You stay low in your serve.
- You see the ball and racquet come together at full extension.
- You finish with a complete follow-through and in good balance, with most (but not all) of your weight on your front foot.

Score Your Success

Complete 10 repetitions. Have a qualified observer, such as a coach or experienced player, evaluate your technique.

1 to 4 attempts with perfect service mechanics = 1 point

5 to 7 attempts with perfect service mechanics = 3 points

8 to 10 attempts with perfect service mechanics = 5 points

Your score ___

Misstep

The ball hits the floor before getting to the short line, resulting in a fault serve.

Correction

Stay low on the serve, hitting out and around, not up and down. Be sure the racquet face is perpendicular to the floor on ball contact, not closed or facing down. Raise the intended ball-contact point on the front wall; it may be too low for you to hit consistently.

Misstep

The ball hits the back wall before the first bounce, or the first bounce is deep in the backcourt, causing the ball to set up off the back wall near center court.

Correction

Stay low during the serve and don't rise before striking the ball with the racquet. Swing out and around, not low to high. Be sure the racquet face is perpendicular to the floor on ball contact, not open or facing up. Lower the ball-contact point on the front wall; it may be too high.

Drive Serve Drill 3.   *Recovery*

After you have all the elements of the drive serve down, practice your recovery to center court. In order to recover quickly, you will need to ensure that you do not have too much weight on your front foot at the end of the serve on the follow through. You will also have to stay balanced. If your service motion caries you forward past the service line, or if you fall off to the side while serving, you will have to get rebalanced before you can recover to center court. Recovery to center court should take no more than three or four steps. Keep in mind that the harder the ball is hit, the sooner it will be returned. This means less time to get out of the service box and into your receiving location and position. Additionally, the more power the ball has on the serve, the more power it will generate on the return. Keep that in mind when you are serving to a hard-hitting receiver.

Success Check

- You are balanced at the end of the serve.
- Most, but not all, of your weight is on the front foot.
- You recover to center court with three or four steps.

Score Your Success

Give yourself points based on how many times out of 10 repetitions you are able to stay balanced on the follow-through and recover to center court with three or four steps.

1 to 3 times = 1 point

4 to 7 times = 3 points

8 to 10 times = 5 points

Your score ___

Misstep

Your back foot comes off the floor during the serve follow-through.

Correction

You are tossing the ball too far forward or allowing your upper body weight to carry you forward during the follow-through. Adjust your toss and balance as necessary.

Misstep

You fall off balance to one side during the follow-through.

Correction

You are tossing the ball too far away or too far out to the side, causing you to overreach or step across rather than forward to hit the ball.

JAM SERVE

The jam serve is virtually the same as the low drive serve. The only difference is the height and angle of the ball. With this serve, you want the ball to hit the front wall at a higher point. If you are hitting your low drive serves correctly, then you want to raise the contact point on the front wall about 6 inches (15 centimeters) for a good jam serve. For a wider angle toward the side wall, you will want to move the ball left or right approximately 12 inches (30 centimeters) of where you hit your normal drive serve to the back corner. This will vary depending on the location you are serving from in the service box. The ball must contact the side wall on the fly, angling toward the receiver in such a way as to hit the floor at your opponent's feet, thus jamming the ball into your opponent (figure 3.7).

Another option is to have the ball jam and hit your opponent on the fly, but this carries a risk: If the ball is hit too high and hard, and if it does not hit the receiver or get immediately returned by the receiver, then it may wrap around off the back wall, come into center court, and give your opponent an easy shot.

The jam is an excellent serve to use after you have hit a few low drive serves to the back corner and your opponent is getting a jump on the serve. Additionally, it is a good serve to use when your opponent is off balance or flat footed in the receiving position, or has his or her shoulders turned toward the side wall for the serve. The jam serve may be used from any of the three basic serve positions in figure

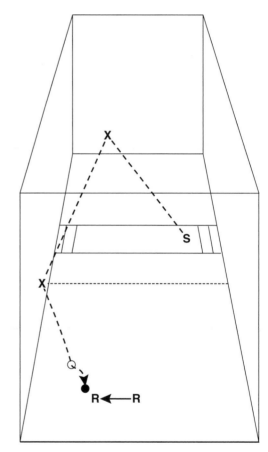

Figure 3.7 A jam serve causes the ball to hit the floor at the opponent's feet, making a return more difficult.

3.4 (page 36). However, serving from location 2 to the left side places you in direct line for a down-the-wall return and increases the possibility you will get hit on the return. (See The Sport of Racquetball on page xv for more information on avoidable hinders.)

Jam Serve Drill.   *Jam Repetition*

Using the three different locations in figure 3.4 (page 36), practice hitting jam serves to the left and right. Begin in location 1 and progress to location 3. For each location, hit 10 serves to each side, for a total of 60 serves (3 sets of 10 to each side).

Success Check

- Remember to stay low.
- Drive (push) with your back leg.
- Hit out and around.
- Stay balanced at the end of the serve so you can recover quickly and move out of the service box to center court.

- The ball strikes the side wall on the fly and bounces on the floor before hitting the back wall.

Score Your Success

Give yourself points based on how many times out of 10 repetitions you hit an effective jam serve.

1 to 3 times = 1 point

4 to 7 times = 3 points

8 to 10 times = 5 points

Your score ____

Misstep

The ball hits the floor before it hits the side wall.

Correction

This slows the ball and may set it up for a point-ending kill shot (see step 5) by your opponent. Raise the contact point of the ball on the front wall so the ball flies more to the side wall. Hit the ball harder. The jam serve is a hard-hit serve and does not work well when hit softly.

Misstep

The ball hits the side wall in front of the service line and angles to center court.

Correction

The angle is too wide off the front wall. Move the contact point of the ball on the front wall closer to the center, narrowing the angle. Check the ball-contact point in the power zone; it may be too far forward or your wrist snap may be too early.

Z SERVE

The Z serve is usually executed from location 1 or 2 in figure 3.4 (page 36). Location 3 makes this serve nearly impossible for the inexperienced player to execute, since the ball path's angle from front wall to side wall brings it across the center of the court and it may hit the server.

The footwork, racquet angle, ball drop, and power zone are similar to those of the drive serve. The Z serve typically requires a lot of pace and angle in order to be effective. However, changing the pace of the ball gives it a different look, just as the change-up pitch does in baseball. The deeper the ball goes into the backcourt, the harder it is to return if the receiver allows it to Z off the side wall (figure 3.8).

For a change from the forehand Z serve to the back left side, you can use a reverse Z serve (figure 3.9) to the right side (if right handed; figure 3.8 for lefties). The reverse Z is considered an advanced serve, but it is worth the effort to develop it.

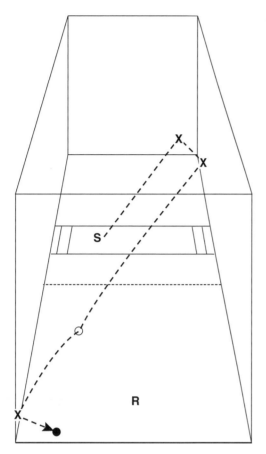

Figure 3.8 Z serve.

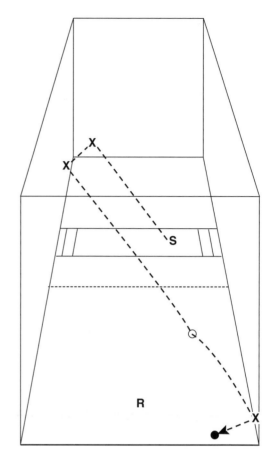

Figure 3.9 Reverse Z serve.

Z Serve Drill. *Z Repetition*

Begin Z serve practice in location 1, then move to location 2. For each location, hit 10 serves to each side, for a total of 40 serves (2 sets of 10 to each side). Practice hitting the ball with different degrees of pace.

Success Check

- Remember to stay low.
- Drive with your back leg.
- Hit out and around.
- Stay balanced at the end of the serve so you can recover quickly and move out of the service box to center court.

- Hit the ball low, hard, and deep into the backcourt.

Score Your Success

Give yourself points based on how many times out of 10 repetitions you hit an effective Z serve to the deep backcourt.

1 to 3 times = 1 point

4 to 7 times = 3 points

8 to 10 times = 5 points

Your score ___

Misstep

The ball hits the second side wall on the fly.

Correction

This is a fault serve. Move the contact point down on the front wall. Don't hit the ball so hard; take a little off the pace.

Misstep

The ball angles off the first side wall directly to or behind the receiver.

Correction

Move the ball-contact point on the front wall closer to the corner of the front wall and side wall for a narrower angle. You may be hitting the ball too far forward in the power zone. Move the contact point farther back in the power zone. Turn your body more in the direction of the ball path for a more direct serve to the corner. Note, though, that this may give away your serve. Move closer to the side wall in the service box for a better angle. The closer you are to the center of the service box, the harder it is to get an effective angle for the Z serve.

LOB SERVE

So far we have discussed and worked on typical first serves. However, if you fault on the first serve, you will need a reliable second serve. Lob serves are excellent second serves because they are more easily controlled and, when executed properly, seldom result in a second fault or side-out. The lob serve is also a great way to control the opponent who loves the drive serve and uses the power to his or her advantage. The other advantage of a good lob serve is that it usually elicits a ceiling return and gives you plenty of time to move to center court.

There are several types of lob serves to choose from:

- High lob
- Half lob
- Z lob
- Nick lob

There are also many advanced variations of these serves, including backhand lobs, but these four are the foundation. All of these lob serves are used for specific reasons to either negate a particular return, exploit a weakness, or just get the ball in play on the second serve.

The stroke mechanics for the lob serve are much different from any other shot in racquetball, varying from a semipendulum swing to little or no wrist snap and little or no arm swing.

The grip for the forehand lob serve is different from the drive serve grip. For the purpose of learning the lob serve, choke up on the handle and hold the racquet in a backhand grip, with about a 45-degree open face to the front wall (figure 3.10a). The open face of the racquet will help with the loft of the ball without your having to change the angle of the wrist. Choking up on the handle gives you more control. Your arm should be bent, with your elbow close to your body, and your wrist should be firm.

Figure 3.10   Lob Serve

a

b

READY POSITION AND GRIP

1. Stand square to the side wall
2. Feet are shoulder-width apart
3. Stand relaxed, with knees slightly bent
4. Use a backhand grip (forehand serve)
5. Choke up on the racquet handle
6. Wrist is firm
7. Elbow is close to body
8. Racquet is in backswing position at waist height

BALL DROP AND STEP

1. Hold ball in front, toward side wall, at shoulder height, with palm down
2. Drop ball slightly forward; don't throw or toss it
3. Step toward front wall with toe of front foot toward front corner
4. Ball is in power zone after step

You will want to be in the backswing position when you drop the ball. The ball drop (figure 3.10b) is usually from about shoulder height in the power zone, with the ball bouncing to a height just above your waist. The basic footwork for the lob serve is typically a no-step or one-step motion in the direction of the front wall, and it incorporates hip and shoulder rotation for control.

As you step and rotate with your hips and shoulders, your arm, wrist, and racquet also rotate forward, and you strike the ball at the peak of the bounce, lofting it to the front wall (figure 3.10c). This motion is much like closing a gate. Imagine a post extending from the top of your head down through the middle of your body and into the floor. If the racquet side of

c

d

ROTATION AND CONTACT

1. Rotate hips and shoulders
2. Bring racquet out and around parallel to floor
3. Rotate in a controlled manner
4. Keep elbow close to body
5. Keep wrist firm
6. Make ball contact at apex of bounce or slightly after
7. Keep eye on ball and racquet at contact

FOLLOW-THROUGH

1. Continue rotation through contact
2. Follow through with slight upward motion
3. Finish with hips and shoulders facing the front wall
4. Racquet is to side at or slightly above shoulder height, but in front, not behind

your body is the gate, your hips, shoulders, arm, and wrist rotate on the post, swinging the gate closed. After the follow-through (figure 3.10d), your hips and shoulders end up toward the front wall with the racquet moving slightly upward. The racquet finishes in front of your body at shoulder height.

Keep in mind that the lob is a finesse serve, not a power serve. Therefore, it is imperative that you make as little arm and wrist movement as possible. Depending on where you want the ball to go, you will drop the ball in different hitting zone locations and use the racquet face to direct the ball.

The lob serve can be served from any location in the service box. There is no possibility of a screen serve or being hit by your own serve and you have ample time to move out of the service box to center court unless you have an opponent who short-hops or cuts off the lob.

There are certain keys elements to the success of the lob serve. First, this is a soft, controlled, finesse serve. Second, the ball should bounce in the safety zone to prevent the ball from being cutoff in the air by the receiver. Third, the ball should fall to the floor after the first bounce in the backcourt as close to the back wall as possible. Do not let the ball set up for an easy return by deflecting off the back or side wall or bouncing too short in the backcourt.

High Lob

The high lob is the easiest lob serve to master. It is hit about 2 to 4 feet (0.6 to 1.2 meters) from the ceiling on the front wall and should bounce in the safety zone (figure 3.11). The ideal bounce location is just past the short line. The bounce trajectory should take the ball high where it will fall rapidly to the floor in the backcourt as close to the back wall and corner as possible.

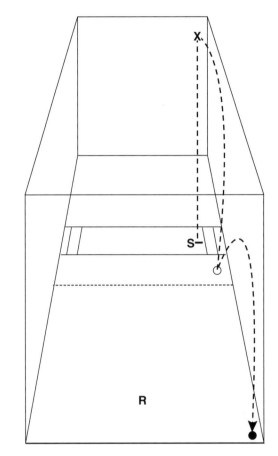

Figure 3.11 High lob.

Lob Serve Drill 1.   *High Lob*

Begin the high lob practice in location 1, then move to location 2, and finish at location 3 (figure 3.4, page 36). Hit 3 sets of 10 serves. Remember, the high lob is a finesse serve.

Success Check

- Stand relaxed. Keep your wrist firm while choking up on the handle in a backhand grip.
- Drop the ball from shoulder height in the proposed power zone.
- Execute the proper rotation of your hips and shoulders, keeping your elbow close to your body.

- Follow through at shoulder height.
- The ball bounces in the safety zone and dies in the backcourt.
- Move out of the service box and into center court once the ball passes the short line.

Score Your Success

Give yourself points based on how many times out of 10 repetitions the ball bounces in the safety zone and dies in the backcourt.

  1 to 3 times = 1 point

  4 to 7 times = 3 points

  8 to 10 times = 5 points

Your score ___

Misstep

The ball bounces past the safety line and off the back wall.

Correction

Slow down and use a softer rotation and stroke. Don't use your arm to hit the ball; rotate at your hips and shoulders. Maintain a firm wrist. Check your grip and racquet angle.

Half Lob

The half lob is a variation of the high lob. The ball makes contact with the front wall approximately 10 to 12 feet (3 to 3.7 meters) up, midway between the floor and the ceiling (figure 3.12). The ball should bounce in the safety zone and take a trajectory to the backcourt. Because the ball is not traveling as far, you will want to hit the half lob with even less power and more finesse than the high lob. The idea is to force the receiver to return the ball around chest to shoulder height in mid backcourt.

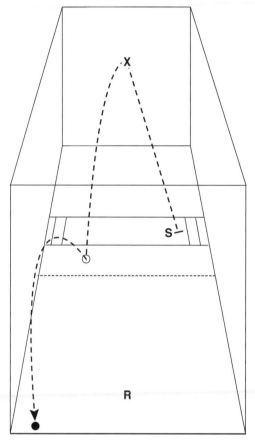

Figure 3.12   Half lob.

Lob Serve Drill 2.   *Half Lob*

Begin the half lob practice in location 1, then move to location 2, and finish in location 3 (figure 3.4, page 36). Hit 3 sets of 10 serves. Remember, half lobs are soft, controlled, finesse serves.

Success Check

- Stand relaxed. Keep your wrist firm while choking up on the handle in a backhand grip.

- Drop the ball from shoulder height in the proposed power zone.

- Execute the proper rotation of your hips and shoulders, keeping your elbow close to your body.

- Follow through at waist height.

- The ball bounces in the safety zone and dies in the backcourt.

- Move out of the service box and into center court once the ball passes the short line.

Misstep

The ball bounces past the safety line and off the back wall.

Correction

Slow down and use a softer rotation and stroke. Don't use your arm to hit the ball; rotate at your hips and shoulders. Maintain a firm wrist. Check your grip and racquet angle.

Z Lob

Z lob serves are hit much like the normal lob serve and can be tricky and difficult to execute. The Z lob is also a dangerous serve if not executed correctly. The ball must contact the front wall about 1 to 2 feet (0.3 to 0.6 meter) from the front-and-side-wall crack and at the correct height. For a high Z, the contact point should be about 2 to 4 feet (0.6 to 1.2 meters) from the ceiling, and for the half Z it should be about 10 to 12 feet (3 to 3.7 meters) up, or midway between the floor and the ceiling (figure 3.13). As the ball comes off the side wall, it travels across the court and behind you if you are serving from the right side of the court. The ball should contact the floor in the safety zone and take a trajectory to the back corner, bouncing a second time as near the back corner as possible.

Be careful not to get in the way of the ball as it travels close to you. The ball must bounce first in the safety zone, as close to the short line as possible, and it may make contact with the opposite side wall after the first bounce as it travels into the backcourt. This is okay as long as the ball falls rapidly to the floor in the backcourt near the back wall.

The easiest way to practice the Z lob serve is to stand with your front and back feet in line (that is, with an imaginary line from one foot to the other) toward the front corner you are serv-

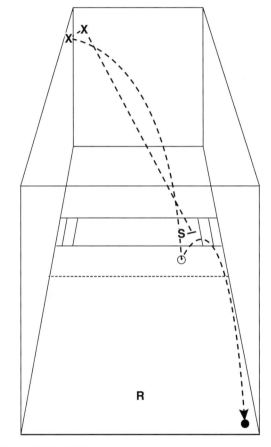

Figure 3.13 Z lob serve.

ing to. This may give the serve away, but it will support proper execution and greater success. As you get more skillful you can experiment with different stances.

Lob Serve Drill 3. **_Z Lob_**

Begin Z lob practice in location 1, then move to location 2, and finish in location 3 (figure 3.4, page 36). Hit 3 sets of 10 serves. Remember Z lobs are finesse serves.

Success Check

- Stand relaxed with your feet in line toward the front corner.
- Keep your wrist firm while choking up on the handle in a backhand grip.
- Drop the ball at shoulder height in the proposed power zone.
- Execute the proper rotation of your hips and shoulders, keeping your elbow close to your body.

- Follow through at waist height for the half Z lob or shoulder height for the high Z lob.
- The ball bounces in the safety zone and dies in the backcourt.
- Move out of the service box and into center court once the ball passes the short line.

Score Your Success

Give yourself points based on how many times out of 10 repetitions the ball bounces in the safety zone and dies in the backcourt.

1 to 3 times = 1 point

4 to 7 times = 3 points

8 to 10 times = 5 points

Your score ___

Nick Lob

The nick lob (figure 3.14) is the most difficult of all lob serves to execute and master. There is no room for error. If this serve is not perfect, it will result in a setup and a potentially easy kill shot for your opponent. The ball is hit on the front wall at approximately the same height as for the high lob, but farther left or right so as to angle to the side wall. It is also hit harder in order to travel past the safety line. The ball should contact the side wall approximately 8 to 12 feet (2.4 to 3.7 meters) off the floor and approximately 3 to 9 feet (0.9 to 2.7 meters) out from the back wall on its downward trajectory. As the ball nicks off the side wall it will fall rapidly to the floor and bounce toward the middle of the backcourt, bouncing a second time near the back wall. The idea is to get the ball as close to the back wall as possible so there is no room for your opponent to swing the racquet.

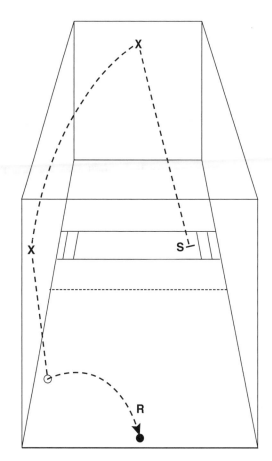

Figure 3.14 Nick lob serve.

Lob Serve Drill 4.   *Nick Lob*

Begin nick lob practice in location 1, then move to location 2, and finish at location 3 (figure 3.4, page 36). Hit 3 sets of 10 serves. Remember, nick lobs are finesse serves.

Success Check

- Stand relaxed with your feet in line with the front wall.
- Keep your wrist firm while choking up on the handle in a backhand grip.
- Drop the ball from shoulder height in the proposed power zone.
- Execute the proper rotation of your hips and shoulders, keeping your elbow close to your body.
- Aim for a contact point on the front wall approximately 12 inches (30 centimeters) left or right of where you would hit a normal high lob serve.

- Follow through at shoulder height.
- The ball hits the side wall approximately 8 to 12 feet (2.4 to 3.7 meters) off the floor and approximately 3 to 9 feet (0.9 to 2.7 meters) out from the back wall.
- Move out of the service box and into center court once the ball passes the short line.

Score Your Success.

Give yourself points based on how many times out of 10 repetitions the ball nicks the side wall and dies in the backcourt.

1 to 3 times = 1 point

4 to 7 times = 3 points

8 to 10 times = 5 points

Your score ____

Misstep

On a nick lob serve, the ball hits the floor before contacting the side wall.

Correction

Hit the ball a bit harder, using a little more arm and wrist movement. Widen the angle by moving the front wall contact point slightly toward the targeted side wall away from the center of the front wall.

Misstep

On a nick lob serve, the ball nicks the side wall, bounces, and caroms off the back wall for a setup before the second bounce.

Correction

Hit the ball softer, using less arm and wrist movement. Move the side wall contact point closer to the front wall.

SERVE SELECTION

Deciding on which serve to hit can be as easy or difficult as you wish to make it. The primary thing to remember in serving is to keep the receiver guessing and force a weak return. If you constantly hit the same serve with the same pace, your opponent will never have to guess where the ball is going and can always get a good jump on returning the ball.

As we will discuss later in more detail, having more tricks in your bag helps you make it harder for your opponent to anticipate what you will do next. You will also want to keep track of what your opponent is not returning well and work that to your advantage (table 3.1). However, if you don't try different serves, you will never know what your opponent can and cannot return well. So, mix your serves up and keep the receiver guessing.

Table 3.1 Serve Selection

Serve	When to use it
Drive serve to backhand	Opponent is weak when returning the drive serve on the backhand side
	Game is fast paced and opponent is tired; use to keep opponent off balance
	Opponent is good when attacking the lob serve
Drive serve to forehand	Opponent is weak when returning the drive serve
	Game is fast paced and opponent is tired; use to keep opponent off balance
	Opponent is good when attacking the lob serve
	Opponent is looking for the drive serve to the backhand
	You want to change the pace of the game
Jam serve	Opponent is weak when returning the jam serve
	Game is fast paced and opponent is tired; use to keep opponent off balance
	Opponent is good when attacking the lob serve
	You want to change the pace of the game
	Opponent is looking for the drive serve to the forehand or backhand
	Opponent is off balance or flat footed
Z serve	Opponent is weak when returning the Z serve
	Game is fast paced and opponent is tired; use to keep opponent off balance
	Opponent is good when attacking the lob serve
	Opponent is looking for the drive serve to the backhand or forehand
	You want to change the pace of the game
	Opponent is weak at tracking the ball and cannot adjust or react to the Z ball action off the side wall
	Opponent has difficulty returning balls that come across his or her body
Lob serve	You want to slow down the game
	Opponent is weak at returning the lob serve
	You want to take away from the receiver the power return off the drive serve
Half-lob serve	Opponent is weak at lob returns and ceiling shots
	You want to keep the opponent from cutting off the high lob serve
Z lob serve	Opponent is good at attacking the drive serve
	You are slow getting out of the service box
	Opponent is weak at returning the Z lob serve

Service Game 1.   *15-Point Game*

With a partner, play a serve-only game to 15 points. Serve 10 points in a row playing out the point, regardless of who wins the rally, before you switch to receiving. If you fault on the first serve, then you get a second serve. However, use the same serve for the second serve that you did on the first. Once you have served your 10 serves, you will receive, and your partner will serve. Use rally scoring; either the server or the receiver scores depending on who wins the rally. The game is over once the first player gets to 15.

This game allows you time to work on serving and receiving. Keep in mind that we haven't covered receiving yet (see step 4); the emphasis here is on the serve. I prefer to have my players work on only one serve during the 10-serve rotation. This gives you enough serves to work on difficulties and make corrections. It also makes it more challenging since the receiver knows what serve you are going to use.

An alternative is to use a different serve each time you serve. In other words, you cannot use the same serve twice during the game. This forces you to work on different serves. However, the best way to work on a serve is to use it over and over again. Repetition is the key to consistency.

Be sure to work on all your serves. Don't just work on the serve that is your best or the easiest to win with against your opponent. This is a practice drill to improve your serve. It won't do you any good to pound a serve to a receiver who cannot return it. Work on your weaknesses, not your strengths.

Success Check

- Visualize your serve before you execute it.
- Take your time and execute the best possible serve you can.
- The goal of the serve is to get a defensive return, weak return, or ace.
- If you are having difficulty with any of the serves, be sure to go back to the drills and review the mechanics.

Score Your Success

Give yourself points based on how well you serve in a normal game to 15. An effective serve for the purpose of this drill is one that does what you want it to, keeps the receiver off balance, or creates a weak return or an ace.

1 to 6 effective serves = 1 point

7 to 15 effective serves = 3 points

16 or more effective serves = 5 points

Your score ___

Service Game 2.   *3-Point Serve Game*

In this game, you must score 3 points in a row in order to win. You can score only when serving. If you score 0, 1, or 2 points, it is sideout and you do not win. This is a great way to simulate a match. It helps you work on your focus and intensity. You will find this is not an easy task. In fact, you may go a long time playing this game before anyone wins.

The better you get and the better your opponent is, the more difficult the game. Mix up your serves and have fun with this difficult game.

To Increase Difficulty

Play to 5 or even more points depending how evenly matched you are with your opponent.

Success Check

- Visualize your serve before you execute it.
- Take your time and execute the best possible serve you can.
- The goal of the serve is to get a defensive return, weak return, or ace.
- If you are having difficulty with any of the serves, be sure to go back to the drills and review the mechanics.

Score Your Success

Give yourself points based on how many service points you get in a game to 5.

1 service point won = 1 point

2 to 3 service points won in a row = 3 points

4 to 5 service points won in a row = 5 points

Your score ___

SUCCESS SUMMARY OF SERVE

The serve is the most important shot in racquetball. If you can't get the ball in play or you set up your opponent for a solid return, you will have a difficult time winning. Few players spend as much time on their serve as they should. You now have the tools to practice the fundamental mechanics of the serve. What you do with this information and how you use the drills and practice games will define you as a server. You have also been given some tools to help you decide (during your practice and your matches) when and where to use the various serves.

You will be a successful server if you focus on each and every serve. Don't rush your serves. Be methodical and plan each serve as you would a move in a chess match. Pay attention to your receiver. Watch how your opponent sets up to receive your serves. Watch how your opponent moves to return the serve. Pay attention to your opponent's strengths and weaknesses in returning the serve. Find your opponent's weakness and exploit it. Treat each serve as though it is the last point of the game. If you approach serving this way, you will be much more successful and will have fewer serving errors. In addition, what you learned here will help you become a better receiver.

Review your scores for each of the serve drills. Enter your scores and tally them up to rate your serving success.

Drive Serve Drills

    1. Ball Toss   ___ out of 5

    2. Dry Serves to Full Serves   ___ out of 5

    3. Recovery   ___ out of 5

Jam Serve Drill

    1. Jam Repetition   ___ out of 5

Z Serve Drill

    1. Z Repetition   ___ out of 5

Lob Serve Drills

    1. High Lob   ___ out of 5

    2. Half Lob   ___ out of 5

    3. Z Lob   ___ out of 5

    4. Nick Lob   ___ out of 5

Service Games

    1. 15-Point Game   ___ out of 5

    2. 3-Point Serve Game   ___ out of 5

Total   ___ ***out of 55***

If you scored fewer than 35 points, review and practice the drills that were difficult for you before you move on to the next step. If you scored 35 points or more, you are ready to continue to step 4, Return of Serve.

Return of Serve

Don't just return the ball; have a plan and return with a purpose. Planning your return is just as important as planning your serve. Just returning the serve is not the way to win a rally. Be methodical when planning your return. The primary objectives should be

- to get the server out of center court,
- to put the server on the defensive,
- to force a weak return by the server, and
- to neutralize the server's ability to return your shot at all.

Some of the shots referred to in this step have not yet been discussed. The reason for discussing the return before delving into all of the shots is that it will allow you to start playing without having to read the entire book first. Most people want to get on the court and start playing as soon as possible. Therefore, I have given you the basics first—forehand, backhand, serve, and now return. Be sure to refer to the necessary steps to learn more about specific shots, and don't forget to refer back to this step as you progress through the book.

There are a number of different shots you can use for the return of serve, depending on the serve you receive and whether you are on or off balance. Regardless of whether you decide to hit an offensive or defensive shot, your primary objective should be to gain control of center court and win the rally outright or force a weak return by your opponent. Stay low in your stance and on the balls of your feet. Keep your racquet in front of you and stay balanced.

Return of serve is crucial to the game of racquetball. If you are unable to return serve, you will never get into a rally to force sideout. The serve is typically the most difficult shot to return from a set position. Even though you are stationary and ready to return the serve, the server has complete control of all aspects of the serve, including the ball dynamics (speed, height, spin), the direction of the ball (ball angle off the front or side wall), depth of shot into the backcourt, and choice of which part of the court you will return the ball from. (Review step 3, Serve, for more on serving specifics.)

Footwork and anticipation are key to getting into position for returning the serve. If the serve is hit hard and low, your reaction time will make a huge difference in determining whether you get set up on the ball to hit an offensive return or just barely get your racquet on the ball for an ace-saving return.

Practicing your footwork for the service return will greatly increase your winning percentage on return of serve. Whether you use a simple crossover or a quick half step with a crossover is determined by where the serve goes and by your reaction to it. Don't try to outthink the server; wait for the serve and be ready to move when the ball is served. Many people try to guess where the ball will be served only to find themselves out of position, resulting in a weak return or an ace. Remember, the objective of the serve is to force a weak return. Be prepared.

One of the most common mistakes in returning is greed. Many players give away points on unforced errors by going for the winner on the serve return. If you have a perfect setup, go for it. But if you don't, be patient and wait for a better opportunity to shoot the ball later in the rally. If you keep the ball in play, your opponent may very well give you the rally by making an unforced error. Most racquetball players are not patient when it comes to long rallies. So, be unwearied and wait for the setup. It will come if you wait long enough.

MAKING THE RETURN

Stand midway between both side walls, approximately 3 to 4 feet (0.9 to 1.2 meters) out from the back wall. This will give you equal opportunity to return balls served to either your forehand or backhand. You may vary your location slightly in any direction; however, if the server picks up that you favor one side or the other, this may set you up for an ace serve. Be careful not to give away any weakness or intent on your part.

Stand in the basic athletic stance (figure 4.1a for forehand, figure 4.2a for backhand). Your feet should be slightly more than shoulder-width apart, with a slight bend in your knees and at your waist. Your position should be much like that of a defensive basketball player or a baseball shortstop. Hold your racquet in front of you, with the head of the racquet just above your waist and pointing toward the front wall. Stand approximately 3 feet or one arm and racquet length from the back wall, centered between the two side walls. Most of the serves will go to the backhand, but don't cheat too much to the backhand side or your opponent may serve a winner to the forehand.

Misstep

You hit the ball from an open stance, which reduces power and limits shot selection.

Correction

Square off to the side wall. If the ball goes wide, take your first step with the near foot, then cross over. If the ball is shallow, cross over with the opposite foot first. Stay low and balanced.

Misstep

You swing and either miss the ball or hit it off the racquet frame.

Correction

Keep your head down and focus on the ball. Watch the ball and the racquet come together. Do not look where you want the ball to go before you hit it.

Figure 4.1   Return of Serve, Forehand

READY POSITION

1. Assume an athletic stance
2. Stand 3 to 4 feet (0.9 to 1.2 meters) from back wall, centered between side walls
3. Hold racquet in backhand grip
4. Hold racquet in front of you with racquet head above waist
5. Balance on the balls of your feet

a

QUICK HALF STEP

1. Push off opposite foot
2. Step left or right with toe pointing toward side wall
3. Hips and shoulders turn toward side wall
4. Racquet goes to backswing position for forehand

b

CROSSOVER STEP

1. Opposite-side foot crosses in front of body to ball side
2. If this is the first step, racquet goes to backswing position for forehand

c

Figure 4.2	Return of Serve, Backhand

READY POSITION

1. Assume an athletic stance
2. Stand 3 to 4 feet (0.9 to 1.2 meters) from back wall, centered between side walls
3. Hold racquet in backhand grip
4. Hold racquet in front of you with racquet head above waist
5. Balance on the balls of your feet

a

QUICK HALF STEP

1. Push off opposite foot
2. Step left or right with toe pointing toward side wall
3. Hips and shoulders turn toward side wall
4. Racquet goes to backswing position (forehand or backhand)

b

CROSSOVER STEP

1. Opposite-side foot crosses in front of body to ball side
2. If this is the first step, racquet goes to backswing position (forehand or backhand)

c

Balance is the first and most important aspect of service return. If you are not balanced, nothing else you do will compensate. I see many people try to anticipate or cheat to one side or the other. When they do this, they place more weight in one direction. This is a dangerous tactic, because if you guess wrong, you have to stop, get balanced, and go in the other direction. This stance also tips off the server to your intention. If the serve is a hard and low drive serve, and you are cheating to one side, you most likely will not be able to recover and get into position to return the ball.

Pay attention to where the server is in the service zone. Any clues you can pick up during the delivery of the serve may allow you to see where and how the ball will be served. Many players use particular serves from specific places in the service zone. Others limit their serve selection by where they stand in the service zone. Some key things to look for are service location, body positioning, ball drop and delivery, and serve mechanics.

The first step (figure 4.1*b* for forehand, figure 4.2*b* for backhand) is crucial in getting to the ball and having an opportunity to hit an aggressive return. The first step is a quick half step, with the left foot going left or with the right foot going right. This step turns you to the side of the court where the ball is served.

Once you make the quick half step, you are in an open stance. If the ball is hit narrow and coming near you, cross over with your opposite foot to get balanced and in good position to set up and return the ball (figure 4.1*c* for forehand, figure 4.2*c* for backhand).

The success of your return will depend largely on how quickly you get into position and how well the ball is served. If the ball comes off the back wall or is served short and is a setup, you will be able to get into position to return the ball from a setup position. What you do with the return will depend on your setup position and the server's court position. The two best offensive options you have on a setup are a down-the-wall return or a cross-court return. More shot return options will be discussed later in the book.

Misstep
The ball flies off the front wall and hits the back wall before bouncing on the floor.
Correction
Aim 18 inches (45 centimeters) off the floor on the front wall. Your racquet face may be open or angled up. The racquet face should be perpendicular to the floor on contact with the ball.

The mechanics used to return any ball—serve or otherwise—are the same as discussed in the forehand and backhand steps. However, keep in mind that how well you are able to return any ball depends on your position and the ball's location. The basic mechanics give you a foundation to work from. There will be times when you will have to cross over and reach as far as you can to return a ball. At other times the ball may be hit directly at you and you will be jammed. Regardless of what the situation is, the main objective is to keep the ball in play, control the court, and ultimately win the rally.

If you do not have a good setup (due to a good serve or your inability to get into a good position to return the ball), then your best option will be to go to the ceiling (see step 7, Ceiling Shots).

Beginning and intermediate players often make the mistake of allowing the ball to get behind or past them. During the service return, your first thought should be to attack the ball and get to it before it gets to the back wall if at all possible. This approach puts you on offense and allows you to return the ball before the server has a chance to set up in center court. When you are returning a serve, you want to be in position to move forward as you strike the ball. This gives you the opportunity to make an offensive shot. If the ball gets behind or past you, you will have a difficult time even hitting a ceiling ball. At best you may be able to flick the ball to the ceiling, but it will be a desperation shot. So, you must make a split-second decision: Do I attack the ball or set up and wait for it to come off the back wall? Regardless of your decision, be sure to keep your shot options open and set up so the ball ends up in front of you. This may require you to move from your return position to the back wall and then forward to hit the ball as it comes off the back wall. Don't let the ball play you; you play the ball. In other words, keep your feet moving and adjust your setup position.

The final part of the serve return after you hit the shot is getting ready for the next shot by getting to center court. One of the biggest mistakes made by receivers is to admire the serve return and not get ready for the next shot.

This is called spectating on the court. You are either a player or a spectator. Being a spectator on the court is disastrous and leaves unlimited shot opportunities for your opponent. Moving to center court will be covered in more detail in step 9, Court Positioning.

As you practice serve returns, move immediately to center court once you return the ball. You should do this even on a ceiling ball return. By moving to center court you are training your mind and body to perform a task. If you do this instinctively, you will be in the best position to return the next shot, while limiting your opponent's shot options. Keep reminding yourself as you are practicing: "Hit and recover," "hit and recover," "hit and recover." Recover to center court.

Serve Return Drill 1. *Breaking the False-Step Habit*

A common mistake is taking a misdirection or false step. A false step is a short step in any direction before taking that first positive step in the direction you really want to go. To correct the tendency to take a false step, stand with your heels against the back wall and get into the ready position for receiving serve. First, go left, using a quick half step and crossover. Next, go left with only a crossover—that is, without the quick half step. Repeat both movements to the right side. Having the wall on your heels will help prevent the false step and thus help you break the habit. A practice partner or video camera can give you immediate feedback on your performance. Complete 10 moves to the left and 10 to the right.

Success Check

- Stand in an athletic stance.
- Get into ready position for the service return.
- Put your heels against the wall.
- Execute a quick half step with crossover.

Score Your Success

Complete 10 repetitions to each side, for a total of 20 steps.

1 to 8 successful steps without a false step = 1 point

9 to 14 successful steps without a false step = 3 points

15 to 20 successful steps without a false step = 5 points

Your score ___

Serve Return Drill 2. *Footwork*

This is an easy drill to practice alone. Position yourself approximately 3 feet (0.9 meter) from the back wall, centered between the two side walls. Get in a balanced ready position on the balls of your feet. Practice the first quick step to the side wall. Do this 10 times each to the left and right. Next, practice the crossover step to each side 10 times. Finally, practice the combination of first quick step and crossover 10 times to each side.

While you practice this drill, pay close attention to the first step, making sure you do not take a false step. If necessary, have a practice partner watch your movements for the false step.

In addition to practicing your footwork, you should also practice racquet preparation. Be sure to get the racquet to the ready position as soon as you make your first move (either the first quick step or the crossover to the right or left). Don't forget: You are training your muscles and mind to do a particular task. Therefore, it is important to practice your movements as much as possible, but practice them correctly. A practice partner or video camera can give you immediate feedback on your performance.

Success Check

- Stand in an athletic stance.
- Get your racquet into ready position to receive the serve.
- Execute a quick step with a crossover step.

Score Your Success

Complete 10 repetitions to each side, for a total of 20 steps.

1 to 8 perfect steps without a false step = 1 point

9 to 14 perfect steps without a false step = 3 points

15 to 20 perfect steps without a false step = 5 points

Your score ___

SERVE-RETURN SELECTION

Now that you are in position to return the ball, where will you hit it? Remember, you need a plan or objective for returning the ball. Don't just hit it; hit it with purpose.

If you are in good position and balanced, hit an aggressive offensive shot, but not necessarily a kill shot (see step 5). Decide what shot to use on the return based on your return position and what the server is doing after the serve (table 4.1).

There is nothing magical about the return of serve. If you stay focused and practice the thought process of making good serve return decisions, you will have greater success at staying in a rally or winning it on the return. The biggest mistake most players make is trying to win the rally outright on the return by being too aggressive and going for a kill when they are off balance and not set up on the ball. There is nothing wrong with being aggressive on the return. Kill shots on service returns are great crowd pleasers and big ego boosters. However, they are low-percentage shots. Keep track of how good or poor your percentages are and adjust your return strategy accordingly.

Table 4.1 Serve-Return Shot Selection

Server's court position	Receiver's return position	High-percentage serve return
Server goes to center court	Receiver is balanced and set up in the backcourt on either side	1. Down-the-wall pass (pages 65, 78) 2. Wide-angle cross-court pass (pages 65,84) 3. Ceiling shot (page 107)
	Receiver is balanced and set up midcourt (not center court)	1. Down-the-wall pass 2. Wide-angle cross-court pass 3. Ceiling shot
	Receiver is unbalanced in the backcourt	1. Down-the-wall ceiling shot (pages 65, 110) 2. Cross-court ceiling shot (pages 66, 112)
Server goes to left center court	Receiver is balanced and set up in the backcourt on either side	1. Cross-court V pass (pages 65, 81) 2. Wide-angle cross-court pass 3. Down-the-wall pass 4. Ceiling shot
	Receiver is balanced and set up midcourt (not center court)	1. Down-the-wall pass 2. Cross-court V pass 3. Ceiling shot
	Receiver is unbalanced in the backcourt	1. Down-the-wall ceiling shot 2. Cross-court ceiling shot
Server stays in front of the safety line	Receiver is balanced	1. Down-the-wall pass 2. Wide-angle cross-court pass 3. Ceiling shot
	Receiver is unbalanced	1. Down-the-wall ceiling shot 2. Cross-court ceiling shot
Server comes to the backcourt	Receiver is balanced	1. Pinch (page 96) 2. Down-the-wall pass 3. Cross-court V pass 4. Ceiling shot
	Receiver is unbalanced	1. Down-the-wall ceiling shot 2. Cross-court ceiling shot

Misstep

The ball skips before hitting the front wall.

Correction

Aim 18 inches (45 centimeters) off the floor on the front wall. Don't go for the kill shot. Shoot the passing shot. Your racquet face may be closed or turned down. The racquet face should be perpendicular to the floor on contact with the ball.

Typical high-percentage serve returns you will use include the following:

- Down-the-wall pass (figure 4.3a). A ball hit along the side wall toward the front wall that returns as close as possible along the same side wall.
- Cross-court V pass (figure 4.3b). A ball hit from one side of the court to the other, wherein the ball angles off the front wall to the opposite back corner (see step 5, Front-Wall Shots).

- Wide-angle pass (figure 4.3c). A ball hit from one side of the court to the other, wherein the ball angles off the front wall to the opposite side wall near the safety line (see step 5, Front-Wall Shots).
- Down-the-wall ceiling shot (figure 4.3d). A ball hit to the ceiling and front wall along the side wall, wherein the ball comes back as close as possible along the same side wall to the back court (see step 7, Ceiling Shots).

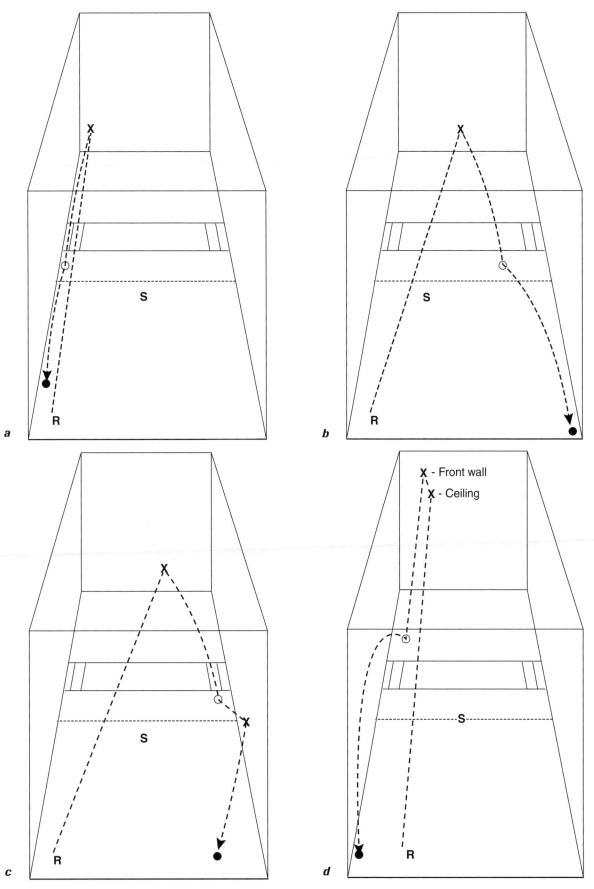

Figure 4.3 High-percentage serve returns: *(a)* down-the-wall pass; *(b)* cross-court V pass; *(c)* wide-angle pass; *(d)* down-the-wall ceiling shot.

- Cross-court ceiling shot (figure 4.3e). A ball hit from one side of the court to the other, wherein the ball angles off the ceiling and front wall to the opposite back corner (see step 7, Ceiling Shots).

- Pinch. A ball hit to the front corner (side wall to front wall) at either the near or far side wall (see step 6, Side-Wall Shots).

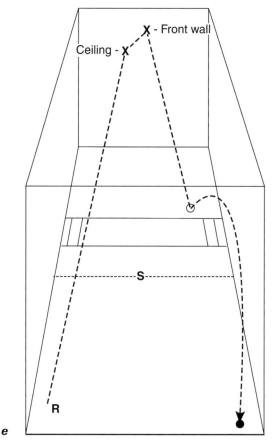

Figure 4.3 *(continued)* High-percentage serve returns: *(e)* cross-court ceiling shot.

Misstep

The ball contacts the side wall before hitting the front wall on a down-the-wall or ceiling return.

Correction

Stay behind the ball and keep it in front of you when you hit it. Either attack it before it gets to the back wall or move out with it as it comes off the back wall. Get your racquet in the backswing position as quickly as possible. You may be hitting the ball in the back of the power zone. Hit the ball in the middle of or in front of the power zone. Wrist snap may be late at ball contact.

Return Selection Drill. *Choosing a Return*

This drill requires a practice partner. Have your partner hit different types of serves in groups of 5 or 10—for example, 5 drive serves to the left corner, 10 half lob serves to the left, 5 half lob serves down the wall to the right, 10 jam serves to the left, and so on. Focus on footwork and getting to your receiving location to set up for the return. Remember, take no false steps and get your racquet in the backswing position on your first step. Practice good split-second decision making as you set up for the return. Remember not to commit to a shot too soon. Committing too early will limit your options and may tip off the server to what your shot will be. Take what is given to you and make the most of it. If you are balanced and set up, shoot a down-the-wall pass or cross-court pass. If you are off balance, hit a down-the-wall or cross-court ceiling ball. The main objective with this drill is to move your opponent out of center court so you can move in and take control of the court for the return of your opponent's next shot. You can play through your return or play the rally out. It's up to you.

To keep things simple, and because we have not yet discussed the ceiling ball, the success checks focus only on the down-the-wall and cross-court shots.

Success Check

- Use a quick half step and crossover step.
- Hold your racquet in backswing position.

- Get into a good setup position for the service return.
- For the down-the-wall return, hit the ball along the side wall to the front wall so it comes back along the same side.
- For the cross-court V return, hit the ball to the opposite backcourt corner.

Score Your Success

Complete 10 down-the-wall returns each to the forehand and backhand sides, for a total of 20 returns.

1 to 8 successful down-the-wall returns = 1 point

9 to 14 successful down-the-wall returns = 3 points

15 to 20 successful down-the-wall returns = 5 points

Your score ___

Complete 10 cross-court V returns each to the forehand and backhand sides, for a total of 20 returns.

1 to 8 successful cross-court returns = 1 point

9 to 14 successful cross-court returns = 3 points

15 to 20 successful cross-court returns = 5 points

Your score ___

Misstep

Instead of angling off the front wall to the side wall (for the wide-angle passing shot) at the safety line, the ball goes to the back corner.

Correction

Widen the angle of the ball as it comes off the front wall by moving the contact point on the front wall closer to the opposite side. Don't go too wide or the ball will come off the side wall into the middle court.

SHORT-HOP RETURN

Another way to approach the service return is to attack the lob serve and cut it off before it reaches the backcourt. This is easier said than done, but with a little practice you can easily go on the offensive by returning the ball before your opponent has an opportunity to get out of the service box and into center court.

High lob serves are the easiest to attack and cut off. Timing is everything with this style of return. Make sure you do not encroach into the safety zone before the ball contacts the floor (see "Basic Rules of Play" in The Sport of Racquetball on page xii). Typically you will want to short-hop the ball when returning the high lob this way. The highest-percentage returns are the down-the-wall pass, cross-court pass, and high Z (discussed in step 5, Front-Wall Shots). No need to go for the kill here: A good passing shot is all you need to force your opponent to the backcourt or even win the rally outright.

Short-hopping the ball is an aggressive way to attack the lob serve. This accomplishes three objectives: It puts you on the offensive, it places the server on the defensive, and it gets the ball past the server before he or she has an opportunity to get out of the service zone and into a ready position in center court.

Hit the short-hop just after the ball bounces on the floor and is just beginning its way back up to the top of its trajectory to the backcourt. You need to be cautious not to encroach on the safety line before the ball bounces on the floor. A short-hop may be as low to the floor as 2 inches (5 centimeters) or as high as chest level.

How you approach the short-hop will have a big effect on how well you are able to execute your shot. A common mistake is to move in a straight line to where the ball will be hit. This may cause you to hit the ball with open hips, limit your shot selection, or create poor ball proximity. You should approach this return with a path that looks similar to a banana

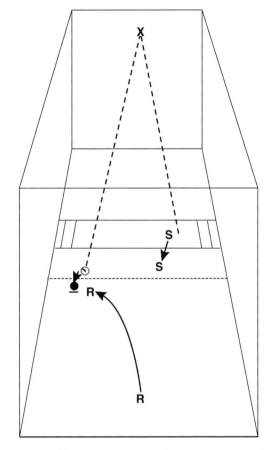

Figure 4.4 The path to the short-hop return is curved like a banana.

(figure 4.4). This approach will allow you to square up to the side wall and keep the ball properly away from your body so you can hit out and around. Refer to step 9, Court Positioning, for a more detailed discussion on how to approach the shot, as well as drills to improve footwork.

If the server hits long lob serves that bounce past the safety line, you may want to attack them even more aggressively, hitting the ball in the air before it hits the floor. Again, be careful of the safety line and encroachment. Your shot selection and approach to the ball will be the same as for the short-hop. This is a very advanced return to control and use effectively.

Short-Hop Return Drill 1. *Solo Practice*

The short-hop is easiest to practice by yourself to get the timing right. Stand close to the side wall and just behind the safety zone line, on either the forehand or backhand side. Lightly bounce the ball off the floor so it hits the side wall and rebounds back to the floor (figure 4.5). As the ball hits the floor off the rebound from the side wall, short-hop the ball by striking it with the racquet just as it bounces up from the floor. This is not easy to do, but with a little patience and practice you will soon master it. The idea is to hit the ball when it is 3 to 4 inches (8 to 10 centimeters) off the floor with a flat, out-and-around stroke and with extreme power. This shot is not hit softly or with finesse; hit it at 90 to 100 percent of full power for maximum effect. Practice all your options by hitting down-the-wall passes, cross-court V passes, and wide-angle passes. Hit 3 sets of 10 repetitions from each side, working on one particular return at a time.

Success Check

- Square off to the side wall.
- Stand in an athletic stance.
- Hold your racquet in backswing position.
- Bounce the ball off the floor to the side wall and back to the floor.
- Hit the ball on the short-hop as it comes back off the floor from the side wall.

Score Your Success

Complete 10 down-the-wall passes off the short-hop to both the forehand and backhand sides, for a total of 20 passes.

1 to 8 successful down-the-wall short-hops = 1 point

9 to 14 successful down-the-wall short-hops = 3 points

15 to 20 successful down-the-wall short-hops = 5 points

Your score ___

Complete 10 cross-court V or wide-angle passes off the short-hop to both the forehand and backhand sides, for a total of 20 passes.

1 to 8 successful cross-court V or wide-angle short-hops = 1 point

9 to 14 successful cross-court V or wide-angle short-hops = 3 points

15 to 20 successful cross-court V or wide-angle short-hops = 5 points

Your score ___

Figure 4.5 On the short-hop, hit the ball when it is 3 to 4 inches (8 to 10 centimeters) off the floor.

Short-Hop Return Drill 2.   *Ball Drops*

Another way to practice the short-hop is to stand just behind the safety zone line and drop and hit the ball (i.e., short-hop it) using the three passing shots. This is good for practicing the short-hop from its actual location as it would come from a high lob serve. Practice all your options by hitting down-the-wall passes, cross-court V passes, and wide-angle passes. Hit 3 sets of 10 repetitions from each side, working on one particular return at a time.

Success Check

- Square off to the side wall.
- Stand in an athletic stance.

- Hold the racquet in backswing position.
- Drop the ball to the floor.
- Hit the ball off the short-hop as it bounces off the floor.

Score Your Success

Complete 10 return shots of your choice off both forehand and backhand short-hops, for a total of 20 returns.

1 to 8 successful short-hops = 1 point

9 to 14 successful short-hops = 3 points

15 to 20 successful short-hops = 5 points

Your score ___

Short-Hop Return Drill 3.   *Gamelike Play*

Stand in the middle backcourt. Hit the ball to the front wall, using a finesse or soft shot so the ball comes back and bounces at or just behind the encroachment line. Short-hop the ball in a game-like replication. This is a highly advanced practice drill, so don't be discouraged if you are unable to accomplish it right away. Practice using all your options by hitting down-the-wall passes, cross-court V passes, and wide-angle passes. Hit 3 sets of 10 repetitions from each side, working on one particular return at a time.

Success Check

- Hit a soft shot off the front wall.
- Square off to the side wall.
- Stand in an athletic stance.

- Hold your racquet in backswing position.
- Adjust your position.
- Hit the return off the short-hop.

Score Your Success

Complete 10 cross-court V or wide-angle passes off the short-hop to both the forehand and back-hand sides, for a total of 20 passes.

1 to 8 successful cross-court V or wide-angle short-hops = 1 point

9 to 14 successful cross-court V or wide-angle short-hops = 3 points

15 to 20 successful cross-court V or wide-angle short-hops = 5 points

Your score ___

DEEP-CORNER RETURN, BACKHAND AND FOREHAND

In the deep-corner return, you have to return a ball that is deep in the backcourt in either the forehand or backhand corner. This is a difficult return because there is very little room to maneuver. Additionally, it is the farthest distance to hit the ball (from deep backcourt to the front wall).

The following two drills are excellent for solo practice of the deep-corner serve return, as well as the deep-corner rally return. It takes skill to toss the ball in the right place, but it is well worth the effort and patience to accomplish. The ball toss will be easier for most people on the backhand side as opposed to the forehand side due to the nature of the arm movement across the body. But be sure to work both corners, not just the backhand side, for strength and balance in your return game.

Deep-Corner Return Drill 1. *Back-to-Side-Wall Return*

Stand one arm's length away from the back wall and approximately 3 feet (0.9 meter) from the side wall. With your nonracquet hand, toss the ball using an overhand or backhand toss so the ball bounces off the floor to the back wall and then hits the side wall. The ball hits the floor off the side wall for the return (figure 4.6). The idea is to toss the ball with finesse so the ball wraps around the corner. Return the ball from deep in the backcourt. Get the racquet in the backswing position before you toss the ball. Additionally, remain balanced and move your feet to get into the proper setup position to return the ball.

Practice all options by hitting ceiling shots, down-the-wall passes, cross-court passes, and wide-angle passes. Hit 4 sets of 10 repetitions, working on one particular return at a time.

To Increase Difficulty

Return the ball as it comes off the side wall, before it hits the floor the second time.

Success Check

- Square off to the side wall in the deep corner.
- Stand in an athletic stance.

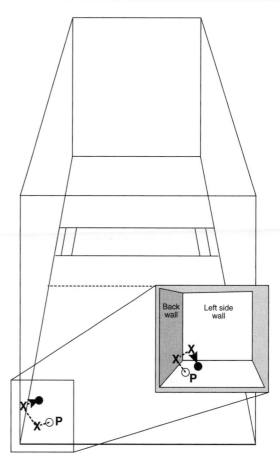

Figure 4.6 The ball hits the floor, then the back wall, then the side wall, then the floor.

71

- Hold the racquet in backswing position.
- Toss the ball to the floor and into the corner of the back and side walls.
- Return the ball after it hits the floor off the side wall, using the down-the-wall pass.

Complete 10 down-the-wall returns using forehand shots and 10 using backhand shots, for a total of 20 down-the-wall passes.

1 to 8 successful returns = 1 point

9 to 14 successful returns = 3 points

15 to 20 successful returns = 5 points

Your score ___

Deep-Corner Return Drill 2. *Side-to-Back-Wall Return*

This is essentially the same as the back-to-side-wall drill, only in reverse. However, because the drill puts the ball closer to the back wall, it makes for a much more difficult return.

Stand one arm's length away from the back wall, approximately 3 feet (0.9 meter) from the side wall. Get the racquet in backswing position before you toss the ball. With your nonracquet hand, toss the ball in an overhand or forehand toss so the ball bounces off the floor to the side wall and then hits the back wall. It then hits the floor for the return (figure 4.7). The idea is to toss the ball with finesse so it wraps around the corner. Return the ball from deep in the backcourt. Be sure to remain balanced and move your feet to get into the proper setup position to return the ball.

Practice all options by hitting ceiling shots, down-the-wall passes, cross-court passes, and wide-angle passes. Hit 4 sets of 10 repetitions from each side, working on one particular return at a time.

To Increase Difficulty

Return the ball as it comes off the back wall, before it hits the floor the second time.

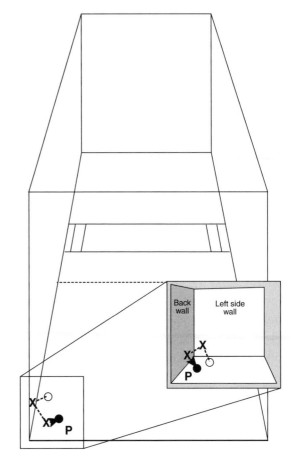

Figure 4.7 The ball bounces off the floor to the side wall, then hits the back wall.

Success Check

- Square off to the side wall in the deep corner.
- Stand in an athletic stance.
- Hold the racquet in backswing position.
- Toss the ball to the floor and into the corner of the side and back walls.
- Return the ball after it hits the floor off the back wall, using the down-the-wall pass.

Complete 10 down-the-wall passes on each side (forehand and backhand), for a total of 20 passes.

1 to 8 successful returns = 1 point

9 to 14 successful returns = 3 points

15 to 20 successful returns = 5 points

Your score ___

Return Game Drill 1.   15-Point Return Game

With a partner, play a return-only game to 15 points. Return serve for 5 or 10 points in a row, regardless of who wins the rally, before you switch to serving. Once you have returned 5 or 10 serves, or the total score of both players is at least 5 or 10, switch the serve. Use rally scoring; either the server or the receiver can score. The game is over once the first player gets to 15.

This game allows you time to work on receiving serve. I prefer to have my players work on only one type of serve return during the 5- or 10-return rotation. This gives you enough returns to work on difficulties. Don't cheat by moving early to return the serve. Focus on the server and try to detect his or her body positioning, ball drop and delivery, and serve mechanics.

Be sure to work on all returns. Don't just work on the return that is your best or the easiest to win with against your opponent. This is a practice drill to improve your return. It won't do you any good to pound a return you already hit well to a server who cannot return it. Work on your weaknesses, not your strengths.

To Increase Difficulty

The server uses a different serve each time. The server cannot use the same serve twice during the game. This forces the receiver to focus on the server and try to detect clues.

Success Check

- Execute a quick half step and crossover step.
- Hold your racquet in backswing position.
- Get into good setup position for the return.
- Return the serve with a successful passing shot.

Play a normal game to 15, but earn points for this drill based on your effective returns. An effective return is one in which you were able to move your opponent to the deep backcourt corner or win the point outright.

1 to 5 effective returns = 1 point

6 to 15 effective returns = 3 points

16 or more effective returns = 5 points

Your score ___

Return Game Drill 2. *3-Point Return Game*

In this game, you must score 3 points in a row in order to win. If you score only 0, 1, or 2 points, then it is sideout and you do not win. This is a great way to simulate a match. It helps you work on your focus and intensity. You will find this is not an easy task. In fact, you may go a long time playing this game before anyone wins. The better you get and the better your opponent, the more difficult the game. Mix up your serves and have fun with this difficult game.

To Increase Difficulty

Play a 5-point return game in which you have to score 5 points in a row to win. Depending on how evenly matched you are with your opponent, you could play to more than 5 points.

Success Check

- Execute a quick half step and crossover step.
- Hold your racquet in the backswing position.
- Get into a good setup position for the return.
- Return the serve with a successful passing shot.

Score Your Success

Give yourself points based on how many effective returns in a row you are able to score in a game to 5. An effective return is one where you move your opponent out of center court to the deep backcourt corner.

1 effective return = 1 point

2 or 3 effective returns = 3 points

4 or 5 effective returns = 5 points

Your score ___

SUCCESS SUMMARY OF RETURN OF SERVE

Return of serve is crucial to the game. You must be able to put the ball in play and have an opportunity to win the rally. Be conservative with your serve returns. Don't be greedy and try to end the rally before it begins. As a receiver, if you make a mistake or skip the ball your opponent wins the point. Serve return is tactical and should be approached with the idea of forcing your opponent out of center court so you can move in for the next shot. If your return is hit well enough, you may force your opponent to hit a weak shot. You may even win the rally outright.

Remember to come back and use the drills and practice games for review as you progress through the book. Continue to build the foundation for a good game of racquetball. These drills and practice games are used by amateurs and pros alike to fine-tune skills for a rock-solid game.

Next, you will progress into the front-wall shots. These shots will add to your return-of-serve skills and will also build the foundation for rally play.

Review your scores for each of the serve return drills. Enter your scores and tally them to rate your serve return success.

Serve Return Drills

   1. Breaking the False-Step Habit   ___ out of 5

   2. Footwork   ___ out of 5

Return Selection Drill

   1. Choosing a Return   ___ out of 10

Short-Hop Return Drills

   1. Solo Practice   ___ out of 10

   2. Ball Drops   ___ out of 5

   3. Gamelike Play   ___ out of 5

Deep-Corner Return Drills

   1. Back-to-Side-Wall Return   ___ out of 5

   2. Side-to-Back-Wall Return   ___ out of 5

Return Game Drills

   1. 15-Point Return Game   ___ out of 5

   2. 3-Point Return Game   ___ out of 5

Total   ___ *out of 60*

If you scored fewer than 35 points, review and practice the drills that were difficult for you. If you scored 35 points or more, you are ready to continue to step 5, Front-Wall Shots.

Front-Wall Shots

Front-wall shots are the meat and potatoes of your racquetball game. The three most basic shots you should use more than any others are the passing shots: down-the-wall, cross-court V, and wide-angle cross-court. With the prime location for the defensive player being center court (see figure 9.1, page 136), passing shots should account for 80 percent of all your racquetball shots.

Front-wall shots are used more than any others because they allow maximum power on the passing shot or kill shot and have the shortest path to the backcourt. Hitting the side wall first will cause a ball to angle to the front wall and eventually toward center court. A pure front-wall shot is a straight shot to the front wall and then toward the backcourt. Anytime the ball hits a wall or ceiling before the front wall, energy is lost and the ball loses some of its speed. Speed is essential for a passing shot, especially if it is not hit perfectly. With speeds ranging from 120 to 150 miles (190 to 240 kilometers) per hour for the average player, you can see how difficult it can be to react to a good passing shot before it gets past.

Even if it is hit too high, a good passing shot with the proper angle will always move the opponent out of center court. Since center court is the prime location, this shot makes it possible

for you to move in and prepare for the next shot. Therefore, practicing your passing shots and achieving a high success rate is critical to the success of your overall game.

The primary reason for occupying center court is that most players are not skilled at hitting the passing shot, or tend to hit too many angle shots, resulting in a ball that eventually angles back toward center court. You can prove this by getting in a racquetball court and hitting the ball anywhere you wish. See where the ball goes. With enough angle or pace on the ball, the ball will eventually pass through or very close to center court. Therefore, you want to be in center court when waiting for a return and be ready for that errant shot to come for a put-away.

Too many racquetball players pinch the ball. (See step 6 for more on the pinch shot). While this shot has its place in the game, it is used far too often. The highest-percentage offensive shot is the front-wall pass. No need to get fancy or go for the bottom board: Just hit a well-placed passing shot and you will be very successful. If you watch a good racquetball game and track the ratio of passing shots to kill shots, you will count many more passing shots. In fact, if you apply the principle of hitting passing shots (down-the-wall, cross-court V, and wide-angle cross-court passes) 80 percent of the time, you will find that you win approximately 80 percent of your rallies.

The well-hit passing shot will move your opponent out of center court and into the backcourt, increasing the chances of a weak return or unforced error. At the same time, a well-placed and well-executed passing shot will seldom result in an unforced error on your part or give your opponent a kill shot. Remember, your primary objective with the passing shot is to move your opponent out of center court and force him or her to return the ball from the farthest distance on the court: the deep backcourt.

Regardless of the outcome, the pressure is on your opponent to hit a good shot. The odds are in your favor because you are in center court and

in control, with your opponent shooting from the backcourt. If your opponent doesn't hit a winner or move you to the backcourt, you will be in excellent position to hit that crowd-pleasing and ego-satisfying winning shot that you have been waiting for.

The keys to successful shots are getting in position quickly, using the correct stance, staying balanced, executing solid swing mechanics, controlling the racquet, and hitting with accuracy. The ball should contact the front wall about 18 inches (45 centimeters) above the floor, or lower, increasing both your rate of high-quality shots and your winning-shot percentage. Even if you are lunging for a ball and cannot get into a good setup position, the passing shot will always be a high-percentage option.

DOWN-THE-WALL PASSING SHOT

The name of the down-the-wall passing shot describes what the ball does. This is an excellent high-percentage shot for passing an opponent who is in center court or out of position on the opposite side of the court. Hit the ball as near as possible to the side wall and straight into the front wall to get the ball to come back down the wall as close to the wall as possible (figure 5.1).

The key to this shot is not so much how low you hit it; rather, you want the ball to hug the wall as it returns to the back of the court. You can hit this ball 18 inches (45 centimeters) off the floor on the front wall and it will usually double-bounce before it gets to the back wall, depending on the velocity and angle of the ball off the racquet. Even if this ball is hit extremely high, the fact that the ball remains close to the wall makes it difficult to return and moves your opponent out of center court.

To execute the down-the-wall passing shot (figure 5.2), square off to the side wall and get in a normal ready stance, with your racquet in the backswing position, as quickly as possible. Adjust your position with small steps and use a flat, out-and-around stroke, hitting the ball in the middle of the power zone. It is necessary to

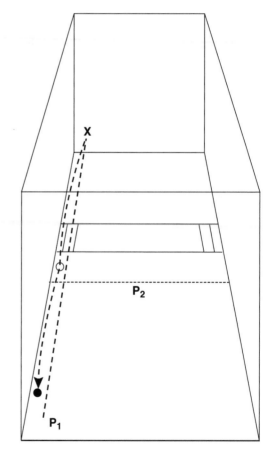

Figure 5.1 Down-the-wall passing shot.

keep the ball from hitting the side wall either on its way to the front wall or on its way to the backcourt. Hitting the side wall may cause the ball to carom toward the center of the court.

The wall is your ally and will act as an obstacle as your opponent tries to return the ball, many times hitting the wall with his or her racquet while attempting the return.

Figure 5.2　Down-the-Wall Pass

a

b

STANCE

1. Anticipate where the ball will go
2. Set up so you can hit the ball in the power zone
3. Get your racquet in the backswing position as quickly as possible
4. Use small steps to adjust your position

SWING

1. Use a flat, out-and-around swing parallel to the floor
2. Rotate with your hips and shoulders
3. Hit the ball in the middle of the power zone

(continued)

79

Figure 5.2   *(continued)*

FOLLOW-THROUGH

1. Follow through in a flat line
2. Stay balanced
3. Move to center court quickly

c

Misstep

The ball contacts the side wall before hitting the front wall.

Correction

You may be hitting the ball in the back of the power zone. Make racquet contact with the ball in the middle of the power zone. You may be using a closed stance. Be sure to square off to the side wall. You may also be late with your wrist snap.

Misstep

The ball caroms off the front wall toward center court.

Correction

You may be hitting the ball in the front end of the power zone. Make racquet contact with the ball in the middle of the power zone. You may be using an open stance. Be sure to square off to the side wall. You may also be early with your wrist snap.

Down-the-Wall Pass Drill.

The down-the-wall passing shot is a fairly easy shot to practice. In fact, competitive players often use down-the-wall pass drills to warm up before play.

You can drop the ball a few different ways to practice:

- Drop it and hit it

Progressive Shots

- Toss the ball off the side wall and let it bounce on the floor before hitting it
- Toss the ball on the floor, let it bounce off the side wall, and hit it before it bounces on the floor
- Toss the ball up and hit it in the air before it hits the floor (more advanced)

Practice from three locations on each side of the court (figure 5.3). You may start with either the forehand or backhand side. Start with position 1 so you will not have to hit the ball as hard; you will be closer to the front wall, and this will give you a higher rate of success. After you complete 10 down-the-wall hits from loca-

tion 1, move to location 2, and then to location 3. Perform this drill in the same order on both sides of the court, using 10 repetitions at each location, for a total of 3 sets of 10 repetitions on each side.

Remember, the keys to a high winning-shot percentage are proper stance, good balance, ability to get the racquet into backswing position quickly, solid swing mechanics, ball contact in the middle of the power zone, racquet control, accuracy, and, follow-through—not power.

Success Check

- Visualize your stroke and shot.
- Set up in the backswing position, squared off to the side wall.
- Drop the ball in the middle of the power zone.
- Hit the ball down the wall.
- Follow through with a flat stroke.

Score Your Success

Complete a total of 30 repetitions of down-the-wall shots, 5 from each of the six positions. If the ball comes back down the wall between your hitting position and the wall, it is considered a successful shot.

1 to 40 percent successful shots = 1 point

41 to 70 percent successful shots = 3 points

71 to 100 percent successful shots = 5 points

Your score ___

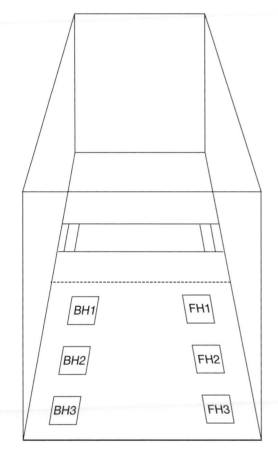

Figure 5.3 Court positions for the down-the-wall drill.

CROSS-COURT V PASSING SHOT

The basic cross-court V pass is another shot you will want to practice often so you can hit it with precision and confidence when required. This shot is best used when your opponent is out of center court on your side and looking for the down-the-wall pass. The cross-court V pass is hit at an angle so the ball travels to the opposite corner in the deep backcourt (figure 5.4). The idea is to have the ball double-bounce before it gets to the back wall or die in the

backcourt as it comes off the back wall at the end of the shot.

When your opponent is in middle center court, this is a lower-percentage shot because it may allow him or her the opportunity to return the ball with an easy step-over shot down the wall or a short-step, open-stance volley. If you are hitting from the deep backcourt, you do not want to give your opponent an easy put-away at mid center court.

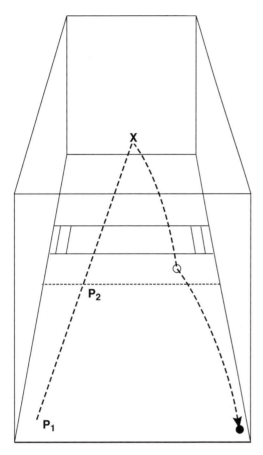

Figure 5.4 Cross-court V passing shot.

To execute the cross-court V pass (figure 5.5), stand in a normal or slightly open stance. A closed stance will make it difficult to hit this shot with any power or accuracy. In the normal stance, you will hit the ball in the forward end of the power zone. If you are using an open stance, you will hit the ball more in the middle of the power zone. Use a level stroke with a full follow-through. Hit the ball against the front wall no higher than 18 inches (45 centimeters) above the floor.

Figure 5.5   Cross-Court V Pass

STANCE

1. Square off to the side wall or use a slightly open stance
2. Assume backswing ready position

a

b

c

SWING

1. Should be a flat, out-and-around motion
2. Swing is parallel to the floor
3. Stay low and balanced
4. Hit the ball in the middle or just forward of the power zone

FOLLOW-THROUGH

1. Follow through is as flat as possible
2. Keep weight balanced through the swing

Misstep

The ball contacts the opposite side wall before hitting the back wall.

Correction

The angle is too wide. Narrow the angle by moving the ball-contact point on the front wall closer to the center of the front wall. You may be hitting the ball at the front end of the power zone or you may be hitting with an open stance. Hit in the middle of the power zone using a normal stance. Square off to the side wall.

Misstep

The ball goes to center court off the front wall.

Correction

Ball contact may be occurring in the back end of the power zone. Ball contact should be in the middle of the power zone. Your stance may be closed. Use a normal stance. An imaginary line connecting your feet would point where you want to hit the ball.

Cross-Court V Pass Drill. *Progressive Shots*

The cross-court V passing shot is not a difficult shot to practice. As with the down-the-wall shot, competitive players often use it to warm up before play. It is important to make sure you are hitting this shot so it ends up within 2 feet (0.6 meter) of either side of the back corner on the opposite side.

Practice from three locations on each side of the court (figure 5.3, page 81). Begin at location 1, nearest the receiving line. It doesn't matter which side you start on. As you practice these drills, be sure to focus on the angle: The ball should hit the front wall about 18 inches (45 centimeters) off the floor, or lower, at an angle to direct the ball within 2 feet (0.6 meter) of the back corner on the opposite side of the court. After you complete 10 cross-court V shots from location 1, move to location 2, and then to location 3. Perform this drill in the same order on both sides of the court, using 10 repetitions at each location, for a total of 3 sets of 10 repetitions on each side.

Success Check

- Visualize your stroke and shot.
- Use a squared-off or slightly open stance toward the side wall.
- Get the racquet in the backswing position.
- Execute a flat, out-and-around stroke.
- Follow through in as flat a line as possible.
- Stay balanced.

Score Your Success

Complete a total of 30 repetitions of down-the-wall shots, 5 from each of the six positions. If the ball comes within 2 feet (0.6 meter) of the back corner, it is considered a successful shot.

1 to 40 percent successful shots = 1 point

41 to 70 percent successful shots = 3 points

71 to 100 percent successful shots = 5 points

Your score ___

WIDE-ANGLE CROSS-COURT PASSING SHOT

No matter where your opponent is in relation to center court, when you hit a wide-angle cross-court pass (figure 5.6), angle the ball so that it hits the side wall directly across from your opponent. Typically this will be at or near the safety line. This makes the return extremely difficult by forcing your opponent to go the farthest distance to get the racquet on the ball.

If the wide-angle cross-court pass is hit with too much angle and the ball caroms off the side wall in front of or toward the opponent, it reduces the distance the opponent has to travel to get the racquet on the ball (figure 5.7). Even worse, if the angle is much too wide off the front wall, your opponent may be able to step across and put away a winner.

What makes this particular shot difficult is the angle of the ball off the front wall. If you don't go wide enough, the ball ends up being a cross-court V pass. If you go too wide, the ball will come back to center court. So practice this shot often if you want to execute it with confidence and accuracy. In fact, you can use this shot most of the time as a cross-court pass.

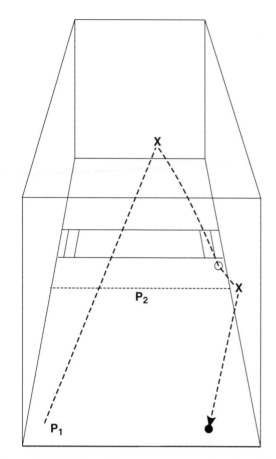

Figure 5.6 Wide-angle cross-court pass (good angle).

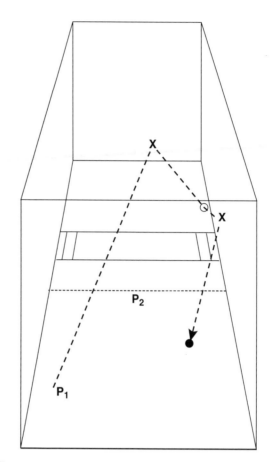

Figure 5.7 Wide-angle cross-court pass (bad angle) with ball too near the opponent.

Misstep

The ball contacts the side wall in front of the service line and caroms to center court.

Correction

The angle is too wide. Narrow the angle by moving the ball-contact point on the front wall closer to the center of the front wall. You may be hitting the ball too far forward in the front end of the power zone or you may be hitting with a wide-open stance. Hit closer to the middle of the power zone. Use a normal stance, with an imaginary line connecting your feet pointing in the direction of the shot.

Misstep

The ball does not contact the side wall before hitting the back wall.

Correction

The angle is not wide enough. Widen the angle by moving the ball-contact point on the front wall farther away from the center of the front wall. Ball contact may be occurring in the back of the power zone, or your stance may be closed. Hit in the middle of or slightly forward in the power zone. Use a normal or slightly open stance, with an imaginary line connecting your feet pointing in the direction of the shot.

Wide-Angle Cross-Court Pass Drill. *Angles, Angles, Angles*

Practice drill locations are the same as for the down-the-wall pass and cross-court V pass (figure 5.3, page 81). There are three locations for practicing these drills on each side of the court. As you practice, be sure to focus on the angle, with the ball hitting the front wall about 18 inches (45 centimeters) off the floor, or lower, and angling to the side wall at the safety line. The ball will carom off the side wall and die at or near the middle of the back wall.

Remember, the ball doesn't have to hit the floor before it hits the side wall. It is perfectly fine for the ball to hit the side wall first, as long as it hits low and doesn't carry so far as to come off the back wall for a setup return.

Begin at location 1, nearest the receiving line. It doesn't matter which side you start on. As you practice these drills, be sure to focus on the angle, with the ball hitting the front wall about 18 inches (45 centimeters) off the floor, or lower, at an angle to direct the ball to the opposite side wall at or near the safety line. After you complete 10 wide-angle cross-court passes from location 1, move to location 2, and then to location 3. Perform this drill in the same order on both sides of the court, using 10 repetitions at each location, for a total of 3 sets of 10 repetitions on each side.

Success Check

- Visualize your stroke and shot.
- Use a squared-off or slightly open stance toward the side wall.
- Get the racquet in the backswing position.
- Execute a flat, out-and-around stroke.
- Make contact with the ball in the middle or just forward of the power zone.
- Follow through in as flat a line as possible.
- Stay balanced.

Score Your Success

Complete a total of 30 repetitions of the wide-angle cross-court pass, 5 from each of the six positions. If the ball comes within 2 feet (0.6 meter) of the safety line and dies at or near the back wall, it is considered a successful shot.

1 to 40 percent successful shots = 1 point

41 to 70 percent successful shots = 3 points

71 to 100 percent successful shots = 5 points

Your score ___

KILL SHOT

A kill shot is an advanced power shot that does what its name implies—kills the rally. This is the shot everyone wants and shoots for in racquetball, but it is not always the best choice. Just like the outright screaming winner in tennis, this is the crowd pleaser of racquetball shots. But be cautious. Hitting the ball too close to the floor will lead to unforced errors (skips), just like hitting the net in tennis when going for the winner.

No matter where you are on the court or what angle your shot takes, if the ball hits the front wall and rolls out or double-bounces before your opponent can hit a return, it is a kill shot. Use this shot with discretion and only when you can afford to take a chance and lose a rally. Kill shots are sometimes a gamble. Many players try to hit kill shots when a higher-percentage passing shot will have the same effect of winning the rally.

Misstep

The ball skips before hitting the front wall.

Correction

Aim higher off the floor on the front wall. Your racquet face may be facing down during contact with the ball. The racquet face should be perpendicular to the floor on contact with the ball. You may be using a pendulum swing. Use a flat, out-and-around stroke.

Misstep

The ball flies off the front wall and doesn't double-bounce before the safety line.

Correction

Aim lower on the front wall. Your racquet face may be facing up during contact with the ball. The racquet face should be perpendicular to the floor on contact with the ball. You may be using a pendulum swing. Use a flat, out-and-around stroke.

Kill Shot Drill.   *Kill the Rally (Advanced)*

There are no specific drills for the kill shot. Rather, as you practice all of your racquetball shots, applying control and accuracy, your power and kill-shot skills will improve. The more you practice your shot skills, the lower you will be able to hit the ball on the front wall. The key ingredients to most kill shots are stance, balance, swing mechanics, racquet control, accuracy, and power.

Use the same locations as used in figure 5.3, page 81. Practice hitting kill shots down the wall on both the forehand and backhand sides of the court. The key to this drill is hitting the ball low in your stroke and low on the front wall.

Success Check

- Visualize the stroke, the location on the front wall, and the finished shot.
- Set up in the backswing position, squared off to the side wall.
- Get low in your stance.
- Drop the ball in the middle of the power zone.

- Use a flat, out-and-around stroke parallel to the floor.
- Keep your eye on the ball and hit it below your knee.
- The ball should contact the front wall 2 to 6 inches (5 to 15 centimeters) above the floor.
- Stay low and follow through low and flat.
- Stay balanced.

Score Your Success

Complete a total of 30 repetitions of down-the-wall shots, 5 from each of the six positions. If the ball comes back down the wall and double-bounces before reaching the safety line, it is considered a successful shot.

1 to 20 percent successful shots = 1 point

21 to 50 percent successful shots = 3 points

51 to 100 percent successful shots = 5 points

Your score ___

OVERHEAD PASS

This shot can be executed from anywhere on the court, but it is primarily hit in the backcourt and with the forehand. It is an advanced, powerful passing shot that has good results if hit properly and used wisely. Remember, it is a low-percentage shot that should be used sparingly.

This shot is best used as a deception in response to a high lob serve or short ceiling ball. Get into position to hit a ceiling ball (see step 7, Ceiling Shots) but instead hit an overhead pass shot. This puts your opponent off guard and may result in a winning shot if executed correctly.

The overhead pass is hit from above the head, much like an overhead smash in tennis. The stance and stroke mechanics are similar to the forehand ceiling shot, except that the racquet contact with the ball will be slightly in front of your body (figure 5.8) and the ball is hit downward with a closed racquet face.

| Figure 5.8 | Overhead Pass |

CONTACT

1. Keep your eye on the ball
2. Hit the ball while stepping forward toward the ball
3. Rotate your hips and shoulders in the direction of the front wall
4. Hit the ball in front of and above your head
5. Aim for a location on the front wall approximately 18 inches (45 centimeters) above the floor

When hitting the ball from the backcourt, begin by squaring up to the side wall, with your shoulders and hips turned slightly forward. Aim for the front wall about 18 inches (45 centimeters) above the floor. The forehand overhead uses the same motion as throwing a baseball overhand or hitting an overhead in tennis.

Many advanced players use the overhead pass when they see their opponent on his or her heels or flat footed and thinking the ball will go to the ceiling. The overhead shot is hit hard to blow by an opponent and should make contact fairly low on the front wall. The idea is to get the ball to double-bounce before hitting the back wall or bounce the second time just after coming off the back wall. Hitting the ball low and hard is important, but the angle of the shot is critical. Keeping the ball off the side wall will help keep it from caroming into the center of the court for a possible setup for your opponent. Make sure the ball is hit to the open side of the court, away from your opponent (figure 5.9).

This shot may be hazardous to your shoulder and should be used with caution and care. Be sure to follow through by rotating your hips and shoulders as you would in throwing a baseball overhand.

The two basic overhead shots are the down-the-wall pass and the cross-court V pass. These are the same as those discussed earlier in this step, with the same angles off the front wall, resulting in the same finish in the backcourt. The only real difference is that the overhead version is hit above the head rather than below the waist—and this shot has a lower success rate.

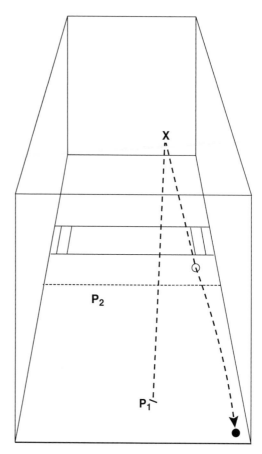

Figure 5.9 Overhead pass.

Misstep

The ball contacts the side wall before hitting the back wall.

Correction

Move the ball-contact point on the front wall closer to the center of the front wall. You may be hitting the ball with the racquet face at an angle toward the side wall. Be sure you are using a flat forehand grip. Check the angle of your stance at ball contact. Rotate your hips and shoulders toward the front wall when hitting the ball. Be sure to follow through.

Misstep

The ball goes to center court off the front wall.

Correction

Check the racquet face angle at ball contact. You may be hitting the ball with the racquet face angled toward the center of the front wall, or possibly with a backhand grip. Be sure you are using a flat forehand grip. Check the angle of your stance at ball contact. Rotate your hips and shoulders toward the front wall when hitting the ball. Be sure to follow through.

Overhead Pass Drill 1.   *Bounce the Ball*

To practice the overhead pass, bounce the ball hard off the floor so it goes high enough for you to execute the overhead pass. This shot is practiced from the two back corners of the court, though it is usually hit from the forehand side or the middle of the backcourt. Aim to hit the ball 18 inches (45 centimeters) off the floor on the front wall. If you are hitting a down-the-wall overhead pass, be sure to keep the ball close to the side wall. If you are hitting a V overhead pass, turn slightly toward the contact point on the front wall and be sure to keep the ball angled so it goes to the back corner on the opposite side of the court (same angle as a normal cross-court V pass).

Practice from the backcourt corner on each side of the court (figure 5.3, page 81). Begin on the forehand side with the forehand down-the-wall shot and then hit the forehand cross-court V pass to the back corner on the backhand side. Next, go to the backhand side of the court and hit the forehand down-the-wall pass along that side wall, and then hit the forehand cross-court V pass to the back corner on the forehand side. Perform 10 repetitions of each shot at each location for a total of 40 repetitions.

Success Check

- Visualize the stroke and shot.
- Square off to the side wall.
- Place your racquet in the overhead backswing position.
- Throw the ball to the floor just in front of your front foot so it bounces high enough to hit above your head.
- Execute the stroke, making contact with the ball above and in front of your head.
- Hit the ball down to the front wall approximately 18 inches (45 centimeters) above the floor for either the down-the-wall or cross-court V pass.
- Follow through.

Score Your Success

Complete a total of 20 overheads, 5 repetitions of each shot from each of the two positions. If the ball comes within 2 feet (0.6 meter) of the targeted back corner, it is considered a successful shot.

1 to 20 percent successful shots = 1 point

21 to 50 percent successful shots = 3 points

51 to 100 percent successful shots = 5 points

Your score ___

Overhead Pass Drill 2.   *Ceiling Setup*

Another way to set yourself up to practice the overhead pass is to hit a ceiling shot that lands short. This is a more advanced technique. Ceiling shots will be covered in detail in step 7. If you don't know how to do ceiling shots yet, don't worry. Just skip this drill and come back to it after you have worked through step 7. This is an excellent drill because it more closely simulates a game situation but doesn't require a partner.

As with the first drill, practice primarily from the backcourt on the forehand and backhand sides. Be sure to hit the ball about 18 inches (45 centimeters) off the floor on the front wall. If you are hitting a down-the-wall overhead pass, be sure

to keep the ball close to the side wall. If you are hitting a cross-court V overhead pass, be sure to angle the ball to the opposite back corner.

Success Check

- Hit the ball to the ceiling so it bounces short in the backcourt.
- Square off and get the racquet in the backswing position.
- Anticipate where the ball will come down in the backcourt.
- Adjust your feet, placing yourself so the ball will be in good contact position.

- Execute the down-the-wall or cross-court V shot.
- Follow through.

Complete a total of 20 overhead pass repetitions, 5 repetitions of each shot from each of the two positions. If the ball comes within 2 feet (0.6 meter) of the back corner, it is considered a successful shot.

1 to 20 percent successful shots = 1 point

21 to 50 percent successful shots = 3 points

51 to 100 percent successful shots = 5 points

Your score ___

FRONT-TO-SIDE-WALL SHOT

This shot usually is the result of a missed pinch shot hit from midcourt to backcourt. (See step 6 for more on the pinch shot.) Advanced players will take this shot occasionally if in the front of the court when their opponent is in the backcourt, but it is not a high-percentage shot from normal hitting locations on the court.

In the front-to-side-wall shot, the ball hits the front wall very close to the corner and then continues to the side wall and caroms to center court. Unless this shot results in a kill, it will bring the ball back to, or near, center court, which sets up an easy return for your opponent. Avoid hitting this shot in the backcourt. Practice pinch shots so this mistake doesn't cost you a rally.

HIGH Z SHOT

The high Z is a great defensive, and sometimes offensive, shot. Unlike the other front-wall shots, the high Z is hit high on the front wall. Using a slightly open stance, with an imaginary line connecting your feet in the direction you are hitting to the front wall, hit the ball so it makes contact with the front wall 6 to 14 inches (15 to 35 centimeters) out from the opposite corner. The contact point should be about two-thirds up the front wall, or about 7 feet (2.1 meters) from the ceiling. This shot must be hit high and fairly hard in order to carry over the opponent's head to the opposite side wall from the front corner. If the ball is not high enough, your opponent may hit the ball out of the air as it comes across center court before it hits the second side wall in the backcourt. The angle and pace of the ball are critical. Proper angle and pace cause the ball to go from the opposite front corner to the backcourt side wall, resulting in a Z pattern (figure 5.10).

If the ball does not contact the backcourt side wall and hits the back wall first, it will carom back to center court. Once the ball strikes the backcourt side wall, it will come off the wall and

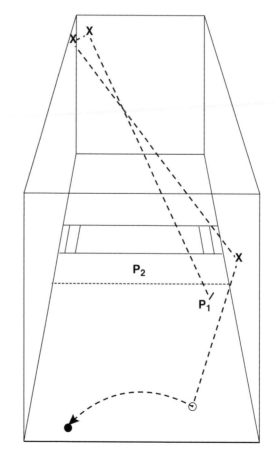

Figure 5.10 High Z.

drop quickly to the floor as it loses velocity after hitting three walls. The ball will be nearly parallel to the back wall and travel across the court to the opposite back corner.

The keys to this shot are the height, pace, and angle of the ball. This is an advanced shot and very difficult to execute unless you practice it. However, it is a very effective shot when used sparingly and can result in poor or weak returns and a few outright winners. You may want to use this shot when you do not have a setup for a good passing shot and as a change of pace from the typical ceiling ball, around-the-court shot, or short high lob serve. This shot gives you an option besides a forced low-percentage shot in the front court when you are trying to get your opponent to the deep backcourt so you have time to recover to center court.

Misstep

The ball contacts the side wall first instead of the front wall.

Correction

The angle is too narrow. Widen the angle by moving the ball-contact point on the front wall closer to the center of the front wall. Hit the ball so it makes contact with the front wall 6 to 14 inches (15 to 35 centimeters) out from the side wall. You may be hitting the ball at the front of the power zone, or you may be hitting with your racquet face angled toward the side wall. Hit in the middle of the power zone. You may also be hitting with too much of an open stance. Use a normal or slightly open stance. It will help to align your feet with each other in the direction you are hitting.

Misstep

The ball hits the back wall before hitting the second side wall and comes to center court.

Correction

The ball angle is too wide or too far out from the side wall on the front wall. Narrow the ball angle. Hit the ball so it makes contact on the front wall 6 to 14 inches (15 to 35 centimeters) out from the side wall. Ball contact may be occurring in the back of the power zone. Make contact in the middle of the power zone. Your stance may be closed. Be sure your stance is normal or slightly open and your feet are in line with the direction you want to hit.

High Z Drill.   *Repetition*

Practice high Z shots from each location shown in figure 5.11. Begin at location 1, nearest the receiving line, with either the forehand or backhand. You will not have to hit the ball as hard from this location since you will be closer to the front wall. This will give you a higher winning-shot percentage. After you complete 10 high Z shots from location 1, move to locations 2, 3, 4, and 5. Locations F/B4 and F/B5 are for both forehand and backhand; be sure to drill with the forehand and backhand from these locations. Perform the drill in the same order starting on the other side of the court. Do 10 repetitions at each location for each side, and do the entire sequence 3 times for intensive practice.

Success Check

- Adjust your feet and open your stance. Feet are in line with each other in the direction of the opposite front corner.

- Get your racquet in the backswing position as quickly as possible.

- Drop the ball so it bounces to a height between your waist and shoulders.

- Hit the ball between your waist and shoulders.

- Rotate your hips and shoulders.

- Follow through above your shoulder.

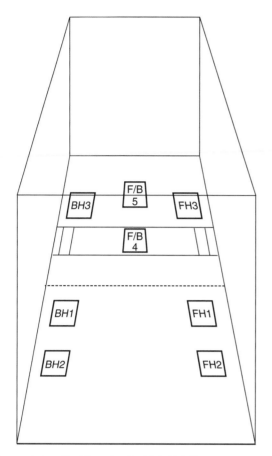

Figure 5.11 Positions for the high Z drill.

Score Your Success

Complete a total of 50 high Z repetitions, 5 repetitions of each shot from each of the positions. If the ball hits the side wall within 6 feet (1.8 meters) of the back corner, it is considered a successful shot.

1 to 30 percent successful shots = 1 point

31 to 60 percent successful shots = 3 points

61 to 100 percent successful shots = 5 points

Your score ___

SUCCESS SUMMARY OF FRONT-WALL SHOTS

Front-wall passing shots will be the main course of your racquetball diet. When hitting a front-wall pass, be sure you are accurate with your shot and keep the ball away from your opponent. The idea is to hit to the open side of the court and move your opponent out of center court and into the backcourt. If your opponent is in the middle, then your best passing options are the down-the-wall and wide-angle shots.

As you progress through the book, you will gain a better understanding of angles, court positioning, and shot selection. You will also develop a game style that is comfortable to you. Be open minded and don't get locked into hitting the same shots all the time. Place as many shot tricks in your bag as possible. Continue to practice all of these shots and use them in game situations.

Review your drill scores. Enter your scores and tally them to rate your front-wall shot success.

Down-the-Wall Pass Drill

    1. Progressive Shots   ___ out of 5

Cross-Court V Pass Drill

    1. Progressive Shots   ___ out of 5

Wide-Angle Cross-Court Pass Drill

    1. Angles, Angles, Angles   ___ out of 5

Kill Shot Drill

    1. Kill the Rally (Advanced)   ___ out of 5

Overhead Pass Drills

    1. Bounce the Ball   ___ out of 5

    2. Ceiling Setup   ___ out of 5

High Z Drill

    1. Repetition   ___ out of 5

Total   ___ *out of 35*

If you scored fewer than 20 points, redo the drills that were difficult for you. If you scored 20 points or more, you are ready to continue to step 6, Side-Wall Shots.

The front-wall shots you have learned in this chapter provide a good foundation to build on as you move to side-wall shots. These new shots will help you continue to build your racquetball résumé and on your way to becoming a complete racquetball player.

Side-Wall Shots

Side-wall shots are a basic part of racquetball. They are used to change the pace of the game and move an opponent around the court, up in the front of the court, and especially out of center court. The pinch shot, in particular, is useful as a setup for the passing shot, and vice versa. However, the side-wall shot is risky: If not executed correctly from the proper position on the court with the opponent in the right position, it may very well bring the ball into center court for a setup kill shot by the opponent.

The keys to hitting side-wall shots are court position and timing. In other words, you and your opponent must be in the right positions in order for the side-wall shot to be effective. If the side-wall shot is hit at the wrong time during the rally or at the wrong location on the court, you may find yourself losing the rally.

The pinch shot is overused in racquetball. Many young players think the pinch shot is the answer to winning all rallies and spend too much time working on the pinch and using it in games. That said, the pinch is an excellent shot and has a time and place on the racquetball court. The pinch shot helps keep an opponent off balance and guessing. Just don't overuse it.

The pinch is especially useful when an opponent is deep in the backcourt and you don't have a passing shot or don't want to risk hitting a bad kill shot. The pinch moves your opponent up to the front of the court, making him or her travel farther to return the ball.

The around-the-wall shot is also a good shot to use against a beginner or intermediate-level player. Most racquetball players in these categories have a difficult time tracking the ball, and the more walls the ball hits the more difficult it is for them to track and return it.

The around-the-wall shot can also be a dangerous shot to use against a well-seasoned player. This shot always passes through center court and will give the opponent the opportunity to cut the ball off in center court. The shot must be hit high and with good touch in order to get it to drop in the backcourt. If it is hit too hard, it will set up the opponent near center court for an easy winner.

Regardless of which side-wall shot you choose, you must be sure you and your opponent are in proper position. A poor decision or improper execution will give your opponent the advantage and possibly the winning shot in the rally.

PINCH SHOT

The pinch shot is a side-wall kill shot of sorts. It has five variations: forehand, backhand, reverse (forehand or backhand), volley (forehand or backhand), and splat. There is a time and place for this shot, but it is not a shot for all occasions.

You will find the greatest success with this shot when you are in center to frontcourt and your opponent is either in the backcourt (figure 6.1*a*) or on the same side of the court you're hitting the ball to (figure 6.1*b*). In the latter case, hit the pinch shot to the near side corner; i.e., the corner of the side wall nearest to you. As you get more comfortable with the pinch shot and your skills improve, your use of it will increase. But remember: It is not a shot for all occasions or the answer for winning every rally.

For all pinch shots, use a normal stance with the imaginary line connecting your feet parallel to the side wall or in line with the direction you are hitting. The problem with lining up the shot with your feet and body is that you give away where you are hitting the shot. Practice these shots initially with your feet in line, then progress to a normal stance, working on hitting the ball in the front, middle, and back of the power zone depending on whether you are hitting a normal or reverse pinch. Use racquet-face angle to direct the ball where you want it to go. Bear in mind that you will sacrifice power anytime you get outside the power zone when executing a shot.

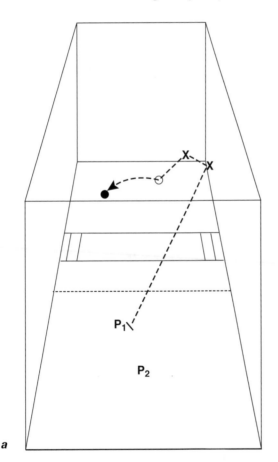

a

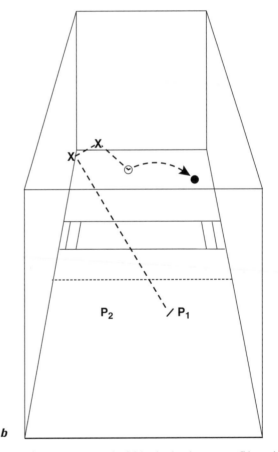

b

Figure 6.1 Hit the pinch shot when you are in center to frontcourt and your opponent is *(a)* in the backcourt or *(b)* on the same side of the court you're hitting the ball to.

Forehand Pinch

When executing the forehand pinch shot on the forehand side of the court, use an in-line or normal stance and a flat, out-and-around stroke. Hit the ball in the middle or back of the power zone, and follow through normally. Hit the side wall a few inches to 4 feet (a few centimeters to 1.2 meters) out from the near front corner and anywhere from a few inches to 4 feet off the floor (figure 6.2). The closer you are to the corner when you hit the ball, the lower the ball can be to the floor. The farther out from the corner, the higher the ball must be in order to reach the front wall before hitting the floor. Ideally the ball should bounce twice before reaching the short line, ending the rally. The ball can be hit hard or soft, depending on what you want it to do.

Figure 6.2   Forehand pinch shot.

 Misstep

The ball hits the opposite side wall before it bounces the second time.

Correction

Hit the ball with a flat, out-and-around stroke, not up and down. Be sure the racquet is perpendicular to the floor and the racquet face is not open or facing up. Ball contact may be too high on the initial side wall. Hit the ball a little lower on the side-to-front-wall combo.

Backhand Pinch

The backhand pinch shot is hit in much the same way as the forehand pinch. Use an in-line to normal stance and a flat, out-and-around stroke. Hit the ball in the middle or front of the power zone. Follow through normally as you would with any other backhand shot. The ball is hit to the near side or backhand side wall and front corner (figure 6.3). Everything else remains the same as in the forehand pinch shot.

Figure 6.3   Backhand pinch shot.

Misstep

The ball flies off the side-to-front-wall combo to the opposite side wall without hitting the floor.

Correction

Aim lower on the side-to-front-wall pinch. Your racquet face may be open or facing up. The racquet face should be perpendicular to the floor on contact with the ball. Swing flat, with an out-and-around stroke, not up and down.

Reverse Pinch

The reverse pinch is hit for the same reason and under the same circumstances as the normal pinch. This more advanced shot, however, is harder to hit. You have to hit the ball across your body to the opposite front corner from the one you are facing (figure 6.4). This shot can be hit with the forehand or backhand and is typically hit in the forward end of the power zone in order to get it to the reverse corner.

Volley Pinch

The volley pinch is also an advanced shot. The ball is hit on the fly as it travels through the air before making contact with the floor (figure 6.5). All other parameters remain the same as with the forehand pinch and backhand pinch. Depending on your stance and where the ball ends up as it comes into your hitting zone, you may take a full swing or volley the ball (as you would in tennis) into the corner. A normal volley is executed with the racquet out in front of the body. The racquet face is directed toward the corner with the wrist. This does not require a swing. The volley uses the energy of the ball and the rebound of the racquet strings to get the ball to the corner. This is a controlled finesse shot.

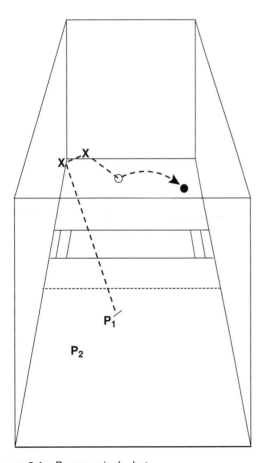

Figure 6.4 Reverse pinch shot.

Figure 6.5 Volley pinch shot.

Splat

The splat is a highly advanced shot. It takes perfect technique to execute properly, is one of the most difficult shots in racquetball, and is normally used only by professionals and other highly skilled players. The splat can be executed only from near the side wall, usually in the deep backcourt. The ball is hit so as to make contact with the side wall in the backcourt with extreme power. The ball contacts the wall slightly in front of your contact point, with the racquet at around a 135-degree angle to the wall. The ball spins and compresses due to the angle and power, making it unpredictable in its flight and angle. It then hits the front wall with a splat sound and dies, rolls out, or double-bounces prior to reaching the service line. If this shot is not executed to perfection, it will probably set up your opponent for a winning shot in the frontcourt.

Due to the advanced nature of this shot, we will not practice it here. The shot is mentioned only because you will hear the term *splat* in racquetball circles. Having an understanding of the term and how the shot is executed will help you in your advancement in racquetball. Keep this shot in mind as you progress. Once you get to that advanced level, you will want to work on this shot and make it part of your repertoire.

Pinch Shot Drill.   *Forehand and Backhand*

Practicing the normal and reverse pinch shots—forehand and backhand—is crucial to proper execution during play. Practice from the three locations shown in figure 6.6. Begin at location 2, center court. After hitting 10 forehand normal and reverse pinch shots and 10 backhand normal and reverse pinch shots from location 2, move to location 3, and then location 1. Perform the entire sequence 3 times for intensive practice.

Begin by aligning your feet and body in the direction you are hitting. Gradually move your feet so that a line connecting them would be parallel to the side wall. Keeping your feet aligned parallel to the side wall will not only disguise your shot; it will open up more shot options for you to use during rally play.

Success Check

- Align your feet in the direction you are hitting.
- Get into a typical ready position.
- Place the racquet in either the forehand or backhand backswing position.
- Drop the ball in the power zone.

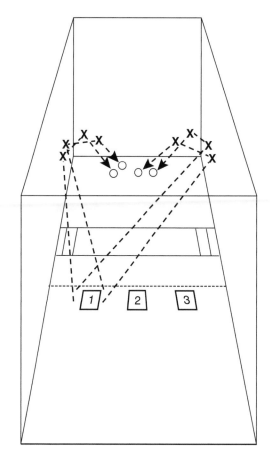

Figure 6.6 Practice the forehand and backhand pinch-shot drill from these three locations.

- Swing out and around, staying as low as possible.
- Hit either a normal or reverse pinch shot.
- Follow through.
- Stay balanced.

Score Your Success

Complete 10 repetitions of the forehand and backhand normal and reverse pinch shots from location 2 for a total of 40 shots. A successful pinch shot is one that double-bounces prior to reaching the short line.

1 to 40 percent successful pinch shots = 1 point

41 to 60 percent successful pinch shots = 3 points

61 to 100 percent successful pinch shots = 5 points

Your score ___

AROUND-THE-WALL SHOT

The around-the-wall shot is a good change of pace from the ceiling ball, but use it sparingly. Hit the ball from the backcourt to the near side wall about two-thirds up the wall from the floor and about midway between the front and back walls (figure 6.7).

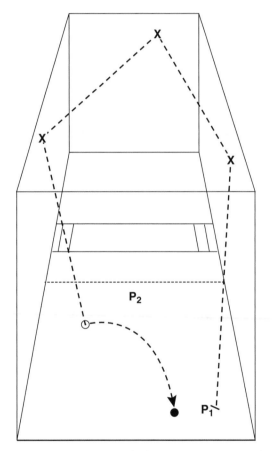

Figure 6.7 Around-the-wall shot.

Misstep

The ball hits the ceiling.

Correction

Hit the ball lower on the side wall, approximately two-thirds up the wall off the floor. Check your racquet face angle; it may be too open or facing up.

Misstep

The ball doesn't hit the second side wall off the front wall.

Correction

Create more angle off the side wall to the front wall. Aim for the center of the near side wall two-thirds up from the floor. You may need more pace on the ball. Hit it harder if necessary.

You will want to practice this shot because it takes a good touch to make the ball die in the backcourt. After the ball strikes the side wall, it hits the front wall, then goes to the opposite side wall. The ball quickly loses velocity and drops to the floor, bouncing toward the back wall and back to the origin of the shot. If the shot is hit too hard, it will create a setup off the back wall. If the shot is too soft, it will create a setup in the middle of the court.

The around-the-wall shot is hit from above the head, much like the overhead pass (see step 5, Front-Wall Shots). The stance and stroke mechanics are similar to those of the forehand ceiling shot (see step 7, Ceiling Shots), except the ball is hit not to the ceiling but to the upper side wall. Make contact with the ball above your head with an open racquet face.

To practice, bounce the ball hard off the floor so it goes high enough for you to execute the around-the-wall shot. Typically you will hit the ball at shoulder to head height. Practice this shot from the two deep court back corners or mid deep backcourt. Hit the ball with the forehand on the forehand side and with the backhand on the backhand side. The around-the-wall shot is primarily hit from the middle to 5 feet (1.5 meters) on either side of the middle of the backcourt. When hitting the ball, begin by squaring up to the side wall, with your shoulders and hips turned slightly forward. Aim for the side wall about 5 feet from the ceiling and about midway between the front and back wall.

Misstep

The ball comes through center court after hitting the second side wall, and your opponent cuts it off in the air.

Correction

The ball is contacting the near side wall too far back in the backcourt, giving it too much angle to the front wall. Hit the near side wall closer to the front wall. Take some velocity off the ball.

Misstep

The ball comes off the second side wall and sets up in the middle of the court.

Correction

Hit the ball with more velocity so it carries to the back wall and dies. The ball may be contacting the near side wall too far back in the backcourt, giving it to much angle to the front wall. Hit the near side wall closer to the front wall.

Around-the-Wall Drill 1. *Around-the-Wall Practice*

Practicing this shot is crucial to its proper execution during play. Practice from the two locations shown in figure 6.8. After you complete 10 around-the-wall shots from location 1, go to location 2. Perform 3 sets of 10 repetitions

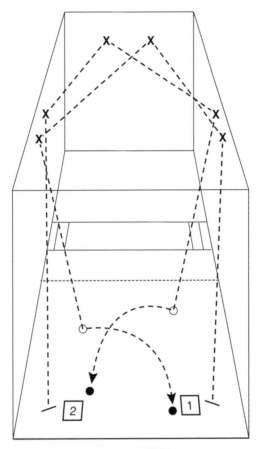

Figure 6.8 Practice the around-the-wall shot from these two locations.

at each location. Control the power of this shot. You want the ball to die in the backcourt. This shot is easier when hit on the forehand side, but, with enough practice, the backhand can be mastered.

Success Check

- Visualize the stroke and shot.
- Square off to the side wall.
- Place your racquet in the overhead or ceiling-shot backswing position.
- Throw the ball to the floor in the middle of the power zone so it bounces high enough to hit between shoulder and head level.
- Hit the ball up on the side wall approximately 5 feet (1.5 meters) from the ceiling and about halfway between the back wall and the front wall.
- Follow through.

Score Your Success

Complete a total of 20 around-the-wall repetitions, 10 repetitions from each of the two positions. If the ball comes within 2 feet (0.6 meter) of the back wall, the shot is considered successful.

1 to 20 percent successful shots = 1 point
21 to 50 percent successful shots = 3 points
51 to 100 percent successful shots = 5 points
Your score ___

Around-the-Wall Drill 2. *Ceiling Setup*

A more advanced way to practice the around-the-wall shot is to set it up by first hitting a ceiling shot. Hit the ceiling ball so that it comes down within 5 feet (1.5 meters) of the middle of the court on either side. Then hit the around-the-wall shot, using your backhand if on the backhand side or forehand if on the forehand side.

Ceiling shots will be covered in detail in step 7. If you don't know how to do ceiling shots yet, don't worry. Just skip this drill and come back to it after you have worked through step 7. This is an

excellent drill because it more closely simulates a game situation but doesn't require a partner.

Success Check

- Hit the ball to the ceiling so it comes down near the middle of the court.
- Square off and get the racquet in the backswing position.
- Anticipate where the ball will come down in the backcourt.

- Adjust your feet, placing yourself so the ball will be in good contact position.
- Execute the around-the-wall shot.
- Follow through.

Score Your Success

Complete a total of 20 around-the-wall repetitions, 10 repetitions from each of the two positions. If the ball comes within 2 feet (0.6 meter) of the back wall, the shot is considered successful.

1 to 20 percent successful shots = 1 point

21 to 50 percent successful shots = 3 points

51 to 100 percent successful shots = 5 points

Your score ___

SIDE-WALL BOAST

The side-wall boast is a shot taken out of the squash playbook. It is an advanced shot and difficult to hit consistently. By nature, it is a defensive shot that produces offensive results. The great thing about this shot is that when it's executed properly, it is a great crowd pleaser and leaves your opponent in awe.

Typically, a player who is too far forward of the ball will hit this shot in a last-ditch effort to save a dying ball. The shot is best executed in the back to middle of the power zone. Hit the ball into the near wall at an abrupt angle, sending the ball across the court to the opposite side wall and then into the front wall (figure 6.9). It will come back toward the near side wall and die. If the ball hits the front wall instead of the opposite side wall first, it may set up your opponent for an easy winner as the ball comes back to center court. This is a high-power shot and is not viable for those who cannot hit the ball hard.

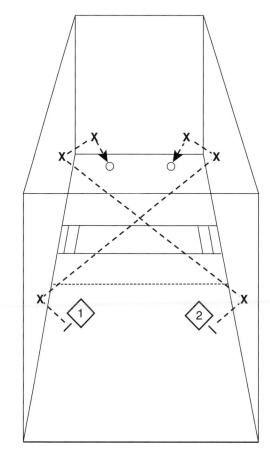

Figure 6.9 Side-wall boast.

Misstep

The ball hits the floor before making contact with the opposite front corner.

Correction

Hit the ball harder. This is a power shot and may require more follow-through or wrist snap.

Misstep

The ball hits the front wall before hitting the opposite side wall.

Correction

The angle of the ball coming off the near side wall is too wide. Move the ball-contact point on the near side wall farther back from the front wall. You may be hitting the ball too far forward in the power zone. Hit the ball in the middle to back of the power zone.

Side-Wall Boast Drill. *Make It Die*

Stand behind the safety line and align your feet with the near side wall at a 45-degree angle toward the front wall, about 3 feet (0.9 meter) out from the side wall. Drop the ball and hit it in the middle of the power zone into the near side wall at approximately a 45-degree angle toward the front wall. With enough power and a flat stroke, you should be able to get the ball to fly off the near side wall, across the court to the opposite side wall, then into the front wall, where it will die coming back toward the near side wall. Power, angle, and height are critical for making this shot work. Your location when you hit the ball in the backcourt will determine the angle of the ball off the near side wall. Experiment with the angle of your feet, body, and ball until you get it right.

Begin just behind the safety line for the best success in learning how to hit this advanced shot. It doesn't matter whether you begin with the forehand or backhand. Square up to the side wall and toss the ball to the floor so it bounces in the middle to forward end of the power zone. Use a normal out-and-around stroke and hit the ball hard. Remember, this is not a finesse shot; it is a power shot. You may need a lot of wrist snap if you are too close to the wall for a full follow-through. Perform 10 repetitions at each of the two locations, and do this sequence 3 times for practice.

Success Check

* Visualize the stroke and shot.
* Line up your feet in the direction of the contact point on the side wall.
* Place your racquet in the backswing position.
* Toss the ball in the middle to the front end of the power zone.
* Use enough power, wrist snap, and follow-through to get the ball to the opposite front corner

Score Your Success

Complete a total of 20 boast shot repetitions, doing 10 repetitions from each of the two positions just behind the safety line. If the ball hits the opposite front corner and double-bounces before the short line, the shot is considered successful.

1 to 20 percent successful shots = 1 point

21 to 50 percent successful shots = 3 points

51 to 100 percent successful shots = 5 points

Your score ___

PRACTICE GAMES

Games are always fun. After all, we practice because we want to get better at playing the game. So why not play and practice at the same time? Here are a couple of games you can incorporate into your practices to help you get better. Keep in mind that these games are designed to work on specific shots, forcing you to concentrate on the key shot. However, it does not prevent you from hitting other shots. The idea is to work on rallies and wait until you get the setup that will allow you to hit the point-winning shot.

Practice Game 1. *Pinch Shot Game*

This game requires a partner. Begin the game with a serve, ceiling ball, or any setup off the front wall. The object of the game is to win the rally with a pinch shot. Although you can win a rally with any shot, you score only if you win the rally with a pinch shot. Set up the game with any game-winning point value you want. I typically use 7, 11, or 15 points. You cannot win the point off your partner's mistake. You must win the point yourself with a winning shot.

Score Your Success

If you set the game-winning value at 7 points,

    1 or 2 points = 1 point

    3 or 4 points = 3 points

    5 or 6 points = 5 points

    7 points = 8 points

    Your score ___

If you set the game-winning value at 11 points,

    1 to 3 points = 1 point

    4 to 7 points = 3 points

    8 to 10 points = 5 points

    11 points = 8 points

    Your score ___

If you set the game-winning value at 15 points,

    1 to 5 points = 1 point

    6 to 10 points = 3 points

    11 to 14 points = 5 points

    15 points = 8 points

    Your score ___

Practice Game 2. *Around-the-Wall Game*

This game requires a partner. Begin the game with a serve, ceiling ball, or any setup off the front wall. The object of the game is to win the rally with an around-the-wall shot. Although you can win a rally with any shot, you can score only if you win the rally with an around-the-wall shot. You can set up the game with any game-winning point value you want. I typically use 7, 11, or 15 points. In this game, you can win the point off your partner if you force him or her to hit a skip off the around-the-wall shot.

Score Your Success

If you set the game-winning value at 7 points,

    1 or 2 points = 1 point

    3 or 4 points = 3 points

    5 or 6 points = 5 points

    7 points = 8 points

    Your score ___

If you set the game-winning value at 11 points,

    1 to 3 points = 1 point

    4 to 7 points = 3 points

    8 to 10 points = 5 points

    11 points = 8 points

    Your score ___

If you set the game-winning value at 15 points,

    1 to 5 points = 1 point

    6 to 10 points = 3 points

    11 to 14 points = 5 points

    15 points = 8 points

    Your score ___

SUCCESS SUMMARY OF SIDE-WALL SHOTS

Now that you have finished this step, you are very close to having all the tools necessary to put together a complete game of racquetball. To this point, you can serve, return serve, and hit passing and side-wall shots. This gives you a good foundation for a good racquetball game, especially one on an outdoor court. Since outdoor courts don't use ceilings or back walls, you now have a fairly complete outdoor racquetball game. If you don't have access to an outdoor court or are not playing on one, then you will want to continue with step 7, Ceiling Shots, and step 8, Back-Wall Shots. If you want to continue to refine your outdoor game, jump to step 9, Court Positioning, and continue in your progress through the rest of the book.

Enter your drill scores and tally them to rate your success at side-wall shots.

Pinch Shot Drill

    1. Forehand and Backhand   ___ out of 5

Around-the-Wall Drills

    1. Around-the-Wall Practice   ___ out of 5

    2. Ceiling Setup   ___ out of 5

Side-Wall Boast Drill

    1. Make It Die   ___ out of 5

Practice Games

    1. Pinch Shot Game   ___ out of 8

    2. Around-the-Wall Game   ___ out of 8

Total   ___ *out of 36*

If you scored fewer than 20 points, review the drills that you found difficult. If you scored 20 points or more, you are ready to continue to step 7, Ceiling Shots, which are a huge part of indoor racquetball. This is a skill you will want to practice and master. Although the ceiling ball may be looked at as a bailout shot, it can actually set you up for an offensive advantage.

Ceiling Shots

The ceiling ball is the most underrated yet most versatile shot in racquetball. Quite often it is regarded as a defensive shot when in fact it can have offensive results. Your intention when hitting the ceiling shot determines whether it is an offensive or defensive shot.

Hit ceiling shots when you don't have an offensive setup to kill or pass the ball. The ceiling shot gives you time to recover and return to center court, an offensive location, to control the rest of the rally. Granted, the ceiling shot is not the crowd pleaser that the pinch or kill shot is, but it does have its place on the court. The only real difference in the ceiling ball and the kill or pass is that the ceiling shot is not aggressive and will most likely not win the point or rally outright.

Most ceiling shots are executed from the back of the court. The ceiling ball is used on serve returns when the receiver doesn't have a good setup to shoot the ball down the line or cross-court. Often, offensive-minded players make the mental mistake of forcing the aggressive offensive shot when they are not in position to do so. Thus they increase their chance of either skipping the ball or setting up the opponent in the frontcourt or center court. The ceiling ball is a good alternative to forcing the aggressive shot from a less than ideal position.

During a rally, if you are faced with an off-balance shot or think you might just barely be able

to save the ball to keep the rally going, then go to the ceiling. Again, many aggressive, offense-minded players will shoot the ball nearly every time they get their racquet on it. These players commit countless unforced errors that may cost them games when scores are close. Don't ever hesitate to use the ceiling ball as an alternative to a low-percentage offensive shot. Remember, if you skip the ball, you give up the rally without forcing your opponent to do anything. However, if you go to the ceiling, you place the pressure on your opponent to try to make the winning shot or at least keep the rally going.

A number of factors influence how hard you will need to strike the ball and where to place the ball on the ceiling in order for it to carry to the back of the court and drop near the back wall. These factors include altitude; the ceiling, and floor composition; inside ball pressure; and ball velocity.

When hitting the ball from the backcourt, aim for the front bank of lights, or around 2 to 5 feet (0.6 to 1.5 meters) out from the front wall on the ceiling. Once again, many factors determine how the ball reacts when it comes to the backcourt, but this will give you a good starting point. As you move closer to the front wall, hit the ball closer to the front wall off the ceiling. Eventually you will reach a point, usually around the service line, at which you need to hit the ball from the front wall to the ceiling in order to get the proper angle and bounce to reach the backcourt.

Caution: Do not overhit the ceiling ball. This will cause the ball to come off the back wall as a potential setup for your opponent.

FOREHAND OVERHEAD CEILING SHOT

This shot (figure 7.1) uses the same basic motion as throwing a baseball from the out-field or hitting an overhead in tennis. The difference is that instead of hitting the ball down, as in tennis, you hit the ball up. This shot is usually hit in returning a well-placed ceiling ball when only a low-percentage kill or pass is available.

Figure 7.1   Forehand Overhead Ceiling Shot

SWING

1. Keep your eye on the ball
2. Hit the ball while stepping forward toward the ball, rotating your hips and shoulders in the direction of the front wall
3. Hit the ball just in front of and above your head
4. Aim for a location on the ceiling about 2 to 5 feet (0.6 to 1.5 meters) out from the front wall
5. Step forward or transfer your weight forward as you hit the ball
6. Don't hit the ball too hard but do hit it hard enough to get the ball to carry to the backcourt

To hit a successful ceiling shot, remember these key points:

- Get back into position and set up before the ball gets there.
- Square off to the side wall with your feet.
- As you relocate to the hitting position, hold your racquet in a forehand grip and in ready position to hit the ball. Hold the racquet behind your head, with the racquet face toward the ceiling.
- Balance with most of your weight on your back foot.
- Keep your eye on the ball. Hit the ball while stepping forward toward the ball, rotating your hips and shoulders in the direction of the front wall.
- Hit the ball slightly in front of and above your head.
- Snap your wrist forward and follow through in a downward motion.
- Relocate to center court.

BACKHAND OVERHEAD CEILING SHOT

This shot (figure 7.2) uses the same motion as throwing a Frisbee to the ceiling. This shot is usually hit in returning a well-placed ceiling ball when only a low-percentage kill or pass option is available.

| Figure 7.2 | Backhand Overhead Ceiling Shot |

SWING

1. Keep your eye on the ball
2. Hit ball while stepping forward toward the ball, rotating your hips and shoulders in the direction of the front wall
3. Hit the ball just in front of and above your head
4. Aim for a location on the ceiling about 2 to 5 feet (0.6 to 1.5 meters) out from the front wall
5. Step forward or transfer your weight forward as you hit the ball
6. Don't hit the ball too hard but do hit it hard enough to get the ball to carry to the backcourt

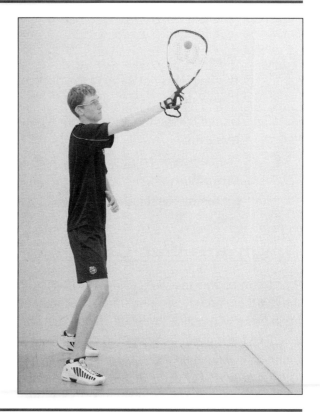

For a successful backhand overhead ceiling shot, remember these key points:

- Move to your return position and set up before the ball gets there.
- Hold your racquet in a backhand grip and in the ready position behind and just slightly below your back shoulder while moving into position.
- Set up facing the side wall.
- Most of your weight should be on your back foot.
- Continue to watch the ball as it comes down. Hit the ball while stepping forward, rotating your hips and shoulders in the direction of the front wall.
- Hit the ball slightly in front of and at about same level as your head.
- Snap your wrist and follow through in a cross-body upward motion to the racquet side of your body.
- Relocate to center court

DOWN-THE-WALL CEILING SHOT

The most common ceiling ball is the down-the-wall ceiling shot. The down-the-wall ceiling ball is ideal when both players have the same dominant hand (both are right handed or both are left handed). The idea is to keep the ball as close to the wall as possible on the backhand or forehand side. This shot is commonly known as a wallpaper ceiling ball. It creates a difficult return for your opponent because you are using the wall to keep your opponent from hitting a high-percentage offensive shot off the sweet spot of the racquet strings. With a good down-the wall ceiling shot, your opponent may not even be able to return it to the ceiling.

Misstep

The ball does not carry to the backcourt.

Correction

Hit the ball harder. Rotate your hips and shoulders to get more weight into the shot.

Misstep

The ball comes off the back wall and sets up for the opponent.

Correction

Hit the ball softer and with more finesse. Don't snap your wrist so hard on ball contact.

Down-the-Wall Ceiling Shot Drill 1.   *Solo Practice*

Practice the down-the-wall ceiling shot drills from the two locations shown in figure 7.3. Set yourself up in order to practice this shot. The easiest way is to toss the ball off the floor hard enough that it bounces above your head.

After you complete 10 down-the-wall ceiling hits from location 1, go to location 2. Perform a total of 3 sets of 10 repetitions at each location.

The down-the-wall ceiling ball is not a power shot but a finesse shot that requires lots of control. You will want to ensure that the ball does not strike the side wall. This will cause the ball to lose momentum and most likely end up short, making it easier for your opponent to set up and hit.

Success Check

- Visualize the stroke and shot.
- Square off to the side wall, approximately one arm-and-racquet length away.
- Get racquet in backswing position.
- Get balanced, with most of your weight on the back foot.
- Toss the ball to the floor so it bounces high enough for you to hit at head height or above.

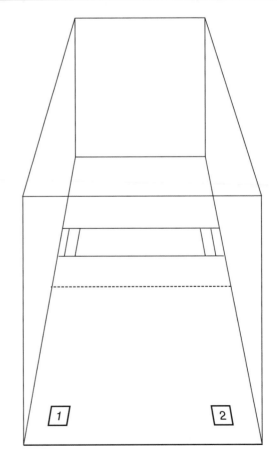

Figure 7.3 Practice ceiling drills from these locations.

- Hit the ball to the ceiling 2 to 5 feet (0.6 to 1.5 meters) out from the front wall.
- The ball should return to the deep backcourt within 2 feet of the crack between the back wall and floor.
- Follow through.

Score Your Success

Complete 10 ceiling shots from each of the two locations (forehand and backhand), for a total of 20 repetitions. A successful shot is one that does not contact the side wall and returns to the deep backcourt within 2 feet (0.6 meter) of the crack between the back wall and floor.

1 to 20 percent successful shots = 1 point

21 to 50 percent successful shots = 3 points

51 to 100 percent successful shots = 5 points

Your score ___

Down-the-Wall Ceiling Shot Drill 2. *Partner Practice*

Use the same two locations shown in figure 7.3 (page 110). For this drill, you will need a partner to hit a ceiling ball from mid backcourt to one of the two backcourt corners. You will then hit a down-the-wall ceiling shot into the same backcourt corner. After you complete 10 down-the-wall ceiling hits from location 1, go to location 2. Perform 3 sets of 10 repetitions at each location.

Success Check

- Visualize the stroke and shot.
- Anticipate where the ball will come down after its first bounce.
- Get your racquet into the backswing position.
- Square off to the side wall and make adjustments with your feet.

- Hit the ball back to the ceiling.
- Follow through and recover to center court.

Score Your Success

In this drill you will add a recovery to center court after you hit the ceiling ball. Complete 10 ceiling shots from each side of the court (forehand and backhand) for a total of 20 repetitions. A successful shot is one that does not contact the side wall and returns to the deep backcourt within 2 feet (0.6 meter) of the back-wall-and-floor crack—and from which you recover to center court.

1 to 20 percent successful shots = 1 point

21 to 50 percent successful shots = 3 points

51 to 100 percent successful shots = 5 points

Your score ___

Down-the-Wall Ceiling Shot Drill 3. *Consecutive Shots*

Use the same locations shown in figure 7.3 (page 110). Toss the ball off the floor hard enough so it bounces above your head. Hit a down-the-wall ceiling shot and then return it back to the ceiling, hitting another down-the-wall ceiling shot. After you complete 5 consecutive down-the-wall ceiling hits from location 1, go to location 2. Perform 3 sets of 10 repetitions at each location.

Success Check

- Visualize the stroke and shot.
- Set up to hit a ceiling ball.
- Toss the ball to the floor so it bounces above your head.
- Hit the ball to the ceiling.
- Move to the return position and return the ball to the ceiling.
- Keep the ball in play, hitting repetitive ceiling balls until you miss.

CROSS-COURT CEILING SHOT

The cross-court ceiling ball is a change-of-direction shot. It is used most commonly when the two players have opposite dominant hands (one is right handed, the other left handed), because each player wants to keep the other in the deep backhand corner.

When executing the cross-court ceiling shot in a back corner, aim at the center of the ceiling, approximately 2 to 5 feet (0.6 to 1.5 meters) out from the front wall. This will angle the ball to the opposite back corner. This shot is hit in the same way as a normal ceiling ball but across the court to the opposite back corner. The biggest difference is getting into a slightly open stance or angling your racquet face to get the ball to go cross-court.

Misstep

The ball hits the side wall.

Correction

Adjust your stance so you are able to hit at the proper angle cross-court. Your racquet face may be turned and is not square with the ball at contact. Adjust your grip.

The cross-court ceiling shot can also be used when both players have the same dominant hand, especially when one favors one side of the court and is looking for the down-the-wall ceiling shot.

Another time to hit the cross-court ceiling shot is when your opponent is already in the backcourt corner you are hitting from, and you want to move him or her to the other side of the court.

Misstep

The ball hits the ceiling midway between the front wall and back wall.

Correction

Aim for a location 2 to 5 feet (0.6 to 1.5 meters) from the front wall. You may be contacting the ball behind your head. You are too far in front of the ball. Move farther back and make contact with the ball slightly in front of your head.

Misstep

The ball hits the front wall before hitting the ceiling.

Correction

Aim for a location 2 to 5 feet (0.6 to 1.5 meters) from the front wall. You may be contacting the ball too far in front. Get under the ball more and make contact with the ball slightly in front of your head. Make sure your racquet face is open enough to give the needed angle to the ceiling.

Cross-Court Ceiling Shot Drill 1. *Solo Practice*

This shot is practiced in much the same way as the down-the-wall ceiling shot. As with the down-the-wall drill, practice from the two locations shown in figure 7.3 (page 110). Set yourself up to practice this shot by tossing the ball off the floor hard enough that it bounces above your head. After you complete 10 cross-court ceiling shots from location 1, go to location 2. Perform 3 sets of 10 repetitions at each location.

Just like the down-the-wall ceiling shot, this is a finesse shot requiring lots of control, not power. You also want to make sure the ball does not strike the side wall. This will cause the ball to lose momentum and most likely end up short, setting up your opponent for a shot.

Success Check

- Visualize the stroke and shot.
- Align your feet in the direction of the center of the front wall.

- Place your racquet in the backswing position.
- Toss the ball to the floor hard enough to bounce it above your head.
- Hit the ball to the center of the ceiling 2 to 5 feet (0.6 to 1.5 meters) out from the front wall.
- Follow through.

Score Your Success

Complete 10 ceiling shots from each of the two locations (forehand and backhand) for a total of 20 repetitions. A successful shot is one that does not contact the side wall and goes to the opposite deep backcourt corner within 2 feet (0.6 meter) of the back wall and side wall and floor crack.

1 to 20 percent successful shots = 1 point

21 to 50 percent successful shots = 3 points

51 to 100 percent successful shots = 5 points

Your score ___

Cross-Court Ceiling Shot Drill 2. *Partner Practice*

Use the locations shown in figure 7.3 (page 110). Have a partner stand in mid center backcourt and hit a ceiling shot into the one of the backcourt corners. Return it back to the ceiling with a cross-court ceiling shot and recover to center court position. After you complete 10 cross-court ceiling hits from location 1, go to location 2. Perform 3 sets of 10 repetitions at each location.

Success Check

- Visualize the stroke and shot.
- Anticipate where the ball will come down after its first bounce.
- Get your racquet into the backswing position.
- Line up toward the middle of the front wall and make adjustments with your feet.
- Hit the ball back to the ceiling cross-court.

- Follow through and recover to center court.

Score Your Success

In this drill, you will add a recovery to center court after you hit the cross-court ceiling ball. Complete 10 ceiling shots from each side of the court (forehand and backhand) for a total of 20 repetitions. A successful shot is one that does not contact the side wall and returns to the deep backcourt corner within 2 feet (0.6 meter) of the back wall and side wall and floor crack—and from which you recover to center court.

1 to 20 percent successful shots = 1 point

21 to 50 percent successful shots = 3 points

51 to 100 percent successful shots = 5 points

Your score ___

Cross-Court Ceiling Shot Drill 3. *Consecutive Shots*

Use the locations shown in figure 7.3 (page 110). Toss the ball off the floor hard enough to bounce it above your head. Hit a down-the-wall ceiling shot and then return it to the ceiling using a cross-court ceiling shot. Complete 10 ceiling shots from location 1, then move to location 2. Perform 3 sets of 10 repetitions at each location.

Success Check

- Visualize the stroke and shot.
- Hit a ceiling ball down the wall.
- Anticipate where the ball will come down.
- Make minor adjustments in your position as needed.
- Align your feet toward the center of the front wall.
- Hit the return to the ceiling cross-court to the opposite back corner.

- Follow through.
- Recover to center court.

Score Your Success

In this drill, you will include a recovery to center court after you hit the cross-court ceiling ball. Complete 10 ceiling shots from each side of the court (forehand and backhand) for a total of 20 repetitions. A successful shot is one that does not contact the side wall and returns to the deep backcourt within 2 feet (0.6 meter) of the back wall and side wall and floor crack—and from which you recover to center court.

1 to 20 percent successful shots = 1 point

21 to 50 percent successful shots = 3 points

51 to 100 percent successful shots = 5 points

Your score ___

RETURNING THE CEILING WALLPAPER SHOT

Possibly the hardest racquetball shot to return is the wallpaper shot, which hugs the wall all the way down the wall. This return is difficult to hit consistently and, therefore, is difficult to practice. It is a difficult shot to hit because the ball is on or very close to the wall, making it impossible to hit the ball in the sweet spot of the racquet. The wall hinders the player returning the ball (figure 7.4).

The two biggest mistakes in returning wallpaper shots are standing too close to the wall and trying to take a full swing and blast the ball. Beginners and intermediate players often try to take a full swing while too close to the wall. The easiest return when a ball is near the wall is a ceiling ball or another ball down the wall. However sometimes just returning the ball, regardless of where it goes, is all you can do. Ball proximity is crucial in this return. Perhaps the easiest way to return this shot is to place your racquet on the wall and try to scrape the ball off the wall while hitting it. You will also have more success if you square off

Figure 7.4 The wall prevents a player from easily returning a down-the-wall ceiling wallpaper shot.

to the wall and hit the ball with 80 percent of full force rather than trying to pound it. This is a controlled swing, not a blast. When you try to blast the ball, the already-low return percentage drops even more. Focus is also crucial to this return. This is no time for a mental lapse if you want a decent chance of returning the shot.

Anytime you hit a ball down the wall, you want it as close to the wall as possible. The biggest problem with trying to get the ball too close to the wall is the chance for error. The ball could hit the side wall and carom toward the center of the court, setting up an easy shot for your opponent. Many elite and pro players are good at getting the ball extremely close to the side wall consistently, but it's not a shot they rely on.

Misstep

The racquet hits the side wall, resulting in a mis-hit or missed shot.

Correction

Don't take a full swing at a ball that is hugging the wall. Use a shorter backswing and follow-through. Place your racquet against the wall and scrape the ball off the wall. Correct your proximity to the ball; you may be too close. Be sure your racquet-and-arm length is correct when you swing at the ball. Keep your eye on the ball and watch it make contact with the racquet.

Misstep

You swing at the ball and miss.

Correction

Don't take a full swing at a ball that is hugging the wall. Use a shorter backswing and follow-through. Correct your proximity to the ball; you may be too far away. Keep your eye on the ball and watch it make contact with the racquet.

Returning the Wallpaper Shot Drill.   *Off the Wall*

Stand next to the wall on either the forehand or backhand side. With the ball in your hand, reach as high as possible, holding it on the wall. Now let the ball drop straight down the wall (figure 7.5) and return it after it bounces off the floor. Practice this for shots to the ceiling and down-the-wall returns.

At first, you will have more success by trying to scrape the ball off the wall. Once you get used to the proximity of the ball to the wall, you can begin taking fuller swings. One thing will become obvious very quickly—if you don't get the proximity of the wall, ball, and racquet right, you will have problems. You will hit the wall, causing the racquet to ricochet off the wall and mis-hit the ball or miss it completely. Or you will just mis-hit or miss the ball altogether (even without hitting the wall). Practice the wallpaper return shot in 3 sets of 5 or 10 repetitions on both sides.

Figure 7.5 Hold the ball on the wall as high as possible.

Success Check

- Visualize the stroke and shot.
- Square off to the side wall.
- Place your racquet in the normal backswing position.
- Hold the ball as high on the wall as possible.
- Let the ball drop to the floor.
- Adjust your position.
- Place your racquet on the wall and scrape the ball off the wall.
- Follow through.

Score Your Success

Complete 10 shots each from the backhand and forehand sides of the backcourt for a total of 20 repetitions. A successful shot is one that returns to the front wall.

1 to 20 percent successful shots = 1 point

21 to 50 percent successful shots = 3 points

51 to 100 percent successful shots = 5 points

Your score ___

Ceiling Ball Game 1. *2-3-4-5 Ceiling Ball Game*

You will need a partner for this game. The game begins with a serve. Whether serving or returning serve, you must hit the ball to the ceiling a certain number of times (2, 3, 4, or 5) in succession before you can shoot the ball. In other words, you will get into a ceiling ball rally. It doesn't matter how you win the rally or what shot you use to win it. The primary function of the exercise is to hit successive ceiling shots during a game. Games can go to any end point. Typically, I set games to 7, 11, or 15 points. This is an excellent way for you to work on your ceiling game during a game situation.

To Increase Difficulty

- If the ceiling ball does not make it to the deep backcourt, the result is a loss of serve or a sideout.
- You must go to center court after each ceiling shot.
- You must alternate between down-the-wall and cross-court ceiling shots.

Success Check

- Line up your feet in the direction of your shot.
- Place your racquet in the backswing position.
- Get in position to hit the return.
- Adjust your position.
- Hit the ceiling ball down the wall or cross-court.
- Follow through.
- Recover to center court.

Score Your Success

Start out with a game to 7 points and two successive ceiling shots. As your skills improve, increase the game points and number of required successive ceiling shots. Keep track of your successive ceiling-ball success rate. If you win the game, you get a 3-point bonus.

1 to 20 percent successful shots = 1 point

21 to 50 percent successful shots = 3 points

51 to 100 percent successful shots = 5 points

Win the game = 3 bonus points

Your score ___

Ceiling Ball Game 2. *Continuous Ceiling Shots*

This game is just what the name implies—a ceiling ball game that continues until someone misses the ceiling. This is not a game for the faint of heart. It is a grueling, difficult game that can last forever. It is a great game for conditioning.

Each rally begins with a serve. The receiver hits a ceiling ball. The rally continues until someone skips or fails to return the ball to the ceiling. The game is scored normally, and games end when a player gets a total of 7 points.

To Increase Difficulty

- If the ceiling ball does not make it to the deep backcourt, the result is a loss of serve or a sideout.
- You must go to center court after each ceiling shot.
- You must alternate between down-the-wall and cross-court ceiling shots.

Success Check

- Anticipate where the ball will come down.
- Set up quickly with racquet in backswing position.
- Focus on the ball.
- Execute the shot.
- Recover to center court.

Score Your Success

Complete a 7-point ceiling ball game.

1 to 2 game points = 1 point

3 to 4 game points = 3 points

5 to 7 game points = 5 points

Your score ___

SUCCESS SUMMARY OF CEILING SHOTS

You will quickly find the ceiling ball to be your friend in indoor racquetball. Although it is similar to the lob in tennis, it has more far reaching effects in racquetball. The ceiling ball is a way to bail out of a potentially rally-ending shot from your opponent. It also allows you time to recover to center court and get ready for the next return, while placing your opponent in the deep backcourt, hitting the ball from the farthest distance to the front wall.

The ceiling ball is a shot you will want to practice and have control over. Use it judiciously. This is a great shot to use against an opponent who is weak in ceiling ball returns or is in poor condition. Constantly forcing your opponent to the deep backcourt with a combination of passing shots and ceiling balls will limit his or her shot options and open up more offensive opportunities for you. Most players are impatient and want to end the rally as quickly as possible. A good ceiling ball player will frustrate the shooter, forcing him or her to make unforced errors.

Record and tally your drill scores to rate your success at ceiling shots.

Down-the-Wall Ceiling Shot Drills

    1. Solo Practice   ___ out of 5

    2. Partner Practice   ___ out of 5

    3. Consecutive Shots   ___ out of 5

Cross-Court Ceiling Shot Drills

    1. Solo Practice   ___ out of 5

    2. Partner Practice   ___ out of 5

    3. Consecutive Shots   ___ out of 5

Returning the Wallpaper Shot Drill

    1. Off the Wall   ___ out of 5

Ceiling Ball Games

    1. 2-3-4-5 Ceiling Ball Game   ___ out of 8

    2. Continuous Ceiling Shots   ___ out of 5

Total   **___ *out of 48***

If you scored fewer than 25 points, go back and practice the drills that gave you the most trouble. If you scored 25 points or more, you are ready for step 8, Back-Wall Shots. Step 8 covers the most difficult racquetball skill to master. Doing so will define you as a racquetball player and will make the difference between being a beginner and becoming an advanced player.

Back-Wall Shots

Playing the ball off the back wall is not easy for the beginning player, who typically has difficulty understanding ball characteristics, allows the ball to get too close to the body (proximity) and does not get back far enough into the backcourt to play the ball off the back wall. Playing the ball—rather than letting the ball play you—is essential to mastering back-wall shots.

Let's define a couple of terms. First, *off the back wall* refers to an offensive shot that is hit directly to the front wall as the ball comes off the back wall. In contrast, *back to the back wall* refers to a defensive shot that is returned directly back to the back wall and then ricochets to the front wall.

Playing either back-wall shot requires quick thinking and strategy at the same time. It also requires anticipation, footwork, and preparation. The biggest problem most beginning players have is failing to get back fast enough to set up for the back-wall return. The player who does not get back quickly ends up with the ball behind himself or herself and therefore must hit the ball back to the back wall to get it to the front wall. Although this is an acceptable way of returning the ball to the front wall, it is less reliable from the standpoint of control and accuracy. It gives your opponent a better offensive opportunity off your return. It also defines your level of play—it separates the beginning player from the advanced player.

Players on the advanced to elite and professional levels rarely hit shots back to the back wall. They want to take every opportunity to return each shot offensively. Most returns back to the back wall are desperation shots on balls that would have double-bounced before even getting to the back wall or are ceiling balls that die in the backcourt, inches off the back wall. These balls are tactically played back to the back wall to save a rally-ending shot.

The average beginning player normally moves with the ball or chases after it. The beginner who starts to follow the ball with his or her eyes and anticipate where the ball is going will see sharp advances in his or her game and in his or her ability to take balls off the back wall straight to the front wall.

Additionally, most beginning players let the ball get too far behind them and end up reaching back to hit the ball, often resulting in a poor or weak return, or one that doesn't even reach the front wall. It is always best to move to the back wall and then move forward as the ball comes off the back wall to return the ball.

Although you can hit the ball into the back wall and have it fly to the front wall, this is a poor approach most of the time. It is a difficult shot to control and quite often results in an easy cutoff or winning return by the opponent. Don't depend on this type of a back-wall return. Work on the offensive back-wall return rather than the defensive one. You will seldom see an advanced player hit the ball into the back wall unless he or she is trying to save a good passing shot or ceiling ball that would otherwise die in the backcourt.

Because the back-wall shot involves so many elements—quick thinking, anticipation, ball speed, ball tendencies and characteristics, footwork, preparation, and strategy—practice is the only way to tame this particular demon. It is even more difficult when you add a glass back wall to the equation. The ball is quite often lost in the dark background of the glass back wall unless you have acute concentration.

The primary reason most beginning players do not advance quickly is that they do not know how to practice the back-wall return. This is a skill that must be developed in order to progress in racquetball. So, let's look at some practice drills to help improve your back-wall shots. Some key areas you will be working on are anticipation, footwork, balance, ball proximity, racquet preparation, timing, concentration, and focus.

The biggest obstacle to overcome is anticipating where the ball will come off the back wall. Quickly anticipating ball location and moving into position as soon as possible will give you the best chance of hitting an off-the-back-wall shot as opposed to a back-to-the-back-wall shot.

Once you have anticipated where the ball will come off the back wall, you will need to get into position to return the ball. Get as close as you can to the back wall. Touch the back wall with your nondominant hand to determine your distance to the back wall on a backhand return. On a forehand return, touch the back wall with your racquet to determine your distance to the back wall. This will give you enough separation from the back wall to swing the racquet and make an off-the-back-wall return if the ball comes out far enough from the back wall.

Once you establish your distance from the wall, get your racquet into the backswing position. Next, determine the ball's proximity and make slight adjustments with your feet in preparation for hitting the ball. Staying focused on the ball will help you make the necessary final adjustments to make the offensive return. Any lapse in focus or in seeing the ball will hurt your ability to make a good return.

The critical point in the off-the-back-wall return is determining whether the ball will come off the back wall far enough to make the return to the front wall. This ability will come with experience and practice. If there is not enough room to make a good swing, you will have to switch to hitting the ball back to the back wall. Again, experience will be the determining factor in this decision.

The final piece of the off-the-back-wall puzzle is timing. The timing of your swing as the ball comes off the back wall will determine where the ball goes. Perfect timing will send the ball to the front wall. Late timing will send the ball out toward the near side wall. Early timing will send the ball cross-court.

OFF-THE-BACK-WALL SHOT

These drills use a progression similar to that of the forehand and backhand drills in steps 1 and 2. This approach helps break down the mechanics of the shot in a logical progression. Omitting steps or progressing from one step to another too quickly may hinder your progress in mastering the shot. Practice and master all toss-and-catch drills before progressing to the toss-and-hit drills.

Back-Wall Toss-and-Catch Drill 1. *Bounce and Catch*

Stand parallel to the side wall in a forehand or backhand position. Stand in a ready position for hitting the ball to the front wall. You should be one arm-and-racquet length away from the back wall on the forehand side or one arm length away from the wall on the backhand side.

In a ready stance, use your nondominant hand to toss the ball to the back wall. Let the ball bounce and catch it with your dominant or racquet hand. The ball should come back to you at arm's length. Catch the ball in the power, or hitting, zone between knee and waist height.

Success Check

- Establish proper proximity to the back wall.
- Get into an athletic stance.

- Toss the ball to the back wall.
- Catch the ball in the power zone after it bounces off the floor.

Score Your Success

Complete 10 repetitions each for the backhand and forehand, for a total of 20 repetitions. A successful repetition is one where you catch the ball in the power zone between your waist and knee.

1 to 19 percent success rate = 1 point

20 to 49 percent success rate = 3 points

50 to 100 percent success rate = 5 points

Your score ___

Back-Wall Toss-and-Catch Drill 2. *Step*

Using the same proximity to the back wall as in drill 1 for the forehand and backhand, toss and catch the ball, adding a step toward the front wall (figure 8.1). In a ready stance, use your nondominant hand to toss the ball to the back wall. Let the ball bounce, then step forward and catch it with your dominant or racquet hand. The ball should come back to you at arm's length. Catch the ball in the power, or hitting, zone between knee and waist height.

Success Check

- Establish proper proximity to the back wall.
- Get into an athletic stance.
- Toss the ball to the back wall.
- Step forward with your forward foot and catch the ball in the power zone after it bounces off the floor.

Figure 8.1 Add a step to the back-wall toss-and-catch drill.

Score Your Success

Complete 10 repetitions each for the backhand and forehand, for a total of 20 repetitions. A successful repetition is one where you catch the ball in the power zone between your waist and knee.

1 to 19 percent success rate = 1 point

20 to 49 percent success rate = 3 points

50 to 100 percent success rate = 5 points

Your score ___

Back-Wall Toss-and-Catch Drill 3. *Shuffle*

With the same proximity to the back wall for the forehand and backhand as in drill 1, toss and catch the ball, adding a shuffle toward the front wall. To shuffle, bring the back foot up to the front foot and then step forward with the front foot (figure 8.2).

In a ready stance (forehand or backhand), use your nondominant hand to toss the ball to the back wall. Shuffle forward as the ball comes off the back wall and bounces. Let the ball bounce and catch it with your dominant or racquet hand. The ball should come back to you at arm's length. Catch the ball in the power, or hitting, zone between knee and waist height.

Success Check

* Establish proper proximity to the back wall.
* Get into an athletic stance.
* Toss the ball to the back wall.
* Shuffle forward and catch the ball in the power zone after it bounces off the floor.

Score Your Success

Complete 10 repetitions each for the backhand and forehand, for a total of 20 repetitions. A successful repetition is one where you catch the ball in the power zone between your waist and knee.

1 to 19 percent success rate = 1 point

20 to 49 percent success rate = 3 points

50 to 100 percent success rate = 5 points

Your score ___

Figure 8.2 Add a shuffle to the back-wall toss-and-catch drill.

Back-Wall Toss-and-Hit Drill 1. *No-Step*

These drills are identical to the toss-and-catch drills except you will hit the ball instead of catching it. The back-wall shot is the most difficult skill to learn in racquetball. The progression from catching the ball to hitting it will help you acquire this skill, so be sure to work through the toss-and-catch drills first.

Forehand: Stand parallel to the side wall, in a forehand position, one arm-and-racquet length away from the back wall. In a ready stance, with the racquet in the forehand backswing position, toss the ball to the back wall using your nondominant hand. Let it rebound off the back wall and bounce on the floor and into the power zone. Hit it to the front wall without taking a step (figure 8.3).

Backhand: From the backhand position, one arm's length away from the back wall, execute this drill as you did the forehand.

Visualize the stroke before you perform it. Check your grip and get into a ready stance. Initiate the backswing. Toss the ball to the back wall so it rebounds and bounces into the middle of the power zone for the forehand, or into the front end of the power zone for the backhand. Keep your eye on the ball. Begin your swing motion. Make contact with the ball between your waist and knees. Hold your pose at the end of the follow-through.

Success Check

- Establish proper proximity to the back wall.
- Get into an athletic stance.
- Place the racquet in the backswing position.
- Toss the ball to the back wall.

Figure 8.3 Hit the ball to the front wall without taking a step.

- After the ball bounces, use an out-and-around swing to hit it in the power zone to the front wall.
- Follow through.

Score Your Success

Complete 10 repetitions each for the backhand and forehand, for a total of 20 repetitions. A successful repetition is one where you hit the ball from the power zone between your waist and knee to the front wall.

1 to 19 percent success rate = 1 point

20 to 49 percent success rate = 5 points

50 to 100 percent success rate = 10 points

Your score ___

Back-Wall Toss-and-Hit Drill 2.   *Step*

Forehand: Stand parallel to the side wall, in a forehand position, one arm-and-racquet length away from the back wall. In a ready stance, with the racquet in the forehand backswing position, use your nondominant hand to toss the ball to the back wall. Let it rebound off the back wall to the floor so it bounces into the power zone as you step forward and hit it to the front wall.

Backhand: From the backhand position, one arm's length away from the back wall, execute the backhand as you did the forehand.

Visualize the stroke. Check your grip and get into your ready stance. Initiate the backswing. Toss the ball to the back wall so it rebounds and bounces into the middle of the power zone for the forehand, or into the front end of the power zone for the backhand. Keep your eye on the ball. Begin your swing motion. Make contact with the ball between your waist and knees. Hold your pose at the end of the follow-through.

Success Check

- Establish proper proximity to the back wall.
- Get into an athletic stance.
- Place the racquet in the backswing position.
- Toss the ball to the back wall.
- Step forward with front foot and use an out-and-around swing to hit the ball in the power zone to the front wall after it bounces off the floor.
- Follow through.

Score Your Success

Complete 10 repetitions each for the backhand and forehand, for a total of 20 repetitions. A successful repetition is one where you step forward and hit the ball from the power zone between the waist and knee to the front wall.

1 to 19 percent success rate = 1 point

20 to 49 percent success rate = 5 points

50 to 100 percent success rate = 10 points

Your score ___

Back-Wall Toss-and-Hit Drill 3.   *Shuffle*

Forehand: Stand parallel to the side wall, in a forehand position, one arm-and-racquet length away from the back wall. In a ready stance, with the racquet in the forehand backswing position, use your nondominant hand to toss the ball to the back wall. Let the ball rebound off the back wall and bounce into the power zone as you shuffle forward and hit it to the front wall.

Backhand: From the backhand position, one arm's length away from the back wall, execute the backhand as you did the forehand.

Visualize the stroke. Check your grip and get into your ready stance. Initiate the backswing. Toss the ball to the back wall so it rebounds and bounces into the power zone for the backhand. Keep your eye on the ball. Shuffle forward and

hit it to the front wall. Make contact with the ball between your waist and knees. Hold your pose at the end of the follow-through.

Success Check

- Establish proper proximity to the back wall.
- Get into an athletic stance.
- Place the racquet in the backswing position.
- Toss the ball to the back wall.
- Shuffle forward and use an out-and-around swing to hit the ball from the power zone to the front wall after it bounces off the floor.
- Follow through.

BACK-TO-THE-BACK-WALL SHOT

In this shot, instead of hitting the ball forward to the front wall off the back wall, you hit the ball back to the back wall, where it then ricochets to the front wall.

The biggest problems beginning players have with this shot are judging the path of the ball, determining where the ball will end up, and getting the correct ball proximity in relation to the body and the hitting zone. The prevalent mistake is allowing the ball to come straight off the back wall directly into the body and then hitting the ball underhand with a pendulum swing. Hitting the ball this way usually does not put enough power on the shot for it to carry to the front wall. In addition to the lack of power, the ball will ricochet off the back wall right back at the player's head, causing the player to flinch and duck while hitting the ball. In contrast, hitting the ball with an out-and-around stroke will give you the necessary power and angle to get the ball to the ceiling and front wall and back to the deep backcourt. It will also keep the ball away from your body as it comes off the back wall.

This out-and-around swing may not be flat, depending on the proximity and angle of the ball coming off the back wall. You may have to adjust the swing toward a down-to-up motion and open the racquet face (turn the face open toward the ceiling) to hit the ball at the correct angle off the back wall to the ceiling and front wall. Experimentation and practice with the following drills will have you hitting this shot with confidence in no time.

All of the key areas learned earlier in this step for hitting the ball off the back wall apply to hitting the ball back to the back wall. The only differences are whether you have enough room to swing the racquet forward and are in the proper position to hit the ball forward. Accordingly, the biggest difference between the off-the-back-wall drills and the back-to-the-back-wall drills will be your proximity to the back wall. You will be working on anticipation, footwork, balance, ball proximity, racquet preparation, timing, concentration, and focus. Please refer back, as necessary, to the beginning of this step for information on anticipating, setting up, and preparing to hit the ball.

Misstep

Your shot does not carry to the back wall.

Correction

Use a down-to-up swing or open the racquet face more toward the ceiling.

Misstep

The ball does not carry to the ceiling.

Correction

Hit the ball harder at the proper angle off the back wall.

Back-to-the-Back-Wall Ceiling Drill 1. *Hit to Back Wall*

Stand about 3 feet (0.9 meter) away from the back wall, parallel to the side wall in a forehand or backhand position, and ready to hit the ball off the back wall (figure 8.4). In a ready stance, with the racquet in the backswing position, drop the ball in the hitting zone. Hit the ball at an angle hard enough to send the ball to the ceiling in the same location as you would for a ceiling shot. The idea is to have the ball respond as a ceiling ball would and come back to the deep backcourt. This is a high-power shot and must be hit hard in order for the ball to travel its intended path.

Figure 8.4 Hit-to-back-wall drill.

Some players may not have the power to get the ball to the ceiling and back to the deep backcourt. In this case, work on getting the ball to the front wall high enough so it bounces to the deep backcourt as it would in a high lob serve.

Visualize the stroke. Check your grip and get into the ready stance. Initiate the backswing.

Drop the ball in the middle of the power zone for the forehand, or in the front end of the power zone for the backhand. Keep your eye on the ball. Begin your swing motion. Make contact with the ball between your waist and knees. Use an out-and-around swing to blast the ball into the back wall at an upward angle so the ball contacts the ceiling on its way to the front wall and returns to the deep backcourt. Hold your pose at the end of the follow-through.

Success Check

- Establish your position about 3 feet (0.9 meter) from the back wall.
- Get into an athletic stance.
- Place the racquet in the backswing position.
- Drop the ball to the floor at arm's length in the power zone.
- Use an out-and-around or slightly down-to-up swing to angle the ball off the back wall to the ceiling about 2 to 5 feet (0.6 to 1.5 meters) out from the front wall.
- Hit the ball hard enough to return it to the deep backcourt.
- Follow through.

Score Your Success

Complete 10 repetitions each for the backhand and forehand, for a total of 20 repetitions. A successful repetition is one where the ball goes back to the back wall, to the ceiling, to the front wall, and finally back to the deep backcourt.

1 to 19 percent success rate = 1 point

20 to 49 percent success rate = 3 points

50 to 100 percent success rate = 5 points

Your score ___

Back-to-the-Back-Wall Ceiling Drill 2. *Toss to Back Wall*

Stand about 3 feet (0.9 meter) away from the back wall, parallel to the side wall in a forehand or backhand position, and ready to hit the ball off the back wall (figure 8.4, page 126). In a ready stance, with the racquet in the backswing position, toss the ball to the back wall and let it bounce off the floor into the hitting zone. Hit the ball at an angle hard enough to send the ball to the ceiling in the same location as you would for a ceiling shot. The idea is to have the ball respond as a ceiling ball would and come back to the deep backcourt. This is a high-power shot; it must be hit hard in order for the ball to hit the ceiling and return to the deep backcourt.

Visualize the stroke. Check your grip and get into ready stance. Initiate the backswing. Toss the ball to the back wall so it rebounds and bounces into the middle of the power zone for the forehand, or into the front end of the power zone for the backhand. Keep your eye on the ball. Begin your swing motion. Make contact with the ball between your waist and knees. Use an out-and-around swing to blast the ball into the back wall at an angle to get the ball to contact the ceiling and front wall and return to the deep backcourt. Hold your pose at the end of the follow-through.

Success Check

- Establish your position about 3 feet (0.9 meter) from the back wall.
- Get into an athletic stance.
- Place the racquet in the backswing position.
- Toss the ball to the back wall. Let it bounce into the power zone and hit it.
- Use an out-and-around or slightly down-to-up swing to angle the ball off the back wall to the ceiling about 2 to 5 feet (0.6 to 1.5 meters) out from the front wall.
- Hit the ball hard enough to return it to the deep backcourt.
- Follow through.

Score Your Success

Complete 10 repetitions each for the backhand and forehand, for a total of 20 repetitions. A successful repetition is one where the ball goes back to the back wall, to the ceiling, to the front wall, and finally back to the deep backcourt.

1 to 19 percent success rate = 1 point

20 to 49 percent success rate = 3 points

50 to 100 percent success rate = 5 points

Your score ___

Misstep

The ball goes to the ceiling or front wall, then comes off the back wall, setting up the opponent for a shot.

Correction

Take a little power off the shot.

Misstep

The ball hits the front wall before hitting the ceiling.

Correction

Rotate with your hips and shoulders to get more weight and power behind the shot. Use a more upward stroke to hit the ball off the back wall. Open the racquet face more toward the ceiling.

Back-to-the-Back-Wall Ceiling Drill 3. *Advanced Practice*

Stand about 3 feet (0.9 meter) away from the back wall, parallel to the side wall in a forehand or backhand position, and ready to hit the ball off the back wall (figure 8.4, page 126). In a ready stance, with the racquet in the backswing position, toss the ball to the back wall and—before it bounces—hit it at an upward angle hard enough to send the ball to the ceiling in the same location as for a ceiling shot. The idea is to have the ball respond as a ceiling ball would and come back to the deep backcourt. This is a high-power shot and must be hit hard in order for the ball to hit the ceiling and return to the deep backcourt.

Visualize the stroke. Check your grip and get into ready stance. Initiate the backswing. Toss the ball to the back wall so it rebounds into the middle of the power zone for the forehand, or the front end of the power zone for the backhand, without bouncing to the floor. Keep your eye on the ball. Begin your swing motion. Make contact with the ball between your waist and knees. Use an out-and-around swing to an upward swing to blast the ball into the back wall at an angle to get the ball to contact the ceiling and front wall and return to the deep backcourt. Hold your pose at the end of the follow-through.

Success Check

- Establish your position about 3 feet (0.9 meter) from the back wall.
- Get into an athletic stance.
- Place the racquet in the backswing position.
- Toss the ball to the back wall hard enough to bounce off the wall and into the power zone without bouncing to the floor.
- Use an out-and-around or slightly down-to-up swing to angle the ball off the back wall to the ceiling about 2 to 5 feet (0.6 to 1.5 meters) out from the front wall.
- Hit the ball hard enough to return it to the deep backcourt.
- Follow through.

Score Your Success

Complete 10 repetitions each for the backhand and forehand, for a total of 20 repetitions. A successful repetition is one where the ball goes back to the back wall, to the ceiling, to the front wall, and finally back to the deep backcourt.

1 to 19 percent success rate = 1 point

20 to 49 percent success rate = 3 points

50 to 100 percent success rate = 5 points

Your score ___

Misstep

The ball hits the side wall before hitting the ceiling or front wall.

Correction

Make sure the racquet face is square to the back wall on ball contact and not angled to the left or right. Adjust ball contact to the middle of the power zone for the forehand or to the front of the power zone for the backhand. You may be contacting the ball too far forward or back in the power zone. Adjust your stance, open or closed, so you are hitting the ball straight into the back wall.

Misstep

The ball comes back at or hits you.

Correction

Hit out and around, not up and down. Make sure the racquet face is square to the back wall on ball contact and not angled right or left, which would send the ball back at you. Adjust ball contact to the middle of the power zone for the forehand or to the front of the power zone for the backhand. Adjust your stance and square off to the side wall.

All of the off-the-back-wall and back-to-the-back-wall drills can be performed in a game-style drill with or without a partner. It is best to perform these game-style drills after you master the drop, toss, bounce, and hit drills. Practice returns with both backhand and forehand shots. Practice 3 sets of 5 or 10 repetitions each.

Game-Style Drill 1. *Solo Ceiling Ball*

Stand in the backcourt. Hit a ceiling ball hard enough that it bounces in the backcourt and comes off the back wall or flies to the back wall and then bounces. Keep in mind, this simulates a game situation. The ball will react differently when hit off the back wall than when it is just tossed or bounced from a standing position. You will have to think quickly, anticipate where the ball will drop, judge ball speed, adjust footwork, judge ball proximity, and decide how to hit the ball.

Success Check

- Hit a forehand ceiling ball on the forehand side or a backhand ceiling ball on the backhand side of the backcourt. Hit it hard enough to carry farther than normal so the ball comes off the back wall.
- Once that ball is hit to the ceiling, anticipate where the ball will come off the back wall.

- Move to the back wall and adjust your proximity and position to receive the ball as it comes off the back wall.
- Depending on the ball's proximity to the back wall, decide whether you will hit an off-the-back-wall shot to the front wall, or a back-to-the-back-wall shot to the ceiling and front wall.
- Hit the ball so it returns to the deep back corner.

Score Your Success

Complete 10 repetitions each for the backhand and forehand, for a total of 20 repetitions. A successful repetition is one where the ball hits the front wall and returns to the deep backcourt.

1 to 19 percent success rate = 1 point

20 to 49 percent success rate = 5 points

50 to 100 percent success rate = 10 points

Your score ___

Game-Style Drill 2.   *Solo Front-Wall-to-Back-Wall Ball*

Stand near center court. Hit the ball hard enough off the front wall that it goes to the back wall. The ball will come off the back wall hard and fast to center or frontcourt. You will need to think quickly, anticipate where the ball will drop, judge ball speed, adjust footwork, judge ball proximity, and decide how to hit the ball.

This is a much different type of off-the-back-wall shot than what you have previously hit. In this drill you will be hitting the ball as it comes off the back wall, bounces on the floor, and travels to near center or frontcourt. This helps simulate a mis-hit ceiling ball that does not go to the ceiling, but goes from the front wall to the back wall. This can be an easy setup to the front wall for you if you anticipate quickly and get in position to hit a good shot.

When hitting a back-wall ball near center to frontcourt, shot selection should be determined first. Base shot selection on your capability to set up on the ball and your opponent's location on the court. Refer to step 10, Shot Selection, for help in deciding where to hit the ball.

Success Check

- Drop the ball and hit it to the front wall so it flies to the back wall without hitting the ceiling or side wall. Use different heights and amounts of power to place the ball in different locations as it comes off the back wall.
- Once the ball is hit, anticipate where the ball will end up once it comes off the back wall.
- Get into position to receive the ball as it comes off the back wall.
- Position your racquet in the backswing position.
- Make minor adjustments in your position.
- Return the ball to the front wall.
- Follow through.
- Recover to center court.

Score Your Success

Complete 10 repetitions each for the backhand and forehand, for a total of 20 repetitions. A successful repetition is one where the ball hits the front wall and bounces twice before reaching the back wall.

1 to 19 percent success rate = 1 point

20 to 49 percent success rate = 5 points

50 to 100 percent success rate = 10 points

Your score ___

Game-Style Drill 3.   *Solo Backcourt*

Stand in the backcourt. Hit the ball into the floor in the frontcourt hard enough that it comes off the front wall, flies to the backcourt, bounces on the floor, and then hits the back wall. (Or the ball might bounce off the back wall and then off the floor.) This is just another way to get the ball into the backcourt and off the back wall to practice off-the-back-wall and back-to-the-back-wall shots.

I especially like this drill because you are setting up the return without hitting a bad shot to do so. Hitting bad shots to set up another shot is not good practice, especially for beginners. This drill uses a setup shot not used during a game.

Success Check

- Drop the ball and hit it to the floor and into the front wall so it flies to the ceiling and back wall. Or hit the ball off the front wall for a rebound straight to the back wall without hitting the ceiling (or side wall). Use different heights and amounts of power to place the ball in different locations as it comes off the back wall.
- Once the ball is hit, anticipate where it will end up once it comes off the back wall.
- Get into position to receive the ball as it comes off the back wall.

- Position your racquet in the backswing position.
- Make minor adjustments in your position.
- Return the ball to the front wall.
- Follow through.
- Recover to center court.

Score Your Success

Complete 10 repetitions each for the backhand and forehand, for a total of 20 repetitions. A successful repetition is one where the ball hits the front wall and bounces twice before reaching the back wall.

1 to 19 percent success rate = 1 point

20 to 49 percent success rate = 5 points

50 to 100 percent success rate = 10 points

Your score ___

Game-Style Drill 4. *Partner Ceiling Ball*

Stand in center court and have a partner hit a ceiling ball so it comes off the back wall. Track the ball, anticipate where the ball will drop, judge ball speed, adjust footwork, judge ball proximity, and decide how to hit the ball. Be sure to practice this drill on both sides of the court, using forehand and backhand shots.

Success Check

- Set up in center court.
- Your partner hits a long ceiling ball.
- Once the ball is hit, anticipate where the ball will end up when it comes off the back wall.
- Get into position to receive the ball as it comes off the back wall.
- Position your racquet in the backswing position.

- Make minor adjustments in your position.
- Return the ball to the front wall.
- Follow through.
- Recover to center court.

Score Your Success

Complete 10 repetitions each for the backhand and forehand, for a total of 20 repetitions. A successful repetition is one where the ball hits the front wall and bounces twice before reaching the back wall.

1 to 19 percent success rate = 1 point

20 to 49 percent success rate = 5 points

50 to 100 percent success rate = 10 points

Your score ___

Game-Style Drill 5. *Partner Front-Wall Ball*

Stand in center court and have a partner hit a front-wall fly ball so it bounces first and comes off the back wall, or comes off the back wall first and then bounces. Track the ball, anticipate where the ball will drop, judge ball speed, adjust footwork, judge ball proximity, and decide how to hit the ball. Be sure to practice this drill on both sides of the court, using forehand and backhand shots.

Success Check

- Set up in center court.
- Your partner hits a ball that flies from the front wall to the back wall without hitting the ceiling or side wall.
- Once the ball is hit, anticipate where the ball will end up when it comes off the back wall.

- Get into position to receive the ball as it comes off the back wall.
- Position your racquet in the backswing position.
- Make minor adjustments in your position.
- Return the ball to the front wall.
- Follow through.
- Recover to center court.

Score Your Success

Complete 10 repetitions each for the backhand and forehand, for a total of 20 repetitions. A successful repetition is one where the ball hits the front wall and bounces twice before reaching the back wall.

1 to 19 percent success rate = 1 point

20 to 49 percent success rate = 5 points

50 to 100 percent success rate = 10 points

Your score ___

SUCCESS SUMMARY OF BACK-WALL SHOTS

There you have it. You now have all the drills to develop the skills for the game of racquetball. Back-wall shots are saved for the last skill step because they are the most difficult for beginners to master. Spend plenty of time working on the back-wall drills. These drills will carry over to nearly all the other shots in the game with the exception of the serve and the normal ceiling ball.

Remember, your ability to master the back-wall shots will define you as a player and will quickly advance you from being a beginner to being an advanced player. To speed this progression, spend time learning how the ball moves on the court and where the ball goes off the ceiling, side walls, back wall, and so on. Anticipation is the key. Knowing where the ball will end up so you can quickly get in position to hit it is what you want to be able to do.

Record and tally your drill scores to rate your success at back-wall shots.

Back-Wall Toss-and-Catch Drills

    1. Bounce and Catch   ___ out of 5

    2. Step   ___ out of 5

    3 Shuffle   ___ out of 5

Back-Wall Toss-and-Hit Drills

    1. No-Step   ___ out of 10

    2. Step   ___ out of 10

    3. Shuffle   ___ out of 10

Back-to-the-Back-Wall Ceiling Drills

    1. Hit to Back Wall   ___ out of 5

    2. Toss to Back Wall   ___ out of 5

    3. Advanced Practice   ___ out of 5

Game-Style Drills

    1. Solo Ceiling Ball   ___ out of 10

    2. Solo Front-Wall-to-
Back-Wall Ball   ___ out of 10

    3. Solo Backcourt   ___ out of 10

    4. Partner Ceiling Ball   ___ out of 10

    5. Partner Front-Wall Ball   ___ out of 10

Total   *___ out of 110*

If you scored fewer than 55 points, repeat the drills that you found difficult. If you scored 55 points or more, you are ready for step 9, Court Positioning. In that step, you will learn where to go on the court after hitting a shot or to get ready to return a shot. This will add one more piece to the puzzle as you develop yourself into a competitive player.

Court Positioning

Court positioning is crucial in racquetball. If you control center court, you will, for the most part, control the game. Think about baseball and basketball; in those sports, if players are not in the proper defensive position, they will leave easy opportunities for the opponent to score. If the third baseman in baseball is playing too far to the left, toward the shortstop, he or she leaves the baseline wide open as an offensive opportunity for the batter. So it is in racquetball: If you are out of position—i.e., out of center court or otherwise not in the optimal position for the highest-percentage shot—you leave offensive opportunities or shots for your opponent to take advantage of. Reading your opponent's offensive posture is part of being able to get in position to ensure you have the best possible opportunity to return the shot. Additionally, controlling the court doesn't mean just being in center court all the time. It is also means keeping your opponent out of center court as much as possible.

Many factors determine where you will go on the court when your opponent is returning the ball. The most obvious factor is ball location. However, as your skill level improves, so must your ability to read your opponent's stance to determine where the next shot will go. Some of these advanced reading skills may include noting your opponent's strengths and weaknesses, as well as observing the opponent's foot, hip, shoulder, and racquet positioning and whether he or she has a setup or is hitting the ball on the run or in a defensive posture. In this step, we will cover positioning based on ball location only. This will give you an excellent starting point for improving your reading skills and court positioning.

The biggest obstacle most people have to overcome when it comes to court positioning is getting hit by the ball. As you will see from most of the diagrams, you will need to get close to the ball's path in order to be in a good position for the return. Depending on your opponent's skill level and how accurate he or she is when hitting the ball, it may or may not be good to get very close to the potential path of the ball!

Misstep

You get hit with the ball or create an avoidable hinder. (See "Basic Rules of Play" in The Sport of Racquetball on page xii.)

Correction

You will reduce your risk by looking over your shoulder and keeping your eye on the ball. Don't let the fear of being hit by the ball keep you from getting into the best court position.

A common mistake made by beginning players and most low-intermediate players is not watching where the ball goes once they hit it. Many of these players are afraid of getting hit in the face by watching the ball. Although there is a possibility of being struck in the face when looking back to see where the ball goes, most players who get hit will either be hit by the ball from behind or hit by the opponent's racquet. There is less chance of being hit by the ball if you watch where it goes than if you simply set up in center court and wait for it to come into your peripheral vision on its way to the front wall. This would be the equivalent of shortstops not watching the batter hit the ball but trying to locate and field the ball once they hear the ball hit the bat. You will have greater success and get hit less often if you watch the shot develop and get in the best position for the return or, if needed, out of the way of the returning ball.

CENTER COURT

It is impossible to have a chapter on court positioning without discussing center court, which is located midway between the two side walls and approximately 18 inches (45 centimeters) behind the safety line (figure 9.1). Center court is not a single point on the court but an area through which approximately 80 percent of all balls, depending on the level of play, will travel. It is where you will have the best opportunity to return the majority of shots—or have the best opportunity to move to a point on the court to do so. This area gives you some latitude in your positioning and best coverage of the court. If your opponent makes a poor decision in shot selection or mis-hits the ball, center court will give you the best opportunity for a rally-winning return. Remember, the keys to court positioning are to control center court and keep your opponent in the back corners.

Now that we have identified center court, let's discuss variations of center court based on an assortment of ball locations and shots. Let's first look at the ball location in the back corner (figure 9.2). This is where you want most of your passing shots to go and where you want to keep your opponent the majority of the time. The reason

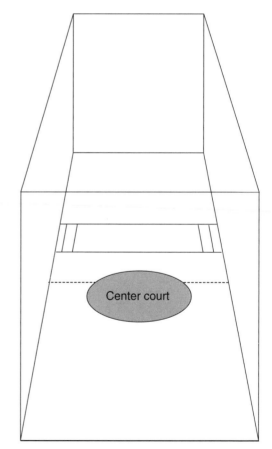

Figure 9.1 Center court.

is that you want your opponent to shoot the ball from the farthest point on the court in relation to the front wall. This means your opponent will have the greatest margin of error in returning the shot, and you will have the most time to react to and return the ball. As discussed in previous steps, you want to move your opponent to the deep backcourt with the highest-percentage shot possible. Most of the time this will be a passing shot or ceiling ball.

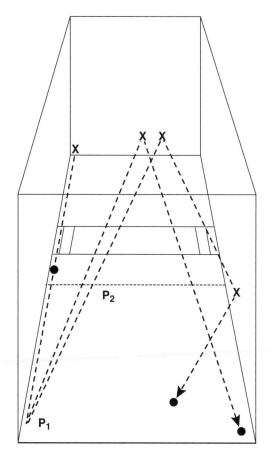

Figure 9.2 Ball in the back corner.

Figure 9.2 shows the returning player positioned slightly left but still in center court. The reason is that the easiest shot for the hitting player in this situation is down the wall. This shot has the highest percentage of accuracy and uses the wall to good advantage. The cross-court V or the wide-angle pass are also options, but they are lower-percentage shots. Either of these shots would give the returning player more time to react due to the ball's length of travel. Keep in mind that the returning player must give the

hitting player enough room to hit the cross-court V in order to avoid creating a hinder.

Figure 9.3 shows a similar situation. The primary difference is that the opponent is set up to hit the ball from mid backcourt. Here the returning player has to move just slightly more to the left because, again, the highest-percentage shot is down the wall. The returning player is hitting the ball up in the court and the ball will travel less distance. This means the defensive player will have less time to react to and get to a down-the-wall shot.

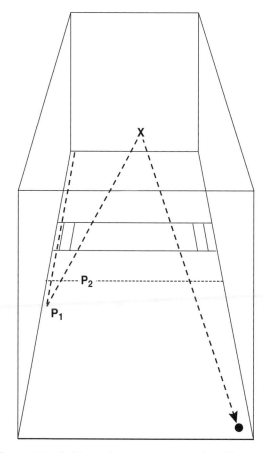

Figure 9.3 Ball in back corner, opponent in mid backcourt.

Setting up your opponent in the middle of the court is the worst situation of all (figure 9.4). Here the opponent has the best possible chance to win the rally. The opponent is in front of you and has many good options to choose from. A right-handed opponent in this position would be able to choose from the three most common, highest-percentage shots (pass right, pass left, and pinch right) to win the rally. (The reverse pinch would also be an option, but it is a low-percentage shot.) You are stuck with having to decide which direction to go. The highest-percentage shot (pass) is to the right side for a right-handed player, so going right makes sense. However, if you go left, you can cover two shots (pass left and right pinch). The choice is yours, so choose wisely. The best option is not to give your opponent the setup in center court in the first place.

keep in mind that the ball may go to the left. It is important to note that you do not want to give away your intentions (the direction you are going) too soon. This will tip off your opponent and give him or her the opportunity to hit behind you (pass left or cross-court if you are moving to the right).

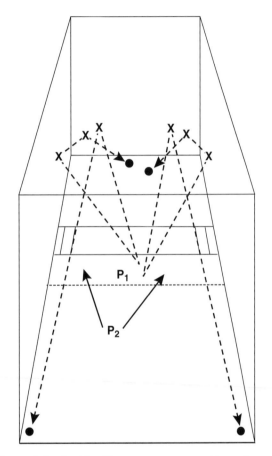

Figure 9.4 Avoid setting up your opponent in center court.

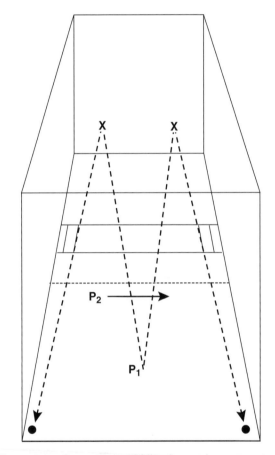

Figure 9.5 Opponent in middle of court, but not center court.

Figure 9.5 shows another situation in which the opponent is set up in the middle of the court, but not center court. This is a better situation for you, especially when you are in front of the opponent. As you can see, the opponent has two good shots. The first is the high-percentage shot to the right side (pass right). The second is the cross-court shot to the left side (pass left). You have a lot of court to cover to get to a well-hit ball to the right side, so get ready to move. But

These are the most common situations that may come up during a game. The biggest mistake most people make is staying in center court or moving completely over to the side and not covering the high-percentage shot. If you want the best opportunity to return the shot, you must cover the shot with the high percentage.

Here is one last thing to keep in mind about court positioning. Do not give your court positioning away too early. A good opponent will see where you are and take the highest-percentage shot by hitting to the open court. Keep your opponent guessing until the last minute.

FOOTWORK

Footwork is a basic element of getting to a position on the court. Understanding how to approach the ball will help you get to your position and set up to hit the ball as efficiently and effectively as possible. The main idea is to be in the right position, in the right place, at the right time.

In steps 1 and 2, we briefly discussed footwork and how to step while hitting the ball. Now, we will discuss how to move around the court to get into position to hit the ball. The most efficient movement patterns on the court are primarily diagonal. Keeping this in mind, we will discuss approaching the ball using a modified straight-line movement known as the banana.

One of the most common mistakes made by the beginning player is moving directly to the ball. Instead, move to the location where the ball will be hit by squaring up to the side wall. Then hit with an out-and-around stroke. The banana is basically a straight-line approach to the ball with a hook on the end during which you square up to the side wall. If you were to approach a ball that was hit short in midcourt from mid backcourt, without the banana approach and squaring off to the side wall, you would end up hitting the ball with open hips and most likely hit the ball too close to your body. The idea behind the banana is to approach the ball with effective ball-proximity spacing so you will be square to the side wall and capable of hitting with an out-and-around stroke.

Figure 9.6 shows how you might approach the ball from the backcourt moving forward or from center court to the back corner. Regardless of where you are on the court, the idea is to use big steps to move quickly, square off to the side wall, make small steps to adjust, and hit the ball from a setup position with a flat, out-and-around stroke.

As you move to the ball, move your racquet from the ready position to the backswing posi-

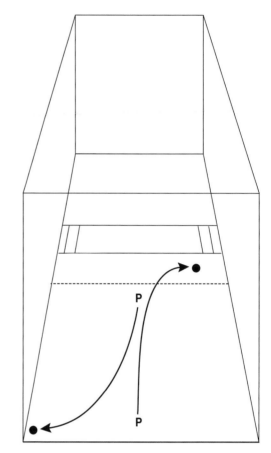

Figure 9.6 Approach from backcourt moving forward and from center court to backcourt.

tion. Keep in mind that you cannot see a racquetball spin. Be ready at any time to return an unexpected freak shot. If your racquet is down, you will not be able to react quickly enough to the carom or bounce from a freak shot. Once you get close to your final position, bring the racquet to the backswing position as you get ready to hit the ball. Your movement to the ball should always be controlled and balanced.

Use the following drills to practice getting from and to various locations on the court. Practice these as often as you wish to increase your court-coverage footwork and cardiovascular conditioning.

Footwork Drill 1. *Ministar Drill*

This drill (figure 9.7) helps you practice your small or minifootwork in center court. If necessary, refer to steps 1 and 2 to refresh your memory of out-and-around swing mechanics.

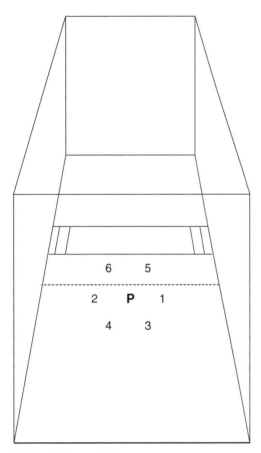

Figure 9.7 Ministar drill.

Begin by standing in center court in ready position. Crossover-step to location 1 and shadow-swing, then return to center court and ready position. Crossover-step to location 2 and shadow-swing, then return to center court and ready position. Shuffle back to location 3 and shadow-swing, then return to center court and ready position. Shuffle back to location 4 and shadow-swing, then return to center court and ready position. Shuffle forward to position 5 and shadow-swing, then return to center court and ready position. Shuffle forward to position 6 and shadow-swing, then return to center court and ready position.

Start slowly and work on your footwork and body movements. As you get better at this drill, you will be able to speed it up and actually get your heart rate up and work on conditioning at the same time. For an excellent workout, complete a total of 10 to 20 repetitions of the movement sequence.

Success Check

- Begin in a good athletic stance.
- Hold your racquet in ready position.
- Make a positive first step—no false steps.
- Bring racquet to backswing position.
- Square off to the side wall.
- Stay low.
- Swing out and around.
- Follow through.
- Stay balanced.
- Recover to the starting location in ready position.

Score Your Success

Complete 1 repetition of the movement sequence times 5 sets. A successful movement is one that fulfills all of the success checks.

1 to 19 percent successful movements = 1 point

20 to 49 percent successful movements = 3 points

50 to 100 percent successful movements = 5 points

Your score ___

Footwork Drill 2.   *Maxistar Drill*

The maxistar drill (figure 9.8) helps you practice your large-step and small-step footwork.

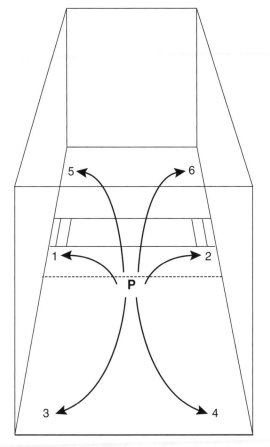

Figure 9.8 Maxistar drill.

As with the ministar drill, begin in center court in the ready position. Move from center court, using the banana approach, to each location, starting with large footsteps and transitioning into small foot step adjustments. Set up, shadow-swing, and return to ready position in center court, moving backward, not forward. Remember to keep your racquet in the ready position as you move. Additionally, keep your hips and shoulders to the side wall and front wall when moving to the backcourt. Do not turn your shoulders and hips to the back wall as you move to the backcourt. As you move to each location, imagine seeing the ball and keep an eye on the imaginary ball. This is especially important as you move to the backcourt.

Move to location 1 with your racquet in front of you. As you approach the mark, bring your racquet into backswing position, square off to the side wall, set your feet, and shadow-swing. Keep your eye on the imaginary ball. Return to center court. Do the same for locations 2, 3, 4, 5, and 6.

Start out slowly and work on your footwork and body movements. As you become more proficient, you can increase the tempo of the drill and get a very good cardio workout in addition to practicing your court movements and footwork. For an excellent workout, complete a total of 10 to 20 repetitions of the movement sequence.

Success Check

- Begin in athletic stance.
- Hold your racquet in ready position.
- Make a positive first step—no false steps.
- Make large steps to the square-off position.
- Bring racquet to backswing position.
- Square off to the side wall and stay low.
- Swing out and around.
- Follow through.
- Stay balanced.
- Recover to center court.
- Keep your hips and shoulders to the side wall and front wall.
- Keep your eye on the imaginary ball.
- Square off to the front wall while in center court in ready position.

Score Your Success

Complete 1 repetition of the movement sequence times 5 sets. A successful movement is one that fulfills all of the success checks.

1 to 19 percent successful movements = 1 point

20 to 49 percent successful movements = 3 points

50 to 100 percent successful movements = 5 points

Your score ___

Footwork Drill 3.   *Court Sprints*

This drill will help you get used to running backward and familiarize yourself with the dimensions of the court. It can also be used as an excellent cardio workout. Begin from the serve-receiving location and in the ready position (figure 9.9). Run to the safety line and run backward to the back wall, keeping your eyes on the front wall or an imaginary ball coming from the front wall. Turn to the forehand side with the racquet in the backswing position and touch the back wall with your racquet as if you were getting ready to hit a ceiling ball.

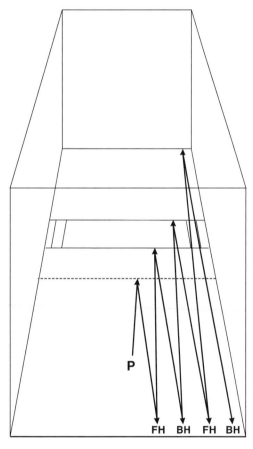

Figure 9.9 Court sprints.

Run to the short line and run backward to the back wall, keeping your eyes on the front wall or an imaginary ball coming from the front wall. Turn to the backhand side, bringing your racquet up into backswing position as if you were getting ready to hit a ceiling ball, and touch the back wall with your nonracquet hand.

Run to the service line and run backward to the back wall, keeping your eyes on the front wall or an imaginary ball coming from the front wall. Do not look back at the back wall. Turn to the forehand side, bringing your racquet up into backswing position, and touch the back wall with your racquet.

Run to the front wall and run backward to the back wall, keeping your eyes on the front wall or an imaginary ball coming from the front wall. Turn to the backhand side, bringing your racquet up into backswing position, and touch the back wall with your nonracquet hand.

You can increase your speed to get a great cardio workout as you get more familiar with the court. Additionally, this is an excellent warm-up when you first get on the court and do your stroke warm-up before a game.

To Increase Difficulty

Each time you come to one of the lines, turn and shadow-swing, then run back to the back wall.

Success Check

- Begin in athletic stance with your racquet in the ready position.
- Go to the safety line.
- Make a positive first step—no false steps.
- Make large steps to the square-off position.
- Bring racquet to backswing position.
- Square off to the side wall and stay low.
- Swing out and around.
- Follow through.
- Stay balanced.
- Run backward as you recover to the back wall.
- Touch the back wall and go to the short line.
- Touch the back wall and move to the service line.
- Touch the back wall and move to the front wall.
- Run backward as you recover to the back wall.

Score Your Success

Complete 5 court sprints (that is, 5 sets of the full sequence). A successful sprint is one that fulfills all of the success checks.

1 to 19 percent successful movements = 1 point

20 to 49 percent successful movements = 3 points

50 to 100 percent successful movements = 5 points

Your score ___

Footwork Drill 4.   Solo Front-Wall Setup Drill

Begin this drill by standing in the safety zone. From either the forehand or backhand position, gently hit the ball straight to the front wall. As the ball returns, adjust your feet, set up, and hit the ball using any shot you want. Don't worry about how many times the ball bounces on its way back. The purpose of the drill is to work on your small footwork, making adjustments to set up and hit the ball. As you get better at this drill, you will be able set up and hit the ball consistently off of one bounce. Additionally, your increased skill will allow you to move farther back in the court and eventually drill from the deep backcourt. This drill should be completed in 3 sets of 10 repetitions each for the forehand and the backhand.

Success Check

- Position yourself in center court.
- Square off to the side wall.
- Gently hit the ball to the front wall so it go to either the forehand or backhand side.
- Get your racquet back in the backswing position.

- Move to the location where you will hit the ball.
- Make adjustments with your feet.
- Stay low.
- Hit the ball in the power zone with an out-and-around stroke without a skip.
- Stay balanced.
- Follow through.
- Recover to center court.

Score Your Success

Complete 10 repetitions each from the forehand and backhand side. A successful repetition fulfills all of the success checks.

1 to 19 percent successful movements = 1 point

20 to 49 percent successful movements = 3 points

50 to 100 percent successful movements = 5 points

Your score ___

Footwork Drill 5. *Partner Front-Wall Setup Drill*

Begin by setting up in center court. Have a partner gently hit the ball straight to the front wall from the service box, angling the ball to the deep back corner. Move from center court to the appropriate backcourt location, set up, and return the ball to the front wall. Don't worry if you can't return the ball before it bounces multiple times. Your skill level will increase with practice, and eventually you will be able to return the ball after the first bounce. Complete 3 sets of 10 repetitions each for the forehand and the backhand.

To Increase Difficulty

Have your partner vary the locations on the court where the ball will go without your knowing where ahead of time. Return the ball after one bounce.

Success Check

- Position yourself in center court in the ready position.
- Determine where the ball is going and get your racquet into the backswing position as quickly as possible.

- Get to your return location, square off to the side wall, set up, and wait for the ball.
- Make miniadjustments with your feet.
- Return the ball to the front wall without a skip.
- Recover to center court.

Score Your Success

Complete 10 repetitions from various locations. A successful repetition is one that fulfills all of the success checks.

1 to 19 percent successful movements = 1 point

20 to 49 percent successful movements = 3 points

50 to 100 percent successful movements = 5 points

Your score ___

SUCCESS SUMMARY OF COURT POSITIONING

With a firm understanding of court positioning and how to move to where the ball is, you are well on your way to advancing your skill level. Here are a few things to remember about court positioning: Control center court as much as you can and relocate to center court as quickly as possible after a shot. Keep your opponent in the deep backcourt corners and force him or her to hit the ball the farthest distance to the front wall. Typically, take the center-court position that covers the high-percentage return, but keep track of your opponent's tendencies

for shot returns. Give your opponent the legal shots to the front wall and cross-court. Don't create an avoidable hinder by getting in the way of the shot.

Work on the drills in this step, which will certainly help you to get to the ball more efficiently. The faster you can get into position, the more time you will have to prepare for the return shot. Anytime you can get into position for a return, the better chance you have of returning the shot with a setup. Record and tally your drill scores to evaluate your footwork.

Footwork Drills

1. Ministar Drill ___ out of 5

2. Maxistar Drill ___ out of 5

3. Court Sprints ___ out of 5

4. Solo Front-Wall Setup Drill ___ out of 5

5. Partner Front-Wall Setup Drill ___ out of 5

Total ___ **out of 25**

If you scored fewer than 15 points, redo the footwork drills to improve your scores. If you scored 15 points or more, you are ready to move on to the next step.

Keep an eye on your opponent and look for weaknesses in court positioning, shot setup, court movement, and so on. All of these things will help you decide where to go on the court and where to hit the ball. The next step, Shot Selection, builds on this one to take you to the next skill level.

Shot Selection

Shot selection is one of the most widely argued areas of racquetball. It is also the most widely ignored aspect of the game. Players love to shoot the ball. Crowds love to see the kill, pinch, and splat. However, if you are a player who is more concerned about winning with high-percentage shots and reducing unforced errors, you will want to pay close attention to this subject and apply what you learn to your game.

There is an old saying in real estate: "If you want to make money, it's all about location, location, location." The same principle applies to racquetball: The money shots are all about location. Here are four basic guidelines for shot location:

1. If your opponent is in front of you, pass.

2. If your opponent is behind you, pinch or kill.

3. Keep yourself between your opponent and the ball or hit to the open court.

4. For ending a rally, a one-wall shot is usually better than a two- or three-wall shot.

Don't forget what you learned about court positioning in the last step. Relocate to center court, or as close to it as possible, after your shot. A good shot doesn't win a rally until the ball double-bounces or your opponent skips the ball. In other words, your best shot is no good if you stand in the backcourt like a spectator and watch while your opponent runs it down, hits a mediocre shot, and wins the rally because you are out of position or not ready to return the ball.

Table 10.1 is a basic introduction to typical shot-selection scenarios. It gives you a foundation for deciding when to use a given shot. Keep in mind that this is only a foundation. As you progress as a player, you will find that you hit certain shots better than others—every player has favorites. The key to using shots is keeping your opponent off balance and guessing. Don't hit the same shot all the time.

Let's look at some basic shot-selection situations.

Table 10.1   Choose Your Shot

Shot	When to use it
Pinch shot	You have a good setup position and are in front of opponent Opponent is in deep backcourt Opponent is offset to one side, and you can pinch to the same-side corner
Kill shot	You have a setup in mid to frontcourt, and opponent is in the backcourt
Down-the-wall pass	You are in good setup position in the backcourt Opponent is in front of you in center court Opponent is out of position Opponent is in center court, and you want to move him or her to the backcourt
Cross-court V pass	You are in good setup position in the backcourt—opponent is in front of you Opponent is looking for the down-the-wall Opponent is in center court, and you want to move him or her to the backcourt
Wide-angle pass	You are in good setup position in the mid to backcourt—opponent is in front of you Opponent is looking for the down-the-wall or cross-court V pass Opponent is in center court, and you want to move him or her to the backcourt You are in front court, and opponent is in center court
Ceiling shot	Choose this shot anytime You are not in a good setup position to hit an offensive shot You want to change the pace of a fast game You want to keep your opponent in the backcourt and out of center court
Around-the-wall shot	Use sparingly as a change of pace from the ceiling shot Opponent is in center court, and you want to move him or her out of center court Opponent has difficulty tracking the ball You want to move your opponent to the backcourt
High Z shot	You are off balance in mid to frontcourt You want to move your opponent to the backcourt You need time to get to center court from the frontcourt Use as an alternative to a ceiling shot when you are in middle to frontcourt Opponent has difficulty tracking the ball

BACK-CORNER SERVE RETURN OR RALLY RETURN

Figure 10.1 shows a typical back-corner serve return, back-corner shot return, or ceiling-ball return. If you have a setup, your highest-percentage shot is down the wall. Your next option would be the cross-court V or even a cross-court wide-angle. Be careful with the cross-court wide-angle, though; if it is left up, it will come back to the center of the court.

The down-the-wall shot is the highest-percentage option because it is a straight shot to the front wall and uses the side wall as a possible hindrance to your opponent's return. If you do not have the setup for a good aggressive, offensive return, then you should go to the down-the-wall ceiling or cross-court ceiling shot to the opposite corner. These shots will move your opponent out of center court to the backcourt corner, and you will be able to relocate to center court. However, if your opponent is off center to the left and waiting for the down-the-wall shot, then you will want to take the cross-court V or wide-angle pass.

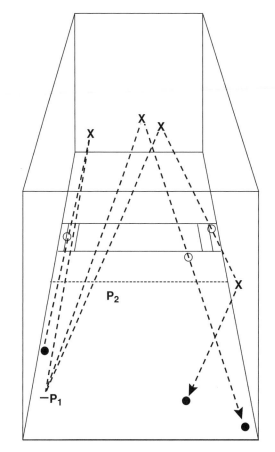

Figure 10.1 Back-corner serve return, back-corner shot return, or ceiling-ball return.

MIDDLE BACKCOURT POSITION

In figure 10.2, your position is in the middle backcourt, with your opponent left of center court. Your first choice on a setup should be to the open court or right side. This is the farthest distance from your opponent and the highest-percentage shot you have. Next you will want to consider the cross-court V, and finally the cross-court wide-angle to the backhand side. Again, be careful with the cross-court wide-angle; if it is left up, it will come back to the center of the court. The V and wide-angle passes to the left are good shots if you pick up that your opponent is going to the right. The reason is that with your opponent's shoulders toward the right side wall, you will have an easy pass behind him or her. For the off-balance shot, the ceiling is your best option. Hit the ceiling shot either left or right, depending on your positioning and that of your opponent.

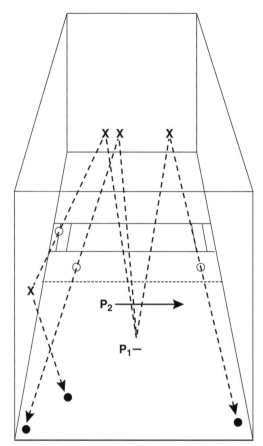

Figure 10.2 In middle backcourt with opponent left of center court.

CENTER COURT POSITION

Figure 10.3 shows you in center court and in front of your opponent, who is in the mid-backcourt. This is the ideal shot in racquetball if you can get in position for the setup. If the pinch is a good shot for you, then it should be your first choice. If you are not hitting the pinch well, then hit the kill shot to the right side, or, as a last choice, to the left. If the ball is coming off the back wall, you will see your opponent and have a better idea where to hit the ball depending on your opponent's movement. If the ball is coming off the front wall, go with your best shot. Don't forget the ceiling or a high Z to bail you out of an off-balance desperation shot. The main idea here is to make your opponent pay for a bad shot so you can win the rally with your best-percentage option.

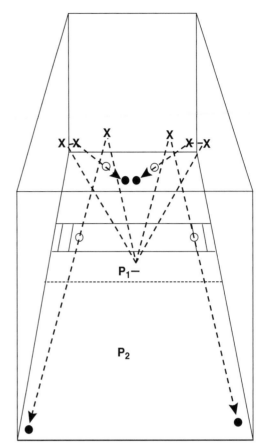

Figure 10.3 In center court, with opponent in mid-backcourt.

FRONTCOURT POSITION

Figure 10.4 puts you in the frontcourt, with your opponent in center court. This can be a good situation for you if you choose the right shot and execute it properly. If you don't execute or you mis-hit the shot, you will most likely set up your opponent for an easy winner, so be careful.

If you are a right-handed player and you are playing a right-handed player, your first option should be to blast the ball past your opponent with a wide-angle pass or kill shot to the right. Your second choice would be to blast the ball past your opponent with a wide-angle pass or kill shot to the left. If the ball is coming off the back wall, be sure to watch your opponent for any clues that he or she is planning to stay in center court or move left or right. This will help you decide which shot to hit. Most beginning and low-intermediate players will opt to stay in center court. Keep in mind that if you don't get the right angle or height on this shot, you can leave your opponent with an easy rally-winning return. Don't be greedy or try to manufacture a shot that is not there. If this is not a clean setup, don't take a chance on the kill or pass. Go to the ceiling or a high Z and get back to center court as quickly as possible. It is always better to punt than go for the first down and come up short.

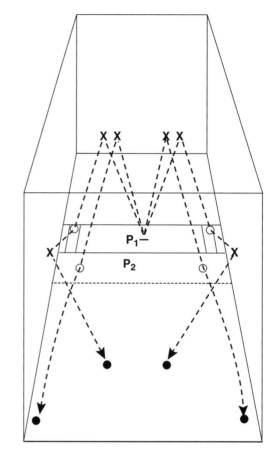

Figure 10.4   In frontcourt, with opponent in center court.

OPPONENT OUT OF POSITION

Figure 10.5 shows a no-brainer. No need to get fancy here: Your opponent is clearly out of position, and you have the entire left side of the court to hit a cross-court shot. Don't go for the kill; go for the pass. Many players make the mistake of trying to shoot too low and end up skipping the ball. It would be better to miss the ball high and leave it up than skip it and end the rally without even making your opponent run cross-court to get the ball. Last but not least, go to the ceiling if the setup shot isn't there.

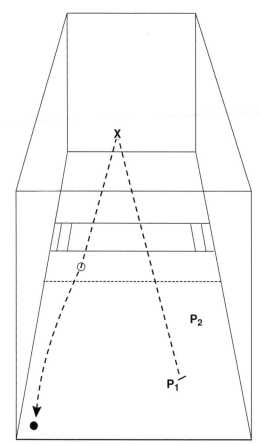

Figure 10.5 Opponent is out of position; left side of the court is open.

OPPONENT PREPARED FOR MISSED SHOT

Figure 10.6 puts you in a difficult position in the frontcourt, with your opponent in perfect position for a missed shot. If you find yourself in the frontcourt and the ball is high or you are scrambling to get to it, one of your best shot options is the high Z. This shot will send your opponent scurrying to get to the ball in the back corner, giving you time to recover and get to center court.

Another shot option is the front-wall ceiling ball to the deep backcourt. We talked about this in step 7, Ceiling Shots. When you are this far forward, you will have to hit the front wall first. Otherwise the ball will come down into the front of the court. Be careful with this shot. If you don't hit the ceiling, the ball will come off the back wall for a setup.

Many players try to create a shot here by trying to kill the ball. This is a mistake if you are off balance and don't have the setup. It is better to save the ball with the high Z or ceiling shot and give yourself a chance to return the next shot than to skip the ball or give your opponent a rally-winning setup. If you do have a setup, then you may want to take advantage by blasting the ball past your opponent (figure 10.4, page 152) or dink a soft shot to the corner.

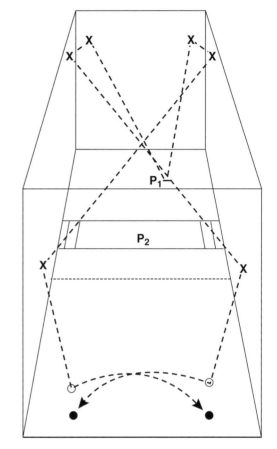

Figure 10.6 In frontcourt, with opponent in position to attack a missed shot.

Shot Selection Drill 1.   *Solo Practice*

This is a good solo drill to prepare you for the partner drill. Begin in center court and hit any shot you want. Move into position to return the shot. While you are moving into position to return the ball, review your shot options and set up to return the ball. Once you are in place and the ball comes into the power zone, make your final decision on which shot to shoot. Don't always take the same shot. Mix up your shots and build your shot selection and execution skills.

Success Check

- Begin in center court.
- Hit a shot.
- Move to the return location.

- Review your shot options.
- Set up on the ball.
- Decide which shot is the best option.
- Hit the shot.
- Recover to center court.

Score Your Success

This drill doesn't have a certain number of repetitions. Keep track of your success percentage. A successful return is one that doesn't skip (or double-bounce before you can hit it).

1 to 19 percent success rate = 1 point

20 to 49 percent success rate = 5 points

50 to 100 percent success rate = 10 points

Your score ___

Shot Selection Drill 2.   *Partner Practice*

Here is a drill I use with my athletes to help them with proper shot selection. You will need a partner. This is a three-hit drill—your partner hits the ball, you hit the ball, and your partner hits the last ball, if possible. This can be done from anywhere on the court.

Your partner begins the drill by hitting any shot except a winning kill shot. Have your partner start out with high shots and ceiling balls that will set up easily off the back wall or into center court. As you get better, you can transition to lower and harder beginning shots. The idea is for your partner to begin the rally by putting the ball in play. You begin in center court and move into position to return the ball. Your partner will next move anywhere on the court, not necessarily into the proper court position, to return your shot. This will force you to keep track of where your opponent is and hit the best shot given your location and that of your opponent. Once you hit the ball, recover to center court. After your partner tries to return your shot, the rally is over. Have your partner mix up the beginning shots and where he or she goes on the court. Have your partner hit the shots you

have the most difficulty with. Don't work on the ones you hit well.

Success Check

- Begin in center court.
- Move to your return position.
- Watch your opponent out of the corner of your eye.
- Decide which shot is the best one to hit.
- Hit the shot.
- Recover to center court.

Score Your Success

This drill doesn't have a certain number of repetitions. Keep track of your success percentage. A successful return is one that you hit before it double-bounces and your opponent either cannot get to or is unable to return to the front wall.

1 to 19 percent success rate = 1 point

20 to 49 percent success rate = 5 points

50 to 100 percent success rate = 10 points

Your score ___

SUCCESS SUMMARY OF SHOT SELECTION

Success in shot selection and execution comes from quickly setting up to hit the ball. The sooner you set up, the more time you have to watch where your opponent goes and decide on the best shot to take. Keep in mind that the highest-percentage shot in general may not always be the best shot to take. You need to determine the best shot you have based on how the ball is set up and where your opponent is on the court.

Don't get greedy with shot selection. In other words, don't go for a kill shot when a good pass-ing shot will work. Don't hit a pinch shot and possibly leave it up when a good passing shot will work. Don't force a shot when you can go to the ceiling or hit a high Z. The biggest mistake a player can make is skipping the ball. A skip ends the rally without making your opponent do anything but watch. Remember, money-making racquetball shots are all about location, location, location.

Record your scores for the two shot selection drills in this step to evaluate your progress.

Shot Selection Drills

1. Solo Practice   ___ out of 10

2. Partner Practice   ___ out of 10

Total   ___ *out of 20*

If you scored fewer than 10 points, perform the drills again to improve your scores. If you scored 10 points or more, you are ready to move on to step 11, Game Management, which describes the essentials of game management. Step 11 brings together everything you have learned to this point. It shows you how to incorporate mental strategies with the physical aspects of the game.

Game Management

Where do you start when putting together a game plan? Here are the two basic questions to ask first: What are your strengths and weaknesses? What are your opponent's strengths, weaknesses, and tendencies?

Many players have no idea that a game plan is as much a part of playing racquetball as are serving and returning, or even rally play for that matter. They go into the court and just play. Not that this is bad, but it means they are not completely prepared to play. Most of those players develop their game plan on the fly or as the game develops. Others never develop one at all.

Have you ever had a hard time beating a particular player? Or, have you ever been in a game and wondered how to change things around, especially when you are getting beat? All of us have.

What is the difference between having a game plan and not having one? If you have watched football or basketball, you have probably noticed the head coach looking at a chart or script. This is a game plan. Coaches spend an enormous amount of time watching video footage of the opposing team to find the strengths and weaknesses in the opponent's game. Then they compare their strengths and weaknesses to their opponent's and come up with a game plan. Most football coaches have the first 25 offensive plays scripted or planned. As the game progresses, the coach notices tendencies and idiosyncrasies in both the opposition and their own team and makes adjustments to the game plan as needed.

Most racquetball players do not have the resources available to get video of their opponents. However, they do have the ability to scout their opponents and watch them play against others. This provides an opportunity to pick up on strengths, weaknesses, and tendencies. If they don't have the opportunity to watch their opponents play, they can at least watch them warm up and develop a game plan based on what they see.

Keep in mind, we are not talking about tournament game planning. However, we all have that competitive instinct and want to do our best. With that said, it is always a good idea to have some idea of how to approach a game. So, let's look at putting together a simple game plan.

PLAY TO YOUR STRENGTHS

You know your game better than anyone else's. Why not play to your own strengths? First, you need to define what your strengths are. Do you have a great drive or lob serve? Are you tireless? Do you get to everything? Do you hit excellent passing shots? Are you mentally tougher than most opponents? Whatever defines you as a player, you must use it to your advantage and make your opponent suffer for it.

But what if your strength is weaker than your opponent's strength? Well, you may want to consider playing to something else. Find a weakness in your opponent and exploit it. You definitely need to find something that works

for you and against your opponent. Granted, playing to your strength may not be the best strategy in every case. But you should start there until you find out that it doesn't work and then formulate a plan that works to your advantage.

One of the advantages you have over an unknown opponent is that you know your weaknesses. Obviously you want to keep this a secret as long as possible. Some weaknesses are obvious, such as body type, but others, such as court positioning, shot selection, stroke mechanics, and mental focus, may not be easily detectable before the match begins.

PLAY TO YOUR OPPONENT'S WEAKNESSES

Weaknesses are those little demons we try to keep hidden in the closet. However, a good player always finds them and exploits them when given the opportunity. It is to your advantage to find those demons in your opponent's game and let them work their magic. What do you look for, and how do you find those demons?

First look for flaws in stroke mechanics: pendulum swing, slice, short compact swing, long looping swing, and so one. Then look for flaws in footwork: light on the feet, or flat footed. Does the player cross over to hit the ball or step forward to hit the ball? Does he or she hit with open hips or closed hips? Finally, look for flaws in stance and ready position: wide stance, narrow stance, low in the stance, upright in the stance. Is the racquet down or in the ready position?

All of these observations will help you work out a strategy and game plan before stepping on the court for game play. Table 11.1 lists some strategies based on the opponent's qualities.

Every player has favorite shots to hit in certain situations. This can work to your advantage in anticipating what your opponent will do. Be observant and store shot data in your memory bank. Remember what your opponent does and when he or she does it. This is all part of game management.

Another aspect of game management is what the ball does on certain shots with a particular player. A Z serve will be different from one player to the next, as will a drive serve or a pinch shot. This is because not everyone hits the ball flat. Some players will cut the ball or slice it. Most players are fairly consistent with their shots, so the ball will generally react the same way from one instance to another. Keeping these things in mind will help you adjust much more quickly to an opponent's game and help you figure out how to position yourself and attack the given shot.

Remember the chapter on shot selection? Well, use what you learned. If your opponent is hitting the ball in front of you, think pinch or kill. If your opponent is hitting the ball behind you, think pass or ceiling ball. Remember, the game is the same for both players. You must assume your opponent knows as much as or more than you do about the game and has equal or better shots.

Another important note is that when your opponent is hitting in front of you, don't go to the center of the court and wait for a bad or mis-hit shot to come to you. Look at your opponent's stance, footwork, body position, shoulders, and so on. Identify the highest-percentage shot, or the shot the opponent hits the most often in that particular situation, and set up for that return. Merely standing in center court will make it very

Table 11.1 Strategies Based on Opponent's Characteristics

Opponent's characteristic	Strategies
Fast	Slow the game down with lob serves Hit off-pace shots Go to the ceiling Use your 10 seconds allowed to put the ball in play Use time-outs Keep shots behind your opponent
Slow	Speed up the game Serve as quickly as possible Don't let your opponent rest Hit hard, low passing shots Use drive serves
Tall player who covers court well	Hit jam serves and jam shots into the body
Short player	Hit very high lob serves deep in backcourt Hit lots of passing shots
Strong backhand	Hit more shots to forehand Go to backhand on defensive shots only, and only when necessary Move opponent to forehand side of the court Serve more to the forehand side
Strong forehand	Hit more shots to backhand. Go to forehand on defensive shots only, and only when necessary Move opponent to backhand side of the court Serve more to the backhand side
Pendulum-style swing	Serve wide Make your opponent reach wide to return shots Hit lots of passes
Out-and-around swing	Serve and shoot into the body Hit lots of jams
Good shooter who hits ball hard	Keep opponent in the backcourt Hit off-pace shots Keep the ball up and make your opponent hit the ball above the waist Hit lots of passing shots and make your opponent hit on the run
Aggressive on serve returns	Hit lob serves Hit off-pace serves
Hits hard drive serves	Jump on serve and return with passes before opponent gets out of service box

easy to pass you. You must commit to a shot and be ready for the return. You will be more successful in returning the ball if you commit to a particular shot.

Don't be predictable. Mix up your shots and keep your opponent off balance and guessing as much as possible. Don't give your opponent the very advantage you are looking to gain.

CONTROL THE GAME

How do you manage a game? Is it all about what serve to hit, or court positioning, or shot selection? Yes, and more. It's a start to understand the rules and how you can use them to your advantage, and to your opponent's disadvantage. But it is also important to understand the tactics involved in playing the game. Table 11.2 lists some ideas for controlling the game in certain situations.

Game management means keeping track of everything that happens on the court. It includes but is not limited to time-outs, game tempo, and strategy. It is like counting cards or keeping track of what combinations have been played in a card game. It is also about how you approach the game mentally. Do you have confidence in your physical and mental games? Are you able to stay cool under pressure, or do you crack? Are you able to look your opponent in the eye and say, "Hit your best shot"? Sometimes controlling the game is about letting it go. In other words, sometimes it's okay to just let things happen naturally rather than striving for total control all the time.

Use Time-Outs

A great game plan includes taking time-outs at precise and calculated moments. You get three time-outs in games to 15 points and two in a tie-breaker game to 11. Why not use them? Time-outs are a great way to catch your breath after a long, tiring rally. Time-outs are also a great way to stop your opponent from gaining momentum. For instance, if your opponent just reeled off 5 points in a row and you are struggling with the service return, take a time-out. Even if it is the beginning of a game, you must try to control the tempo.

Don't let things get out of control at the beginning of the game. If your opponent has rhythm and tempo, break it. This is similar to icing a field-goal kicker in football or a free-throw shooter in basketball. Take that time-out, gather your thoughts and emotions, and formulate a quick plan of attack for the next couple of rallies. In fact, take two time-outs in a row if you feel it is necessary. Time-outs don't do you any good if the game is over and you haven't used them.

Table 11.2 Strategies Based on Game Situation

Game situation	Strategies
You are up 7 points or more	Apply pressure; don't relax
You won the first game	Stay with your game plan
You are down 7 points or more	Hit high-percentage shots only Don't force shots
You lost the first game	Change and control the tempo of the game Change or adjust your game plan
You are in a tie breaker	Go in with energy Believe in yourself Adjust your game plan as needed Control the tempo of the game
You are serving for game or match point	Use your best serve Use a good serve you haven't used yet Take your game-winning shot when it comes
You are receiving serve for game or match point	Hit a high-percentage return only Stay in the rally no matter what Avoid committing unforced errors Keep your opponent in the backcourt Take your shot when it comes

Control the Tempo

Tempo refers to the pace or timing of the game. Everyone has a favorite tempo for walking, hiking, running, and so on. A racquetball game is no different. You will find a game pace that is comfortable for you and allows you to play your best. Your opponent will have a favorite tempo as well. You will want to find out what your opponent's tempo is and disrupt that tempo as much as possible without taking yourself out of your own game.

The men's basketball team at the United States Air Force Academy provides a good example of playing to one's own tempo and taking the opponent out of his or hers. Due to their constraints on recruiting when it comes to body types allowed into the military, the basketball players on the academy's team are much shorter and less athletic than the players at most of the colleges they play. To compensate, they use a precise and calculated approach in which they slow down the ball by running a motion offense to use as much time as possible before taking a shot. By doing this, they play within their athletic ability and take the opposing team out of the popular run-and-gun style of play. They play to their strength and disrupt the opponent's tempo. I have seen many a better team become frustrated and get conquered when confronted with this type of tempo and game plan.

FOLLOW THE SIX RULES OF RACQUETBALL

Regardless of your level of play, the following six fundamental rules of racquetball will help you play your best and keep you out of trouble during a game.

1. **Control center court.** Keep your opponent in the backcourt and stay in center court as much as possible. This will give you the offensive advantage and the opportunity to win the majority of the rallies if you can execute your shots.

2. **Hit to the open court.** Hit away from your opponent as much as possible, using down-the-wall, cross-court V, and wide-angle passing shots when your opponent is in front of you. When you are in front, hit pinches and kills that go away from your opponent. Keep your opponent moving and hitting on the run as much as possible.

3. **Exploit your opponent's weaknesses.** Take the game to your opponent. Don't be shy about releasing that demon that he or she wants to keep caged. If your opponent doesn't return lob serves very well, offer up a steady diet of lob serves. If your opponent is slow in getting out of the service zone and into center court, hit pass after pass after pass. There is no reward for setting up your opponent and giving him or her a chance to kill the ball.

4. **Play to your strengths.** Keep in mind that your strength may be counteracted by your opponent's. If you have excellent drive serves and your opponent returns them well, you may want to go to something else. However, that drive serve may also be just a little bit better than your opponent's return.

5. **Play to the back corners.** Keep the ball deep and in the back corners as much as possible. You want your opponent to return the ball from 38 feet (11.6 meters) as much as possible. There is more chance of error when shooting from this distance, and you have more time to react and return the ball.

6. **Be patient and wait for the shot to develop.** Wait on the ball and, when possible, hit it low (below your waist level). Don't cut the ball off at center court when it is above your waist. Let the shot develop, and you will most likely have a setup to hit off the back wall. Ideally, you want to hit the ball below your waist for kill shots, pinch shots, and passing shots, and above your waist for passing shots and ceiling shots. Play high percentage shots.

Game Planning Drill 1.   *Observe and Learn*

This drill is an exercise in watching a player to identify his or her strengths and weaknesses in stroke mechanics, footwork, stance, and ready position.

Watch another player and note the following:

- Flaws in stroke mechanics: pendulum swing; slice; short, compact swing; long, looping swing
- Flaws in footwork: light on feet, flat-footed, fond of crossover or forward step to hit the ball, open or closed hips
- Flaws in stance and ready position: wide or narrow stance, low or upright in the stance, racquet down or in ready position

Success Check

- Refer to previous steps, if necessary, when evaluating the player's stroke mechanics, footwork, stance, and ready position.
- Record the strengths and weaknesses you identify in your practice notebook.

Score Your Success

Identify one strength and one weakness = 1 point

Identify two strengths and two weaknesses = 3 points

Identify three strengths and three weaknesses, or more = 5 points

Your score ___

Game Planning Drill 2.   *Self-Evaluation*

Identify your own strengths and weaknesses in stroke mechanics, footwork, stance, and ready position. As you play or practice, mentally note the following:

- Flaws in stroke mechanics: pendulum swing; slice; short, compact swing; long, looping swing
- Flaws in footwork: light on feet, flat-footed, fond of crossover or forward step to hit the ball, open or closed hips
- Flaws in stance and ready position: wide or narrow stance, low or upright in the stance, racquet down or in ready position

To Decrease Difficulty

Ask a coach, instructor, or experienced player to evaluate you instead. Your evaluator should record his or her observations in your practice notebook.

Success Check

- Refer to previous steps, if necessary, when evaluating your own stroke mechanics, footwork, stance, and ready position.
- Record the strengths and weaknesses you identify in your practice notebook. Refer back to previous drills to work on areas you identify as weaknesses.

Score Your Success

Identify one strength and one weakness = 1 point

Identify two strengths and two weaknesses = 3 points

Identify three strengths and three weaknesses, or more = 5 points

Your score ___

Game Planning Drill 3.   *Develop a Game Plan*

Using the information you gathered from drills 1 and 2, as well as table 11.1, put together a game plan you can use against the player you observed for drill 1. Write out your game plan in your practice notebook.

Success Check

- Identify ways to play to your strengths.
- Discover how to exploit your opponent's weaknesses.
- Find ways to control the tempo of the game.

Score Your Success

Earn points for your game plan:

Identify one way to neutralize your opponent's strengths = 1 point

Identify one way to exploit your opponent's weaknesses = 1 point

Identify one way to play to your strengths = 1 point

Identify two ways to neutralize your opponent's strengths = 3 points

Identify two ways to exploit your opponent's weaknesses = 3 points

Identify two ways to play to your strengths = 3 points

Identify three ways to neutralize your opponent's strengths = 5 points

Identify three ways to exploit your opponent's weaknesses = 5 points

Identify three ways to play to your strengths = 5 points

Your score ___

Game Planning Drill 4.   *Execute Your Game Plan*

Using the game plan you developed in drill 3, play against the player you observed for drill 1. Evaluate your game plan after the match.

Success Check

- Play to your strengths.
- Exploit your opponent's weaknesses.
- Control the tempo of the game.

Score Your Success

Earn points for executing and adjusting your game plan. If you did not need to adjust your game plan, or if you adjusted your plan as needed, give yourself the appropriate number of points indicated below. If you did not execute your game plan, or if you should have adjusted but did not, give yourself 0 points.

Executed game plan, no adjustments needed = 10 points

Executed game plan, adjusted plan as needed = 5 points

Won the game = 5 bonus points

Your score ___

SUCCESS SUMMARY OF GAME MANAGEMENT

Now that you know how to put together a game plan, you can use this to your advantage. You will see that having a game plan before you play, and being fluid with that game plan, can help you succeed on the court and improve your skills.

It's been said that competing in athletics is 90 percent mental (which is true if you are 100 percent prepared physically). The aspects of the mental game covered in this book are game planning, game management, and strategy. You will find that you need to spend just as much time working on these skills as you do on the physical aspects of your game.

Having a game plan should be your first priority before stepping onto the court for a match. Your first experience with game planning, game management, and game strategy will be similar to your skills experience—there will be plenty of room for improvement. However, the more you practice, the more your skills will improve.

Record your scores for the game planning drills to evaluate your progress.

Game Planning Drills	
1. Observe and Learn	___ out of 5
2 Self-Evaluation	___ out of 5
3. Develop a Game Plan	___ out of 15
4. Execute Your Game Plan	___ out of 15
Total	___ *out of 40*

If you scored fewer than 20 points, perform the drills again. If you scored 20 points or more, you are ready to move on to the next step. Step 12, the final step in this book, is Doubles, Cutthroat, and Outdoor Court Games. This step introduces you to skills other than those used in singles and on an indoor racquetball court.

Doubles, Cutthroat, and Outdoor Court Games

For those who want more than indoor singles racquetball, this step will introduce you to some exciting options. Many racquetball players use these alternatives to help break up the potential monotony of practicing or playing singles. Additionally, these alternatives help make racquetball much more diverse.

Doubles is exactly what the name implies—a game pitting two players against two other players. This is a great game for the competitive player who wants an alternative to singles and is ready for the challenge of playing a game on a 20-by-40-foot court with three other people. Doubles is also a great way for four individuals or two couples to enjoy a workout and good company at the same time. Not everyone enjoys playing doubles, but many players prefer it over singles. Older players who do not have the speed and agility to play singles are turning to doubles so they don't have to give up the game. Doubles is exciting and challenging and will certainly find a place in your racquetball world if you give it a chance.

Cutthroat is a lot like playing basketball lightning or 21. The many variations of this game benefit singles and doubles players alike. Cutthroat is also an option when you have a third player who wants to play without waiting to rotate in for the next singles game. One of the best things about cutthroat is the diversity of the game and the opportunity to play singles and doubles at the same time. In addition, you can make cutthroat as difficult or as easy as you want. Many singles players love to play the countless variations of cutthroat to improve their singles game.

Outdoor racquetball is a luxury not available everywhere. Southern California and Florida have many outdoor courts, so if you are fortunate to live in or visit those areas you will find courts available to play on year-round. Unfortunately, outdoor courts are not found everywhere in the United States, and even fewer are found around the world. If you are fortunate to have an outdoor court in your community, take the opportunity to enjoy the outdoors while playing racquetball. It is truly a rare treat. In fact, many competitive players travel to Florida or southern California every year for an annual outdoor tournament.

DOUBLES

Doubles is a fun game and one of the most challenging in competitive racquetball. It can be a fun social game with all males, all females, or a mixed group. Doubles is even enjoyed with a mixture of young and old on the court. No matter how you mix it up with your doubles teams, you will find it challenging and exciting to play as one of four people on the court at the same time.

The most common mistake made while playing doubles is to have two players on the same team playing singles on their own side of the court. Competitive doubles is a highly complex game played by two partners who both understand the game and know how their partner thinks and plays. Two good singles players do not always make the best doubles partners, especially when egos get in the way. The best doubles partners are those who are more concerned about the outcome of the game than whether they were the one who got the rally- or game-winning shot. In fact, finding a compatible doubles partner can be a very difficult thing. Many nationally ranked doubles partners don't even live in the same region of the country.

When two players are contemplating playing doubles together, they need to decide who will play the forehand and who will play the backhand side of the court. This is an easy decision if one is left handed and the other right handed. Typically, the player with the strongest backhand plays the backhand side. However, much of the decision depends on compatibility and the ability of the player playing the forehand side to be able to play there confidently. Not all right-handed players play well on the forehand side. Again, you must consider the ability of both players and decide what is best for the team, not necessarily what is best for the ego.

Communication is another huge aspect of doubles team success. Typically one player will become the team leader and call most of the balls either for himself or herself or for the other player. This is important because each player must know the partner's intentions at all times. The biggest mistake a doubles team can make is

not communicating and having players go after the same ball. This puts both players in the same area on the court and leaves a lot of open court for the opponents to hit into. It also puts you at risk of hitting your own partner with either the ball or your racquet.

Two good players can play excellent racquetball together if the chemistry is right. In fact, many elite competitors playing doubles together have been taken down by less talented players who understand and play the game as one rather than two.

Some of the best doubles teams in the world play without ever uttering a single word to each other. These players know how their partner thinks and what he or she will do in each situation, making their team truly one in mind, spirit, and motion.

Rules in doubles are similar to those in singles. See this book's introductory chapter for a review of the general rules and the exceptions for doubles. Additionally, as appropriate, you may want to follow a few unwritten rules of etiquette to make the game less intensively competitive and more socially enjoyable:

- Serve to your own side of the court.
- Don't isolate your partner and play one-on-two.
- Don't serve only to the weaker opponent.
- Don't hit only to the weaker opponent.

Safety

It is impossible to have a discussion about doubles without talking about safety. With four people on the court and each partner on a team having equal opportunity to hit the ball, things get crowded and hectic. One team is moving out of the way, and the other is trying to get in position to hit the ball. There will be times when one, two, or all three of the players not returning the ball may get in the way. It is always best to hold up and not hit the ball if you are concerned about someone being in the path of the hit ball or your racquet swing.

Communication

Communication is vital to both safety and cooperation. It is necessary to talk and decide which player will play certain balls before you even get on the court. At times, both players will be able to get to a ball that is in neutral territory. Even if it is clear who should return the ball, it is always best to call it so there is no confusion. The simplest words to use in the heat of the moment are one-syllable words. The terms used most often by advanced players are *me, mine, you, yours,* and *switch.*

If both partners call the ball, it defaults to the player with the forehand shot. It is not improper or uncommon to call the ball for one's partner, especially if the ball is coming into your side of the court but you are out of position and therefore feel that your partner may have a better opportunity to get to and hit the ball. Moreover, calling *switch* when retrieving a ball on your partner's side of the court will prevent leaving one side of the court uncovered. If you do switch, you should remain on the new side until the rally is over or the opportunity arises to switch back.

Scoring and Rotation

The first team to serve in doubles at the beginning of each game is allowed only one serve. When that server is out, the team is out and rotates to receive. From that point on, both players on each team serve until the team receives a handout or sideout. The partner on the team that is not serving must remain in the doubles box with his or her back against the wall in an erect position. Both players on the serving team must remain in the service zone until the ball passes the short line. Once the ball passes the short line, they may exit the service zone and take any position on the court not occupied by the receiving team. The server may hit any legal serve to either receiving player. The receiving team must remain on the backcourt side of the safety line until the ball bounces on the floor or crosses the safety line. Additionally, either receiving player can make a play on the ball, and the other team must give ground to the receiving

team to return the ball. Rotation in doubles must remain the same throughout the game. Once the game is over, the rotation may change for the next game. (See also "Basic Rules of Play" in The Sport of Racquetball, page xii.)

Team Formations

Team formations vary depending on the skill level of the team and that of the opponents. Many factors should be considered when choosing a doubles formation. The most important consideration is what is most comfortable for you and your partner and what fits your particular skills as a team. The three basic formations in racquetball are *up-and-back, side-by-side,* and *modified.* Each of these formations is designed to fit the team's playing style and make the most of individual players' skills.

The up-and-back formation (figure 12.1) is likened to and sometimes called the I formation. After the serve and during the rally, one player plays up, covering the middle and front part of

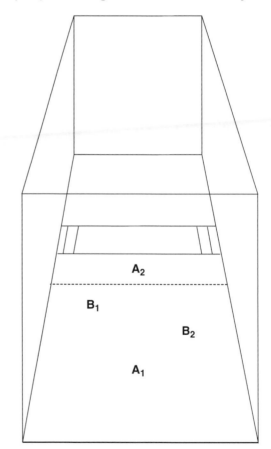

Figure 12.1 Up-and-back formation (A_1 and A_2).

the court. The other player covers the back of the court. This is a logical team formation when one partner is clearly faster than the other. The quicker partner plays up and the slower partner plays back. Additionally, the partner playing up should be good at kills, pinches, and passes. The back partner should be skilled at ceiling shots, passing shots, and pinches from the backcourt. The biggest disadvantage of this formation is it is easy to exploit and play to one player, leaving the other one out. Your opponents can hit pinches and kills to the front of the court to isolate the backcourt player, or hit passing and ceiling shots to the backcourt to isolate the frontcourt player.

The side-by-side formation (figure 12.2) divides the court directly down the middle. This is a great formation when both players possess equal ability. Each player is responsible for his or her side of the court. If both players are right handed, place the player with the strongest backhand on the left side. If one player is left handed

and one is right handed, put the left-handed player in position to play the left side. This is the most common formation for beginning players and those who have not been introduced to competitive doubles. For this type of formation to be played most effectively, both players must communicate well and be ready to back up the other if the ball gets past the partner. It also requires both players to have nearly equal skills in playing up or back. The biggest disadvantage of this formation arises if both players try to cover a ball to the front or back, thus leaving most of the court open for the other team to hit to. The best way to beat this formation is to hit wide passes when both players are at mid court and try to get both players either to the front, back, or one side of the court. Additionally, if the opposing team has a left-hander on the left and a right-hander on the right, you can hit down the middle of the court to both their backhands.

The modified formation is a hybrid of the up-and-back and side-by-side formations. In the side-by-side formation, players play their strongest sides. In the modified formation, if both players are right handed, the player on the left side will play nearly two-thirds of the court and the majority of the balls down the middle. Balls in the middle of the court come to the left-side player's forehand, which typically will be stronger than the right-side player's backhand. If both players are left-handed, the player with the strongest backhand takes two-thirds of the court and the majority of the balls down the middle. One caveat is that if the player taking the majority of the balls down the middle is out of position, then the other player should play the ball if in position to do so. The difficulty with this type of play is one player plays most of the balls, leaving the other player out. This can be a problem, especially if one player hits the ball only once in awhile. It is hard to get into a game and get any kind of rhythm when you aren't consistently involved in the play of the game. It also creates holes in the coverage on the side of the player who is taking most of the balls, thus making it easy for the opponents to exploit. Additionally, one player can get worn down very quickly by chasing down most of the balls.

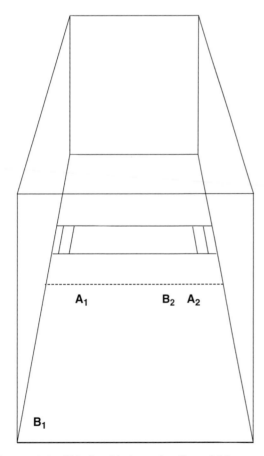

Figure 12.2 Side-by-side formation (A$_1$ and A$_2$).

Figure 12.3 shows examples of various modified formations. The partner in the backcourt should mirror the partner in the frontcourt. If player A goes to position 3, player B should go to position 4. If player A goes to position 1, player B should go to position 2. If player A goes to position 5, player B should go to position 6. If player A goes to position 7, player B should go to position 4. If player A goes to position 8, player B should to position 9. The backcourt partner is able to see where the frontcourt partner is, so it is the backcourt player's primary responsibility to cover the open court for passes.

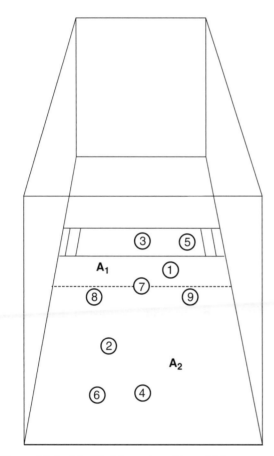

Figure 12.3 Modified formations (A$_1$ and A$_2$).

Court Positioning

In doubles, court positioning can sometimes be confusing. The receiving team has the right to get into a strategic position to return the ball. Therefore, the team who just hit the ball must move if the returning team wants a particular position on the court. At times, one player will

go the wrong direction and bodies will collide. Hinders are very common in doubles; therefore, you must be understanding and patient when playing the doubles game.

Figure 12.4 shows various court positions for both offensive and defensive teams. To help explain court positioning, let's break down a rally piece by piece and see where each player should go under certain circumstances and for particular shot locations.

Serve and return of serve 1: Player A is serving to the left side, with player B in the service box on the right side. Player C is receiving on the left side, and player D is on the right. Player A serves to the back left corner and moves to position 2, looking for the down-the-line shot and moving out of the way of the cross-court pass, while player B moves to position 1, anticipating a cross-court shot from C. As C sets up to hit the ball from the left back corner—most likely down the line, cross-court, or to the ceiling—player D moves to position 3 to get out of the way of a cross-court pass and get

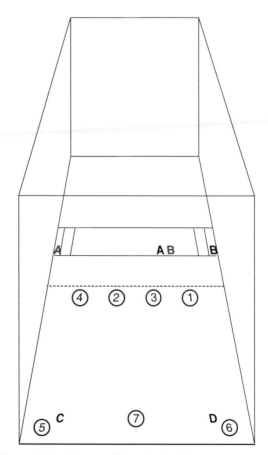

Figure 12.4 Court positions for doubles.

in position for the next return without interfering with A or B on the return.

Rally play 1: Player C has just returned a cross-court ceiling ball to the back right corner and will move up to position 4 in preparation for the return. Player B will move back to position 6 to hit the ball, and D will move to somewhere between positions 3 and 1, depending on where the ball goes and the type of shot player D has for the return. Player A goes to position 2 to get out of the way of a cross-court pass and in position for the next return without interfering with D or C on the return.

Serve and return of serve 2: Player B is serving to the right side, with A in the service box on the left side. Player D is receiving on the right, and C is on the left. Player B serves to the back right corner and moves to position 3, looking for the down-the-line shot and getting out of the way of the cross-court pass, while partner A moves to position 4, anticipating a cross-court shot from D. As D sets up to hit the ball from the right back corner—most likely down the line, cross-court, or to the ceiling—player C moves to position 2 to get out of the way of a cross-court pass and in position for the next return without interfering with A or B on the return.

Rally play 2: Player D has just returned an errant ceiling ball down the center of the court. Player A moves to position 7 to return the ball, while player B moves to position 1, staying out of the way of the return from player A. Player C should move to position 4, and D should move to position 1. If D moves to position 1, B will have to move back behind D to stay out of the way of A's shot to the right side. B needs to be ready to move into position 1 on the next return.

Doubles Strategy

Control center court. This is crucial to effective doubles. Controlling center court gives you the best court coverage and shot selection, and you will also have a better view of the ball without having to get around your opponents. Opt to shoot balls that keep your opponents out of center court and that travel into the front- or backcourt. Take advantage of center court by hitting pinches and kills when the opportunity arises. At least one player should be at mid or center court at all times.

Keep moving. If you are standing in one place during a rally, you are probably out of position. You should always be looking to cover the open court

Remember the lob serve. The lob allows you and your partner time to reposition out of the service zone. If the receiver cuts off or short-hops the lob effectively, then go to the nick lob. If you are serving to a lefty-righty team, with each playing the side wall with the forehand, serve down the middle. Wraparound serves to the middle are good to the lefty-righty team. Don't let the ball wrap around so far that you put your partner in danger of getting hit by the ball. Don't serve to your partner's side of the court unless he or she knows you are going to do it. This sets your partner up to get hit with the return and is not conducive to a good doubles team relationship!

Return wisely. When returning serve, your first choice should be to move the serving team to the backcourt with a ceiling ball or passing shot. If the nonserving partner is slow getting out of the service zone, blast the ball to that side with a hard passing shot. You may cut off or short-hop lobs and hit them to or at the nonserving partner. The high Z is also a good serve return. However, if you have the setup, go for the kill when the opportunity presents itself.

Don't cut off and play every shot in the frontcourt. If the ball is above your waist and you have to reach for it, let it go. Your partner in the backcourt may have a better shot and can see court coverage a great deal better than you can. However, if you have a good shot, take it.

Advanced Court Positioning

In advanced court positioning, the court is divided diagonally. If player A is up, the court is divided to give A the predominantly frontcourt slice on the right, and player B has the predominantly backcourt slice on the left (figure 12.5). If player B were up, then B would have the frontcourt slice on the left and player A would have the backcourt slice on the right. This is a dynamic division and constantly changes depending on where each player is located. Of course, this is only a division for the purposes of responsibility. Either player may get a ball anywhere on the court depending on the situation. This type of court division is good only if both players have equal ability and are good both up front and in the backcourt. This is the best type of court coverage for intermediate to advanced players. Both players must communicate and know what the other is doing. The only disadvantage comes if the two players are not in harmony with each other. This is a difficult formation to break down and exploit unless one player is out of position. It takes patience to play against this formation. But waiting for the right shot at the right time will eventually pay off.

Look for the weak player in doubles. Every team has one. Once you find out who that is and identify the particular weakness, you must take advantage of it. Test the water. Hit different serves and shots to find that demon your opponents are tying to hide. If you are playing to win, don't be shy or polite about where you hit. If you are playing a social game, then take that into consideration and keep the game light and enjoyable for everyone.

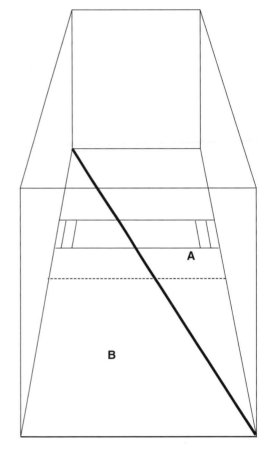

Figure 12.5 Diagonal division of the court for a doubles team.

CUTTHROAT

Cutthroat is a modified game played by three people. It is a great game to play when there are not enough people to play doubles, since it keeps the odd person from having to sit out. Cutthroat comes in three flavors: *one-out, one-on-two,* and *ironman.*

One-out is basically a singles game with an odd person staying in the backcourt and remaining out of the way of the two players in the rally. Once the rally is over, the out player receives and the player who lost the rally goes out. The winner serves to begin the next rally.

One-on-two is a modified singles and doubles game. One player plays against two players who are basically playing doubles. The single player is always the server. When the first single player sideouts, he or she moves to the receiving team and switches positions with the incoming server

who moves to serve as the single player. Once that server sideouts, he or she will move to the receiving team, switching places with the third player in the rotation who will serve as the single player. This rotation continues until a single player reaches the agreed-upon point total, ending the game.

Ironman is the ultimate cutthroat game, pitting one player against the other two throughout the entire game. To keep things fairly even, the single player serves as if he or she were two players. This is a great game to help a single player work on shot selection and learn how to control the court. Any number of handicaps may be applied, depending on the skill level of all the players. Winning ironman as a single player is a difficult thing to do and a great ego booster when accomplished.

One-Out

One-out is actually a singles game played with three people on the court at the same time (figure 12.6). Player A serves to player B with player C standing on the back wall in the out position, out of the way of the serve to the left side. Players A and B will play a singles rally with player C moving out of the way of the ball and any returns off the back wall during play. Once the rally is over, the winner serves next and the loser moves to the out position. This type of rotation continues until the game is over. Games end when a player reaches either 11 or 15 points. For the next game, the first server usually is the player who had the lowest score in the previous game. The first receiver is the player with the second-lowest score. The winner of the previous game is in the out position on the first serve. Normal singles rules apply during one-out cutthroat. Strategy during this game is the same as for a normal singles game.

One-on-Two

This game is played by three players at the same time. Two players play as a doubles team against a single player for one rally or point (figure 12.7). If the server wins the rally, he or she continues to serve. If the server loses, he or she sideouts and one of the other players, in rotation, moves to serve. Once that server loses, he or she is replaced by the next player in the rotation. Players alternate serves to each side of the court. This keeps everyone in the game and prevents a strong server from dominating the game by serving to a weak receiver. The doubles team changes with each sideout as the next player in rotation comes in to serve as the single player. The single player is always the one serving to the doubles team. Normal singles rules apply. The best strategy is to control center court, exploit the weaknesses of the two players, and make good shot selections.

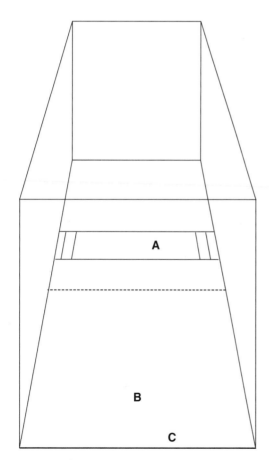

Figure 12.6   Cutthroat one-out.

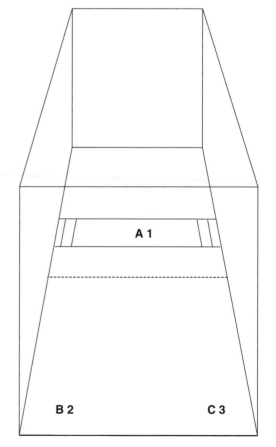

Figure 12.7   Cutthroat one-on-two.

Here is an example of how the rotation and serving order should go. Player A serves to B. Player A wins the rally, so again A serves to B. This time player A loses the rally. Player A goes to position 2, and player B goes to position 1. Player B serves to player A and loses the rally. Player B goes to position 3, and C goes to position 1. Player C serves to B and wins the rally. Player C serves to player A and wins the rally. Player C serves to player B but loses the rally. Player A goes to position 1, and C goes to position 2.

This staggered rotation alternates the side you receive from each time you lose your serve. Another way to remember the rotation is that the outgoing server always replaces the next player to serve. A player who loses serve always goes to the side opposite the one he or she came from.

Games end when one player reaches either 11 or 15 points. The player with the lowest score usually begins the next game as the server. The second player to serve will be the player who had the next-lowest score, and the winner will serve last.

Ironman

Ironman is the ultimate hybrid cutthroat game, pitting one player against the other two for an entire game. This is excellent singles practice because you have to be more precise with your shot selection and court coverage.

Ironman is similar to one-on-two with special serving rules. The single player serves twice, with a two-fault serve for the first serve. If the single player loses the first rally, he or she serves again, this time with a no-fault serve (single serve). If the singles player wins the first rally, he or she continues to serve (single serve, no fault) until the next rally is lost and the server sideouts. Then the singles player moves to receive serve. The singles player must also alternate sides with each subsequent serve. Each doubles player will get one single serve (no fault) each. Games end when the single player or the team reaches 7, 11, or 15 points. The service rules can be modified to suit your needs and how you want to play the game. Singles rules apply, and the strategy is the same as for one-on-two cutthroat.

OUTDOOR COURT GAMES

If you are lucky enough to have access to outdoor racquetball courts, I envy you. Outdoor racquetball is a great way to enjoy the game and be outdoors at the same time. See The Sport of Racquetball for discussion of the special rules associated with outdoor courts. The two biggest differences are the absence of a ceiling and the fact that the side walls are either absent or shorter (in height and length). This makes the game offensive in nature. Although the ball must bounce the first time inside the boundaries of the 20-by-40-foot court, the lack of side walls nearly doubles the width and increases the length of the playing surface of the court. This makes for an interesting game and will surely improve your wide-angle passing game. Another difference is the use of the lob shot off the front wall, which is not used in indoor racquetball. Cutting the ball off on the fly (volleying) is common. Additionally, rallies are typically much shorter than on the four-wall indoor court with ceiling.

One-Wall

The biggest difference in the one-wall game is the removal of the side walls. This eliminates the pinch and all Z shots. Now, the wide-angle passes are the shot of choice, with the occasional front-wall lob or long shot to the backcourt and kill. The ball must always bounce off the front wall inside the court boundaries. One-wall can be played with singles or doubles. The idea is to spread your opponent out with wide passing shots. Wide serves are best to get your opponent outside the court boundaries from the very beginning. When you move your opponent wide, then you can go to the other side or use a touch lob shot off the front wall to the deep backcourt. Moving your opponent from side to side or to the deep backcourt is your best strategy. You are able to hit the ball higher off the front wall to the backcourt due to the fact that there is no back wall to redirect ball to the middle of the court where your opponent might have a setup. Keep 'em wide and deep. You will seldom need to kill the ball. This is primarily a wide-angle passing game. Normal singles and doubles rules apply, with the exceptions noted in the "Basic Rules of Play" in The Sport of Racquetball (page xii). Just remember, the court has no ceiling or side or back walls.

Three-Wall

The three-wall game allows for pinches and Z shots of sorts. The ball is usually played higher than in the indoor game due to the partial side walls (on most outdoor courts) and the absence of a ceiling or back wall, which allows the ball to travel beyond the 20-by-40 foot boundaries. This gets the ball outside the court boundaries and forces the receiver to hit a long shot back to the front wall. Wide-angle passes are the typical offensive shot of choice, with the high lob off the front wall being the main defensive choice. Singles and doubles can be played on this court. The strategy for playing three-wall is primarily the same as for one-wall. Normal rules apply, with the exceptions noted in the "Basic Rules of Play" in The Sport of Racquetball (page xii). Remember, the court has no ceiling or back wall and only a partial front side wall.

SUCCESS SUMMARY OF DOUBLES, CUTTHROAT, AND OUTDOOR COURT GAMES

If you are a doubles player, you've probably learned a few tricks to help you and your partner become better. If you aren't a doubles player, I hope I have inspired you to at least try it. I personally prefer playing doubles over singles. The doubles game is much more challenging at the advanced level, and I like the challenge and camaraderie associated in playing with a partner.

Cutthroat is always an option when there is an odd person. It gives everyone an opportunity to play, regardless of what type of cutthroat you decide on. The dynamics of playing two players with different styles can be fun and challenging.

I personally prefer ironman cutthroat for the ultimate challenge and workout.

Outdoor games are a great alternative to playing indoors, especially when the weather is nice. These games are much different and will change your way of thinking and choosing shots. If you are a purist favoring either indoor or outdoor racquetball, you may find it difficult to switch back and forth. However, I like the change and challenge of having to think through shot selection and strategy in different ways.

Although there are no specific success checks in this step, most of the skills and drills you have learned may be applied here if you wish.

TOP OF THE STAIRCASE

Now that you have completed all of the steps in *Racquetball: Steps to Success*, you should have a good foundation for building an excellent racquetball game. Remember, perfect practice makes perfect players. How you practice will define your game. Setting racquetball goals will help you become the type of player you want to be.

If you want to take your racquetball game to the next level, I encourage you to find a coach or instructor certified by the American Professional Racquetball Organization (AmPRO) or the International Professional Racquetball Organization

(IPRO). These professionals know what it takes to be the best and will help you to become the best racquetball player you can be.

I have never found a person who was introduced properly to this great game who didn't enjoy it. Racquetball is truly a lifelong sport. I have been playing this game longer than any other sport. I have made it my athletic life. The many different clubs and locations I have played and coached at have taken me all over the world. The many friendships I have made while playing and coaching will last a lifetime. The opportunities I have had to play and coach have extended and cemented my love of the game. Sharing with you what I have learned about this game is my ultimate racquetball dream. This is my way of giving back to the sport that I love so much.

I hope you enjoy this game as much as I do. It is my desire for you to learn, play, and have fun. Regardless of what your racquetball goal is, this book has given you the foundation to get started on your journey and enjoy playing with some measure of skill and knowledge. Make the most of your racquetball experience. But more than anything else, have fun doing it and share it with others.

◨ About the Author

Dennis Fisher is head coach of the Brigham Young University racquetball team, which has won four combined-team and eight women's-team national collegiate championships during his tenure. He is a certified level II coach through the American Professional Racquetball Organization (AmPRO)/International Professional Racquetball Organization (IPRO), an AmPRO/IPRO professional instructor, a United States Racquet Stringers Association racquet technician, and a Wilson racquet technician. In 1999, the U.S. Racquetball Association (USAR) and the United States Olympic Committee (USOC) named Fisher Developmental Coach of the Year; and in 2006, Volunteer Coach of the Year for Racquetball. He is a member of Wilson's Racquetball Advisory Staff and past chairman of the USRA Intercollegiate Council. Coach Fisher also coaches at the USRA-sponsored high performance/elite game each year at the USOC in Colorado Springs, CO. Fisher also has a business that specializes in coaching, training, and instructing racquetball for all levels of players around the world. He has played racquetball for almost 40 years, competing at the Open level nationally and internationally. In his spare time, Fisher likes to cycle, fly fish, snow ski, snowboard, and guide canyoneering trips.